CANTERBURY STUDIES
IN ANGLICANISM

Anglican Women on Church and Mission

D1320156

Also available in the same series

Apostolic Women, Apostolic Authority:
Transfiguring Leadership in Today's Church
Martyn Percy & Christina Rees, Editors

Calling on the Spirit in Unsettling Times:
Anglican Present and Future
L. William Countryman

Christ and Culture: Communion After Lambeth
*Martyn Percy, Mark Chapman, Ian S. Markham
& James Barney Hawkins IV, Editors*

Worship-Shaped Life: Liturgical Formation and the People of God
Ruth Meyers & Paul Gibson, Editors

CANTERBURY STUDIES
IN ANGLICANISM

Series Editors: Martyn Percy and Ian Markham

Anglican Women on Church and Mission

Edited by Kwok Pui-lan
Judith A. Berling
and Jenny Plane Te Paa

Morehouse Publishing
NEW YORK · HARRISBURG · DENVER

CANTERBURY
PRESS
Norwich

Morehouse Publishing
4775 Linglestown Road, Harrisburg, PA 17112

Morehouse Publishing
445 Fifth Avenue, New York, NY 10016

Morehouse Publishing is an imprint
of Church Publishing Incorporated.
www.churchpublishing.org

Cover design by Laurie Klein Westhafer
Typeset by Denise Hoff

Library of Congress Cataloging-in-Publication Data

A catalog record of this book is available from the Library of Congress.

ISBN-13: 978-0-8192-2804-8 (pbk.)
ISBN-13: 978-0-8192-2805-5 (ebook)

Printed in the United States of America

CONTENTS

Part 2
Anglican Women and God's Mission

ACKNOWLEDGMENTS

This book is the result of friendship and collaboration in the work of the Anglican Communion and the academy for many years. The idea of the book originated at an inaugural conference of Anglican female theological educators at Canterbury, United Kingdom, in the spring of 2009. Organized by Clare Amos, former director of Theological Education for the Anglican Communion, the conference brought together leading female theological educators from the global North and global South to discuss mentoring, pedagogy, leadership development, and the need for collaboration of Anglican women in the Communion. Judith A. Berling, Beverley Haddad, Kwok Pui-lan, Esther M. Mombo, and Jenny Plane Te Paa met in Hong Kong in early spring of 2010, and some of them met again at Atlanta in October of that year to formally establish the book project and the mentoring of Anglican women leaders of the two-thirds world.

We would like to thank the authors for sharing our vision for this volume and for their contributions. We are grateful to the St. Boniface Trust, St. Augustine's Foundation, and the Graduate Theological Union for providing support and research funds to enable the production of this pioneering volume. We are much indebted to the Right Reverend Ian T. Douglas, Bishop of the Diocese of Connecticut of the Episcopal Church of the United States, who has been very supportive of the project and his diocese has provided us with much needed additional funds. Michele Waldinger offered invaluable assistance in editing the manuscript. We appreciate the meticulous care and sensitivity she brought to this anthology, which made the book more readable and consistent. We also want to thank Davis Perkins, our editor at Church Publishing, for his enthusiasm about the book from the beginning and for his guidance throughout. It was a blessing working with the staff at Church Publishing, who shepherded the manuscript through the production process with patience and professionalism. We are grateful to Cluster Publications for permission to reprint a revised and shortened version of Denise M. Ackermann's "Tamar's Cry: Re-reading an Ancient Text in the Midst of an HIV/AIDS Pandemic," in *Grant Me Justice! HIV/AIDS & Gender Readings of the Bible*, ed. Musa W. Dube and Musimbi R. A. Kanyoro (Pietermaritzburg: Cluster Publications, 2004), 27-59. Esther M. Mombo's chapter was originally entitled "Religion and Materiality: The Case of Poverty Alleviation," in *Religion and Poverty: Pan-African Perspectives*, ed. Peter J. Paris (Durham: Duke University Press, 2009), 213-27. Copyright by Duke University Press and reprinted by kind permission of the publisher. Proceeds from the book will be used to support mentoring the upcoming generation of women from the two-thirds world as academic leaders for the future global Anglican Communion.

ABOUT THE CONTRIBUTORS

Dr. Denise M. Ackermann, from South Africa, is Extraordinary Professor of Christian Theology at the University of Stellenbosch, South Africa. She is a research fellow of the Center of Theological Inquiry in Princeton, New Jersey, member of the International Academy for Practical Theology, member of the Circle for Concerned African Women Theologians, a licensed preacher in the Anglican Church, and an associate of the Black Sash Trust. Ackermann is the author of *After the Locusts: Letters from a Landscape of Faith* and coeditor of *Women Hold Up the Sky: Women in the Church in Southern Africa*; *Liberating Practices: Feminist Practical Theologies in Different Contexts*; and *Claiming our Footprints: South African Women Reflect on Context, Identity and Spirituality.*

Dr. Clara Luz Ajo Lázaro is a Cuban Anglican theologian and professor of systematic theology at the Theological Evangelical Seminary in Matanzas, Cuba. She also works with the biblical-theological formation programs for the Episcopal Church in Cuba. She received her doctorate from the Faculta Ecuménica de Post-Grafo of the Universidade Metodista in Sãn Paulo in Brazil. Her research is related to interreligious dialogue between the Episcopal Cuban tradition and Santería, a Cuban religion of African origin. Her publications include *Teología Género: Seleccíon de Textos* and other articles.

Judy Berinai, from Malaysia, is a doctoral student at the Oxford Centre for Mission Studies/Middlesex University, London. She has been seconded by the Anglican Church of Sabah to teach in the Sabah Theological Seminary, Kota Kinabalu, Sabah, Malaysia, since 1991. Apart from full-time teaching, she is involved in publication, specifically in translating English theological books into the Malay language. She is the editor of *Matang dan Sempurna* (Mature and Perfect) and *Bercambah dan Berbunga* (Sprouting and Flowering).

Dr. Judith A. Berling is a professor at the Graduate Theological Union in Berkeley, California, where she has also served as Dean and Vice President of Academic Affairs. She teaches and writes in the fields of East Asian religions, Asian Christianities, and Interreligious Learning. She is a past president of the American Academy of Religion and of the American Society for the Study of Religion. An active lay Episcopalian, she is currently Senior Warden of St. Mark's Episcopal Church in Berkeley. Her publications include *Understanding Other Religious Worlds: A Guide for Interreligious Education* and *A Pilgrim in Chinese Culture: Negotiating Religious Diversity.*

The Revd Dr. Wendy Fletcher is Professor of History of Christianity at Vancouver School of Theology where she also served as Principal and Dean for twelve years. Prior to that, she was Professor of Church History and Historical Theology at Huron University College of the University of Western Ontario. Her research interests have focused on the intersection of culture and Christianity in the twentieth century, with particular reference to the role and place of women, relations with Canadian First Nations persons, and the decline of Christianity in Canadian culture, all set in conversation with the formulation of a postcolonial missiology. She is the author of *Beyond the Walled Garden: Anglican Women and the Priesthood* and *Like Water on Rock: Gender Integration in Canadian Anglicanism,* as well as chapters in many books.

The Revd Dr. Gulnar E. Francis-Dehqani, was born in Isfahan, Iran, and moved to England following the events of the 1979 Islamic Revolution and has, to date, been unable to return to Iran. A Nottingham University music graduate, she worked at BBC World Service radio and Domestic Radio's Religious Department. Her PhD from Bristol University was awarded in 1999, and soon after she was ordained in the Church of England. Francis-Dehqani has written and spoken in particular on the areas of feminist theology and interfaith studies. She is currently Curate Training Officer in the Diocese of Peterborough and is the author of *Religious Feminism in the Age of Empire: CMS Missionaries in Iran, 1869–1934.*

Dr. Kwok Pui-lan was born in Hong Kong and is the William F. Cole Professor of Christian Theology and Spirituality at the Episcopal Divinity School in Cambridge, Massachusetts. She is past president of the American Academy of Religion. Her publications include *Postcolonial Imagination and Feminist Theology*; *Introducing Asian Feminist Theology*; and

Discovering the Bible in the Non-Biblical World. She is the editor of *Hope Abundant: Third World and Indigenous Women's Theology* and *Women and Christianity* in four volumes.

Dr. Esther M. Mombo is Deputy Vice Chancellor (Academics) at St. Paul's University, Limuru, Kenya, and holds a PhD from the University of Edinburgh and an honorary doctorate from Virginia Theological Seminary. She is a member of the Circle of Concerned African Women Theologians and has made significant contributions to developing women's ecclesial leadership in Africa. Her passion is to make the voices of women heard in theological circles within the context of Western and African patriarchies. This has meant making creative moves to have more women study theology and serve in positions of leadership within the Church and its institutions. She is the coeditor of *If You Have No Voice Just Sing!*

Dr. Cordelia Moyse was born in the United Kingdom and is a social historian specializing in both church and women's history. Her PhD from the University of Cambridge was on marriage and divorce law reform in twentieth-century Britain. She is the author of *The History of the Mothers' Union: Women, Anglicanism and Globalization, 1876-2008.* Since moving to the United States in 2008, she has taught at Lancaster Theological Seminary and Franklin & Marshall College in Pennsylvania. She is a board member of the Historical Society of the Episcopal Church. She currently works as Director of Development and Communications for the Lancaster Cleft Palate Clinic.

The Very Revd Dr. Jane Shaw is the Dean of Grace Cathedral, San Francisco. Prior to her appointment there in 2010, she was Dean of Divinity and Fellow of New College, Oxford, and taught history and theology at Oxford University for sixteen years. She was also Canon Theologian of Salisbury Cathedral and an honorary canon of Christ Church Cathedral, Oxford, and has served as Theological Consultant to the Church of England House of Bishops. Her publications include *Miracles in Enlightenment England*; *Octavia, Daughter of God: The Story of a Female Messiah and her Followers*; and *A Practical Christianity.*

Dr. Jenny Plane Te Paa has taught at St. John's College in Auckland, New Zealand, since 1992. In 1995 she was appointed as Ahorangi, or Principal, of Te Rau Kahikatea, becoming the first indigenous lay woman to head an Anglican theological college anywhere in the Anglican Communion. Since 2002, Jenny served as a member of the Lambeth Commission, the Inter-Anglican Theological and Doctrinal Commission, and the Theological Education for the Anglican Communion, and she was a founding member of the Global Anglican Theological Academy. She received her PhD from the Graduate Theological Union in Berkeley, California, and honorary doctorates for her contributions to theological education from the Episcopal Divinity School and the Virginia Theological Seminary.

The Revd Dr. Ellen K. Wondra is Professor of Theology and Ethics at the Bexley Hall Seabury Western Seminary Federation and Academic Dean for the Seabury campus in Chicago, Illinois. The author of numerous articles, she is the editor of *Reconstructing Christian Ethics*, by F. D. Maurice, and author of *Humanity Has Been a Holy Thing: Towards a Contemporary Feminist Christology*. From 1992 to 2010, she was an official representative of the Episcopal Church on the Anglican-Roman Catholic Consultation in the United States. She has been the Editor in Chief of the *Anglican Theological Review* since 2006. She is working on a book on the theology and practice of authority in the Episcopal Church and the Anglican Communion.

INTRODUCTION

The Anglican Communion is in crisis. The battle over homosexuality, with its intense media coverage, threatens to rip the Church apart. The debates on women bishops in the Church of England caused anger and frustrations among female clergy and their supporters. Some conservative Anglican bishops and their followers have formed a Fellowship of Confessing Anglicans, chastising the Church as having gone astray from true biblical teaching. These controversies epitomize the challenges facing the Communion and touch on fundamental issues such as the crisis of Anglican identity, the nature of authority and provincial autonomy, contrasting views on biblical interpretation, and ecumenical relations with other churches. The tenor of the debates is also influenced by the shift of Christian demographics from the global North to the global South. If the contentious issue of women's ordination did not break the Anglican Church apart in the 1970s, some are less optimistic that the Communion can weather the present storm and find ways to remain together.

The Anglican Communion is a worldwide body of churches with about eighty-five million people in more than 165 countries. Divided into thirty-eight regional or national churches called provinces, the Communion was formed as a result of the expansion of the British Empire and the missionary legacy of the Church of England. Today's Anglican Communion is multicultural and multilingual, with the more vibrant and fast-growing churches found in the global South. Cultural differences and the wide spectrum of theological leanings exert pressures on the unity of the Communion, which does not have a clear hierarchy and bureaucratic structures like those of the Roman Catholic Church. The unity of the Communion relies on four Instruments: the Archbishop of Canterbury; the Lambeth Conference (the meeting of bishops every ten years); the Primates' Meeting; and the Anglican Consultative Council, which consists of bishops, clergy, and lay people. These latter two instruments, though frequently mentioned, have not been formally adopted by the Lambeth Conference or other Anglican communion-wide organs.

The Primates' Meeting and the Anglican Consultative Council were constituted fairly recently in the 1970s, largely in response to the "urgent" matter of women's ordination.[1]

Because of the nature of this dispersed authority, the provinces are interdependent but autonomous in deciding their own affairs and adapting their polity and church life to local contexts. There are no clear mechanisms for resolving tensions and conflicts that are deeply divisive and have the potential to cause schisms. The Anglican Church has often prided itself for its *via media* approach and for its ability to hold together different contrasting elements: being catholic and reformed in its legacy, being episcopal and synodical in its polity, and being comprehensive without being fragmented or relativistic.[2] The Archbishop of Canterbury Rowan Williams has said that the strength of the Anglican tradition has been in maintaining a balance between the priority of the authority of the Bible, a catholic loyalty to the sacraments, and a habit of cultural sensitivity and intellectual flexibility. But he also acknowledged the gravity of the present crisis and said, "there is no way in which the Anglican Communion can remain unchanged by what is happening at the moment."[3]

Many of the conflicts that have divided the Church in recent years have involved issues of gender and sexuality. Women have struggled for equal opportunities for ministry and leadership in the Anglican Church for a very long time. Although more and more provinces are open to women's ordination, there are still many bishops and church members who refuse to accept women priests. Since the consecration of Bishop Barbara Harris in Massachusetts in the United States in 1989, women have become bishops in New Zealand, Canada, Cuba, Australia, and most recently in South Africa. But the debates on women and the episcopacy are far from over, as evident in what is happening in the Church of England. The divisiveness of the issue of homosexuality was brought to the fore at the 1998 Lambeth Conference. Although the resolution on human sexuality called on all people to minister to all irrespective of sexual orientation, it did not advise the blessing of same-sex unions or ordaining those in same-sex unions. Moreover, the conservatives pushed to include the clause "homosexual practice as incompatible with Scripture" in the resolution.[4] Fierce debates ensued after the Lambeth Conference, highlighting the differences between the transnational alliances of African bishops and their supporters in the North and the more liberal bishops and leaders of the Church.

Intra-Communion relations soured in 2003, when the Diocese of New

Hampshire elected Gene Robinson, a gay man in a same-sex relationship, as bishop, and the Canadian Diocese of New Westminster authorized rites for same-sex blessings. Because of the uproar created by these incidents, Archbishop Williams appointed a Lambeth Commission on Communion and the Windsor Report was published in October 2004. The Report suggests a "common Anglican Covenant" to be adopted by the churches of the Communion, which would "make explicit and forceful the loyalty and bonds of affection which govern the relationships between the churches of the Communion."[5] The Covenant would spell out the common heritage of the Church, relationships in the Communion, and means of conflict resolution among member churches. The Covenant Design Group produced an initial draft in 2007 and comments and feedback were solicited from various constituencies. In December 2009, the final version was sent to member churches for formal consideration for adoption through appropriate processes.[6] The Anglican Covenant not only generated heated arguments, but also created suspicion among the member churches.[7] Some objected to the disciplinary provisions in the proposed pan-Anglican agreement and expressed concerns over the centralization of authority in London. Several provinces, including the Church of England, the Anglican Church of Aotearoa, New Zealand, and Polynesia, and the Episcopal Church in the United States, have rejected the Covenant or declined to endorse it. It is highly unlikely that the Covenant in its present form would serve as a new basis for Anglican unity.

These various developments affect the life of the whole Church and the future unity of the Communion. Yet even as gender and sexuality issues remain at the heart of these debates, voices of women from the Communion have not been clearly heard or appreciated. Media coverage and church pronouncements tend to focus on the opinions of bishops, as if they could represent the range of diversity within the member churches, or of spokespersons of various Anglican networks and agencies, who are mostly male and clergy. The voices of lay people and women are marginalized, even though women make up the majority of many churches. This groundbreaking volume attempts to fill this gap by inviting female church leaders, scholars, and theological educators from across the Communion to share their reflections on the Anglican Church and its mission. An anthology such as this makes a unique contribution because there are very few substantial works by women from different parts of the Communion. It is even rarer for the majority of the book's authors to have grown up in the global South, bringing with them the rich textures and multilayered experiences of the Anglican Church.

The book is divided into two parts. Part one provides Anglican historical and theological perspectives on the Church. In the opening chapter, Kwok Pui-lan offers an analysis of the tensions within the Anglican Church as it transitioned from the established Church of England to a global Anglican Communion in our postcolonial world. Taking into consideration race, gender, class, and sexuality, she places the current issues facing the Anglican Communion, such as the crisis of identity and church unity, in a longitudinal view of the cultural politics of the Church. She argues that the Anglican Covenant is problematic and offers her visions of the future of the Communion. Ellen K. Wondra follows this discussion by elucidating the problems of authority within the Anglican Communion. When discussing authority in the Communion, Wondra notes that many refer to Scripture or to official reports and resolutions, often without critical studies of their origins or contexts of interpretations. Such an approach gives priority to the voices of the bishops or church leaders, while ignoring or marginalizing the contributions and roles of the laity. She argues that in concrete practice, the distribution and dispersal of authority is much more complex, involving the exercise of both formal and informal authority and different modes of decision making. Within the Communion, there are also local and regional variances. An adequate account of contemporary authority, therefore, must attend to the contributions of social sciences and must be grounded in the analyses of gender, race/ethnicity, and class.

The next chapter is devoted to the most controversial issue of the Communion today—human sexuality. Jane Shaw provides the historical and cultural backgrounds to the debates on sexuality in the Anglican Communion since the Lambeth Conference of 1888. She reminds us that long before homosexuality became the central focus, issues such as polygamy, divorce, and birth control had preoccupied the Church. In each of these cases, the Church has either reversed or changed its initial position, showing that the Anglican tradition is dynamic and Scripture is necessarily interpreted in relation to the context in which it is read. She discusses the gay and lesbian movements in the British and American churches and bemoans that some of the principles that the Communion has used to deal with the earlier issues have been forgotten or ignored in the homosexuality debate.

The last two chapters in part one focus on women's struggle for leadership in the Anglican Church. Wendy Fletcher places the issue of women's ordination and leadership in the larger contexts of changing gender roles and religious sensibilities in the West since the Victorian era. She discusses women's ordination at the macro level by tracing successive debates at the Lambeth Conferences from 1920 to 1998, when a slim majority of the provinces decided to ordain women. She then turns her attention to the present controversy on women and the episcopacy. Using the Anglican Church of Canada as an example, she elucidates the change of attitudes toward women priests at the micro level and what the ordination of women means to the Church. Jenny Plane Te Paa, the first indigenous woman to head an Anglican theological college, has served in leadership positions on the Anglican Communion's commissions and committees. Her chapter pinpoints the problems of underrepresentation of women in the top-level decision-making bodies of the Anglican Church. Although women have pushed for more equal representation, the progress has been slow and tortuous. To remedy this situation, she and other Anglican women have formed professional networks to support and nurture the younger generation of women, especially those from the two-thirds world, so that they will be able to exercise greater leadership in the future. One example is the formation of the Global Anglican Theological Academy, which seeks to provide mentoring and advanced theological educational opportunities for younger women.

Part two of the book discusses Anglican women and God's mission from a plurality of social and cultural contexts. Gulnar E. Francis-Dehqani assesses the complicated relations among gender, empire, and the missionary movement using the work of the Church Missionary Society (CMS) in Iran as an example. Situating the CMS within the context of Victorian feminism and the dominant evangelical culture, the chapter highlights the ambiguous legacies of British missionary women, who were able to identify with native women on some level, while trying to maintain their superior status in terms of race and class in the mission fields. Even with good intentions, these missionary women often displayed an Orientalist bias toward Persian culture, thus reinforcing a presumption of Western cultural superiority. The historical review pushes us to reimagine the mission of the Church and mutuality and partnership in carrying God's mission in our globalized world.

A successful institution that spread from England to the rest of the Communion is the Mothers' Union, founded by Mary Sumner in a rural parish church in Winchester in 1876. Initially set up to champion the sanctity of marriage, the Mothers' Union today has four million members in more than eighty-four countries. In her chapter, Cordelia Moyse describes the ways the Mothers' Union provides women a model of female Christian discipleship and ideals of marriage, family, and motherhood, as well as networking between the metropole and the colonies. She discusses how the Mothers' Union negotiated changing attitudes toward divorce and remarriage and had to open its membership to women with different kinds of marital status. As the movement has grown, the Mothers' Union has tried to move away from a centralized colonial model of organization and broaden its mission to include educational programs combating HIV and AIDS and promoting literacy. At a time of crisis for the Anglican Communion, the Mothers' Union has grown and flourished to become an instrument of unity with its concern for family life.

The next two chapters focus on Africa, a continent that has experienced phenomenal church growth but bisected by poverty and other social problems. In 2025, the number of Christians in Africa will outnumber that of Europe and Latin America to become the continent with the most Christians. The Anglican churches in Africa have been involved in programs and projects that address grinding poverty, famine, ethnic and religious conflicts, violence, and HIV and AIDS. In her chapter, Esther M. Mombo discusses the Church's involvements in poverty alleviation in Africa. She explicates why the mission societies' approach and their modernization projects did not help alleviate poverty because they did not fit into the indigenous legacy. The Jubilee 2000 campaign for debt relief advocated the cancellation of debts for poor nations and offering them the hope for a new beginning. The Lambeth Conference of 1998 addressed debt cancellation and called for an economy that enhanced full humanity. She describes how the Anglican Provinces in Africa have cooperated with the World Bank to reach the most vulnerable group in society—women in rural communities. It is imperative, she says, for the churches to help those who are most in need and address the structural issues that keep them poor.

The HIV and AIDS pandemic has wreaked havoc on the African continent. According to the Joint United Nations Programme on HIV/AIDS, at the end of 2010, an estimated 34 million people were living with HIV worldwide. Among them 68 percent live in Sub-Saharan Africa, a region with only 12 percent of the world's population. The epidemic is most serious in southern Africa, with about 5.6 million living with HIV in South Africa, about one out of nine of South Africa's population. Denise M. Ackermann, in her chapter, rereads the story of Tamar (2 Sam. 13:1-22) for clues for resistance and hope to address the current pandemic. She discusses the link between women's vulnerability, gender violence, poverty, and HIV and AIDS, and calls the Church to accountability and to stand prophetically on the side of gender justice. She says that the Church as the Body of Christ has AIDS, and must develop moral and pastoral resources to help people understand issues surrounding embodiment, sexuality, and life and death. She sees the Eucharist, which remembers and celebrates the Body of Christ broken for us, as a powerful symbol for Christian solidarity with all those who suffer.

The last two chapters of the book explore diversity within the Anglican Church and women's witness to Christ in a religiously pluralistic world. In her chapter, Clara Luz Ajo Lázaro discusses the diversity and plurality within the Anglican tradition, as illustrated by the experience of women in the Afro-Caribbean church. Many people in the Anglican Communion do not speak English as their first language and the Anglican tradition is shaped by the interaction with local cultures and religious practices. In Cuba, for example, women's spirituality is shaped by a transculturation process, in which Christian ideas and practices are combined with those of Santería, a religion of African origin, to form something new. Her chapter presents an interesting discussion of intrafaith dialogue and hybridization of cultures, in which multiple traditions are practiced and embodied by one person.

Judy Berinai's chapter turns our attention to interreligious relations and the challenging task of women witnessing Christ in a Muslim country. The so-called war on terrorism highlights the importance for Christians to know more about Islam and about the interactions between Christians and Muslims. Using the case of Malaysia as an example, Berinai describes the Islamization in Muslim countries, which touches on many areas, such as education, media, the role of government, and dietary and dressing practices. The Islamic resurgence has alienated and created an oppressive atmosphere for non-Muslims living in these countries. Despite such limitations, Anglican women have continued to bear witness to Christ and contribute to ministries, especially through women's organizations and fellowships. She challenges them to come out from their comfort zones to work with non-Christians to address social concerns, such as human trafficking, migrant workers, sexually abused women, and the poor and the elderly.

We hope that this book will promote dialogue and scholarship on women in the Communion. We are grateful to those faithful Anglican women who have gone before us, and we hope that women in the upcoming generation will be given greater responsibilities and leadership opportunities in the Church.

Kwok Pui-lan
Feast of Michael, Gabriel, and Raphael, 2012

Notes

1 Fredrica Harris Thompsett, "Inquiring Minds Want to Know: A Layperson's Perspective on the Proposed Anglican Covenant," in *The Genius of Anglicanism: Perspectives on the Proposed Anglican Covenant*, ed. Jim Naughton (Chicago: The Chicago Consultation, 2011), 31, http://www.chicagoconsultation.org/site/1/docs/Genius_of_Anglicanism_final.pdf.

2 Paul Avis, "Anglican Ecclesiology," in *The Routledge Companion to the Christian Church*, ed. Gerard Mannion and Lewis S. Mudge (New York: Routledge, 2008), 214.

3 Rowan Williams, "The Challenge and Hope of Being an Anglican Today: A Reflection for the Bishops, Clergy and Faithful of the Anglican Communion," June 27, 2006, http://www.archbishopofcanterbury.org/articles.php/1478/the-challenge-and-hope-of-being-an-anglican-today-a-reflection-for-the-bishops-clergy-and-faithful-o.

4 Lambeth Conference 1998, Resolution 1.10, http://www.lambethconference.org/resolutions/1998/1998-1-10.cfm.

5 Lambeth Commission on Communion, The Windsor Report 2004 (London: Anglican Communion Office, 2004), http://www.anglicancommunion.org/windsor2004, Para. 118.

6 Material of the Anglican Covenant is available at http://www.anglicancommunion.org/commission/covenant/index.cfm.

7 For the background of the Anglican Covenant and different perspectives about it, see Mark D. Chapman, ed., *Anglican Covenant: Unity and Diversity in the Anglican Communion* (London: Mowbray, 2008).

PART 1

ANGLICAN HISTORICAL
AND THEOLOGICAL PERSPECTIVES
ON THE CHURCH

1

FROM A COLONIAL CHURCH TO A GLOBAL COMMUNION

Kwok Pui-lan

The Anglican Communion was formed as a result of the expansion of colonialism and mission work in the colonies. Beginning in the seventeenth century, Anglican churches were established in the settler colonies in Australia, New Zealand, Canada, South Africa, and the eastern part of the United States. By the mid-1860s, a large number of overseas Anglican dioceses were effectively independent of the Church of England, having their own patterns of government and discipline and procedures for electing bishops. Controversy over the position of churches in the colonies led the Canadian bishops to request Archbishop of Canterbury Charles Longley to convene a meeting of all the bishops of the Anglican Church, both at home and abroad. Lambeth Conference 1867 marked the beginning of Anglican churches coming together to discuss their common concerns and affairs. Of the seventy-six bishops gathered at Lambeth Palace, many shared very similar backgrounds, as the colonial bishops and the English bishops had mostly gone through an education at Oxford or Cambridge.[1]

The idea of an Anglican Communion slowly took root and became more popularized in the first half of the twentieth century. After the Second World War, the diversity within the Communion was heightened, when many African and Asian countries regained political independence and struggled to assert cultural autonomy. Lambeth 1948 endorsed the United Nations' proposed Covenant on Human Rights and declared that these rights belong to all men (sic) irrespective of race and color.[2] The Conference also discussed the relation between the Church and the modern state.

Since the end of the Cold War, the term "globalization" has been widely used in the 1990s to describe changes brought by the neoliberal market, the information highway, and the use of new technology. The global character of the Anglican Communion has been recognized and strengthened by more connections between member churches in the North and in the South. While membership in mainline denominations in the North Atlantic has continued to decline, churches in the South experience growth and vitality. The global breadth was shown at Lambeth 1998, attended by nearly 750 bishops, including 224 from Africa, 177 from the United States and Canada, 139 from the United Kingdom and Europe, 95 from Asia, 56 from Australia, 41 from Central and South America, and 4 from the Middle East.[3] The voices of churches in the global South could no longer be ignored. They have significantly changed the discussion in the Communion.

Within the academy, the study of world Christianity has gained momentum, with prominent scholars such as Andrew Walls and Lamin Sanneh pushing for more attention to be paid to African churches. Several important works on the Anglican Communion have been published, which study the history of the Communion, the trajectory from colonial to national churches, and the struggles from a church of the British Isles to become a postcolonial and multicultural church.[4] Several of them feature authors who are lay and ordained scholars across the Communion.[5] In recent years, the controversies over women priests and bishops and homosexuality have generated poignant conversations on the identity, authority, and future of Anglicanism. This chapter begins with a discussion on the crisis of Anglican identity. Using the examples of polygamy and homosexuality, it examines how race, gender, and sexuality have shaped the cultural politics of the Anglican Church. The final section offers some comments on the future of the Anglican Communion.

The Crisis of Anglican Identity

An important challenge facing the Anglican Communion is how to be accountable to each other, when controversies and conflicts arise. Archbishop of Canterbury Rowan Williams acknowledged that the issues that threaten to divide the Communion are not limited to human sexuality, but could include "developments about how we understand our ordained ministry; how we understand our mission; the limits of diversity in our worship; even perhaps in the public language we use about our doctrine."[6] That the Anglican Church has not come to some common understanding on so many fundamental aspects of the Church and its mission points to the deep crisis of Anglican identity.

The crisis of Anglican identity can be attributed to many causes. The Anglican Church is not a confessional church and does not have the equivalent of the Augsburg Confession and the body of official doctrines similar to those of Lutheranism. It was formed more out of political expediency by Henry VIII, rather than out of rigorous theological arguments similar to those advanced by Luther and Calvin. The Thirty-nine Articles, which served to define the doctrine of the Church of England during Reformation, are not officially normative in all Anglican churches. The Chicago-Lambeth Quadrilateral adopted by Lambeth 1888 laid out the broad consensus of the Church: the Scripture as containing all things necessary to salvation, the Apostles' Creed as the sufficient statement of Christian faith, the two sacraments of baptism and Eucharist as ordained by Christ himself, and the emphasis on the historic episcopacy as the basis of Christian unity.[7] While the Quadrilateral can serve as a foundation to discuss Christian unity and ecumenism with other churches and denominations, it does not spell out the uniqueness of Anglicanism.

Some of the most prominent Anglican theologians even debated whether Anglicanism has special doctrines of its own. Several modern interpreters, such as Michael Ramsey, Stephen Neill, and Henry McAdoo, insist that the Anglican Church is a part of the historical Christian tradition that embraces the creeds and doctrines of the early church and does not have unique doctrines of its own. Such a claim emphasizes the intention of Anglicanism to be Catholic, to remain in the mainstream, and to be part of the whole.[8] Others, such as Stephen Sykes, argue that "the no special doctrines" claim is a fallacy, for every Church must have a doctrine of the Church to legitimize its existence and maintain its integrity. Sykes writes, "While it may have been true that there is no specifically Anglican Christology or doctrine of the Trinity, or even (though it could be disputed) doctrine of justification, it cannot be the case that there is no Anglican ecclesiology."[9]

But even if one wishes to study the doctrine of the Church in the Anglican Church, as Paul Avis notes, one is immediately faced with the issues of the diversity of Anglicanism and the problem of selectivity.[10] The Anglican Church does not have a teaching office similar to that of the Roman Catholic Church and it is not easy to appeal to certain texts or writers as "typical" or "representative." The historical scope and geographical extent of Anglicanism further undermine any easy generalizations. There is no single period of Anglican history that can be seen as definitive and can serve as the paradigm for developing Anglican ecclesiology. In addition, Anglicanism is a global phenomenon, existing in many social and cultural contexts. While the historical texts developed in sixteenth- and seventeenth-century England and Ireland constitute a common legacy, member churches in the Communion have developed their Anglican theology to address their own issues. Richard Hooker's classic text, *Of the Laws of Ecclesiastical Polity*,[11] written in the sixteenth century in the context of the established Church of England, cannot be easily applied to other churches with totally different church-state relations.

If it is not easy to define Anglican identity by its doctrines and theological locus, many turn to its common liturgy, because Anglicans are fond of saying *lex orandi, lex credendi* (the law of prayer is the law of belief). The Book of Common Prayer serves for some as a pointer to conformity and *koinonia* (communion) of member churches. Yet the provinces have freedom in revising their Book of Common Prayer and many modern revisions have come out. It was often difficult to balance between historical continuity and cultural relevance. By Lambeth 1958, it was acknowledged that the Prayer Book was no longer the basis for unity.[12] New liturgies emerged to meet the needs of different cultures. For example, the widely acclaimed New Zealand Prayer Book is bicultural and bilingual (Maori and English), and includes the cosmological worldviews, idioms, and languages of the Maoris.[13] Another example can be found in one of the Eucharistic prayers of the Episcopal Church's Book of Common Prayer, which includes modern language in its reference to God's creation. It addresses God as ruler of the universe, who creates "the vast expanse of interstellar space, galaxies, suns, the planets in their courses, and this fragile earth, our island home."[14]

Even the elements used for Eucharist could be controversial, as the question of substitution of bread and wine has arisen. Some churches consider bread and wine to be "foreign" imports; others claim that there are elements in their local culture to convey the notion of the celebratory meal better than bread and wine. In Islamic countries, the government outlaws all alcoholic drinks and it is hard to obtain wine. Some churches need to respond to concerns of recovering alcoholics and the needs of those who have gluten allergies. The discussion of food and drink at Eucharist touches on theological issues, but also on cultural authenticity and adaptability, given the diversity of the Communion.[15]

The discussion of theology and liturgy has already touched on the complex issues of cultural difference in the Communion. Some scholars attribute the crisis of Anglican identity to the difficulties of the transition of an English church to a global multiracial, multicultural, and multilingual Communion. Writing in 1993, before the heated debates erupted in recent decades, William L. Sachs already noted: "The deepening of local influences upon the Church brought forth a profusion of religious forms, all claiming historic precedent and religious validity, which shattered the unity of Anglican identity. The modern question became one of mediating between diverse forms of Anglican experience."[16] Ian T. Douglas, a member of the Design Group for Lambeth 2008, has gone one step further in his critique of the cultural domination and the continued colonial patterns of power in the Anglican Communion. For him, the crisis in the Anglican Communion is not so much about structure and instruments of unity, but about relationships and mission. In order for the Church to advance God's mission of reconciliation and restoration, the Church must respect and embrace what he has called "different incarnational realities."[17] He writes, "Communion is thus primarily based upon relationships of mutual responsibility and interdependence in the body of Christ across the differences of culture, location, ethnicity, and even theological perspective to serve God's mission in the world."[18]

The issue of cultural difference has arisen in the Anglican Communion since its inception. Lambeth 1867 was convened in part to settle the "Colenso Affair." John Colenso, Bishop of Natal in South Africa, was criticized for undermining the authority and inerrancy of Scripture by using the historical method to study the Bible. Sympathetic to Zulu culture, he challenged the missionaries' condescending attitudes toward the "heathens." He insisted that God is revealed to all humanity and that revelation is not confined to one nation and to one set of books. Colenso approached the Bible through wider and comparative lenses and insisted that Christ redeems all people everywhere whether they have heard his name or not.[19] Colenso was tried for heresy and appealed his case all the way to England. The Colenso affair brought into focus questions that would engage the Anglican Communion for years to come, such as Gospel and culture, diversity in biblical interpretation, the nature of Church, relations in the Communion, and the authority of the Lambeth Conference. In the following section, I use the examples of polygamy and homosexuality to examine the intersection of race, gender, and sexuality in the cultural politics of the Anglican Communion. It underlines the twists and turns of the transition from a colonial church to a global Communion.

The Cultural Politics of Polygamy and Homosexuality

During the colonial days, differences in marriage, sexual norms, and family structures served to reinforce cultural superiority of the colonizers over the colonized. English missionaries, shaped by their Victorian marriage norms and domesticity, found polygamous marriage troubling and against their Christian upbringing. Although polygamy was practiced in most societies encountered by missionaries in the nineteenth century, it was in Africa that polygamy became most problematic for the churches, including the Church of England.[20] Traditional African marriages were arranged between families and often involved the exchange of bride wealth in the form of cattle. Multiple wives served as a sign of wealth, children, power, and status.

Missionaries and the mission societies frequently raised the question of how to deal with polygamy. While the majority of missionaries upheld the monogamous ideal, a small minority, including Bishop Colenso, argued that polygamy should not be a barrier for baptism and exclude a person from becoming a full member of the Church.[21] Lambeth 1888 allowed for the baptism of polygamous wives, but resolved that "persons living in polygamy be not admitted to baptism, but that they be accepted as candidates and kept under Christian instruction until such time as they shall be in a position to accept the law of Christ."[22] The resolution did not resolve the issue, but rather created further problems, because it implied that a polygamous husband had to divorce all but one of his wives in order to receive baptism. But the churches at the time opposed divorce in general. In the African familial system, women deserted by their husbands had little means of supporting themselves and their children.

Throughout the twentieth century, polygamy continued to be an issue for the Anglican Church. The matter was brought up repeatedly at various Lambeth Conferences. The Archbishop of Canterbury commissioned a survey of the treatment of polygamous converts in the Anglican Communion leading up to Lambeth 1920. The Conference maintained the ban on the baptism of men living in polygamy. Timothy Willem Jones notes that the tone of church proclamations regarding polygamy softened after the Second World War, when the African countries became decolonized.[23] Lambeth 1958 maintained that monogamy is the divine will, but recognized that "the introduction of monogamy into societies that practice polygamy involves a social and economic revolution and raises problems which the Christian Church has as yet not solved."[24] The 1968 Conference reaffirmed monogamous lifelong marriage as God's will and acknowledged that polygamy posed "one of the sharpest conflicts between the faith and particular cultures."[25]

The issue of polygamy was also brought up in the meetings of Mothers' Unions in Africa. The Mothers' Union, an Anglican organization begun in England, spread to Africa and had a strong presence in the continent. The Union was set up to strengthen Christian marriage and to promote the well-being of families. Anglican scholar Esther Mombo notes that in Kenya, the Mothers' Union discussed marriage and polygamy in their early meetings beginning in the late 1950s.[26] The missionaries who founded the Mothers' Union spoke against polygamy and argued that Christian marriage should be based on the teachings of the Bible. Many women did not want to be one of several wives of the same husband. But the leaders of the Mothers' Union also recognized that polygamy had its social and economic causes and could not be easily abolished.

Polygamy became a focal point of debate about cultural imperialism, when African people wanted to reassert their cultural identity after decolonization. In reaction to the colonial mentality of the Church, some African theologians began the project of inculturation, using African worldviews and idioms to express Christian faith. They challenged European domination in theology and church practices. Writing in 1976, Felix Ekechi questioned whether monogamy as the only ideal Christian family life reflects the imposition of European values. He said monogamy conforms to Western nuclear family structure, as opposed to the African extended family system.[27] A. O. Nkwoka reported that quite a number of the first Nigerian converts saw "the imposition of monogamy on the African Church as one of the whitemen's oppressive measures and a sign of white supremacy."[28] Some Africans argued that the Bible is not univocal against polygamy, since some of the patriarchs, such as Abraham and Jacob, had multiple wives.

In contrast, African women theologians argue that African cultures are not monolithic and criticize the androcentric biases in the interpretation of African traditions. For Esther Mombo, polygamy raises the deeper question of the position of women in a patriarchal society. The Bible should be interpreted in a way to support the dignity and worth of women and not to abuse them.[29] Musimbi R. A. Kanyoro further argues that inculturation is not sufficient, if the culture reclaimed reinforces patriarchy and does not lead to the promotion of justice and support for the life and dignity of women. Citing studies that show that polygamy is an institution that oppresses women, she writes: "Polygamy has been the basis of exploitation of women and children's labor because polygamy is justified as a means of enhancing the productivity of property for men. Polygamy also depicts women as weak and in need of the constant protection of men."[30]

Within the Anglican Church, some African bishops worked to lift the ban against the polygamists. The ban has created many pastoral and practical problems. Families were broken up and the wives and children expelled from polygamous marriages became social concerns. In addition, responding to the Church's ban, several indigenous African churches were founded, which accepted polygamous members and competed for converts. In 1988, the East African bishops came to the Lambeth Conference determined to have the ban on admission to the sacraments of polygamists lifted. The strength of representation from Africa at the Conference was keenly felt. Of the 518 bishops who attended, 175 came from Africa, compared to 80 in 1978.[31] The Conference finally reversed the one hundred years' ban and allowed a polygamist to be baptized and confirmed with his believing wives and children.[32] For Jones, this means that polygamy is now tolerated as "a permissible alternative marriage structure by many Anglican provinces."[33]

The Anglican Church's long debate on polygamy provides useful background and insights for looking at the cultural politics of the controversy on homosexuality that threatens to divide the Communion. Although the missionaries and mission bodies had insisted on monogamy as the ideal family structure, different marriage patterns and sexual norms continue to exist, showing that it is difficult to prescribe universal norms that fit all cultures. The demographic shift within the Communion means that African bishops have increasingly played significant roles in setting the terms for the Communion. They shaped the debates on evangelism and culture, polygamy, relation with other faiths, and homosexuality at the 1988 Conference. The debate on polygamy also points out there are diverse perspectives on this complex issue, especially when gender and women's concerns are brought into the picture. The cultural politics at the level of Lambeth Conference was quite different from what was happening at the local level.

When Lambeth 1988 reversed the ban on the baptism of polygamist converts, it also discussed homosexuality and placed the issue within the context of human rights and pastoral care for people with homosexual orientation. From today's perspective, the wording of the resolution was quite mild and respectful. The Conference did not make any moral judgment, but recognized the continuing need for "deep and dispassionate study of the question of homosexuality, which would take seriously both the teaching of Scripture and the results of scientific and medical research."[34] It also recognized that sociocultural factors might lead to different attitudes in the Communion. However, the conciliatory tone changed in the decade leading up to Lambeth 1998. Miranda K. Hassett, in her detailed study of the crisis in the Anglican Communion, documents the global alliance formed between the church leaders of the South and dissident conservative Northerners, who felt that their churches had become too liberal. Several pre-Lambeth meetings were held in Kuala Lumpur, Dallas, and Kampala, with the goal to strengthen conservative alliances and to influence the outcome of Lambeth 1998.[35]

Even before Lambeth 1998, tensions were high when American Bishop John Spong of the Diocese of Newark was reported as having said that African Christians are "superstitious, fundamentalist Christians" who have "moved out from animism into a very superstitious kind of Christianity" and have yet to face the intellectual revolution of Copernicus and Einstein of the modern world.[36] The African and Southern bishops came to Lambeth already feeling insulted and defensive. Tensions and suspicions between the North and the South could not be contained. An unforgettable scene was that of Nigerian Bishop Emmanuel Chukwuma attempting to exorcise the English deacon Richard Kirker, a gay activist. Kirker's sin was that he was gay. Chukwuma's words to Kirker were direct: "God did not create you as a homosexual. That is our stand. That is why your church is dying in Europe—because it is condoning immorality."[37]

The resolution on human sexuality at Lambeth 1998 upheld the faithfulness in marriage between a man and a woman. It recognized that there are people with homosexual orientation, who seek pastoral care and moral direction from the Church. The Conference committed to listening to the experience of homosexual persons and affirmed that all baptized, regardless of their sexual orientation, are full members of the Body of Christ. Yet the Southern bishops with their Western supporters pushed for the inclusion of the clause that referred to "homosexual practice as incompatible with Scripture." The resolution also did not advise the blessing of same-sex unions and the ordination of those who engaged in same-sex unions.[38] The controversy caused by Lambeth 1998 was still roaring, when several incidents added fuel to the fire. In 2003 the Diocese of New Hampshire elected Gene Robinson, a gay man in a same-sex relationship, as bishop. The Diocese of Westminster in the Anglican Church of Canada authorized rites for same-sex blessing. In the Church of England, Jeffrey John, a gay man, was nominated as bishop, though he later had to withdraw due to mounting pressure. Responding to the outcry coming from the Communion, Archbishop Rowan Williams appointed a Lambeth Commission to explore the polity, relationships, and accountability of the Communion. The Commission produced the Windsor Report in 2004.

Commentators have used different explanations to elucidate the cultural politics of the homosexuality debate. Many employ the narrative of demographic shift of Christianity from the North to the South, popularized by Philip Jenkins's book, *The Next Christendom: The Coming of Global Christianity*.[39] Citing this global shift, critics are quick to point out that the majority of Anglicans now live in the South: the Church of Nigeria has approximately 17 million members, the Church of Uganda 8 million, while the Episcopal Church in the United States has only 2.5 million. Membership in mainline churches has been in decline in Europe and North America. The next Christendom, according to Jenkins, will be defined by the Southern churches, which tend to be theologically more conservative, while the influences of liberal mainline denominations will continue to decline. He further warns that if the Northern churches proclaim a moral stance more in line with progressive secular values, they are heading for a collision course with their Southern counterparts.

Conservative Episcopalians and many Southern Anglicans have used Jenkins's writings to bolster their position. But Jenkins's observations have received much criticism from other astute scholars of world Christianity. Vietnamese-American theologian Peter C. Phan has criticized Jenkins's use of the trope "Christendom" to describe Southern Christianity, for the term has exaggerated the power and influences of the South. Phan says that Christianity is still a small minority religion in Asia, and the prospects of Asian Christians forming political and ecclesiastical alliance with their counterparts in Latin America and Africa to build Christendom are remote.[40] Phan also faults Jenkins for his generalization of Southern Christianity as conservative and traditional, in sharp contrast with the more progressive and liberal Northern Christianity.

The criticism that Southern Christianity is conservative and traditional not only points to theological divergence, but carries with it vestiges of colonial conceptions of cultural difference. In colonial ideology, the colonized are depicted as "uncivilized," "savage," "childlike," and having yet to catch up with modernity. Some of these colonial stereotypes resurfaced in the homosexuality debate, as evident in Bishop Spong's condescending remarks toward Africans. Yet the binary construction of "tradition" and "modern," or "underdeveloped" and "developed," can also be deployed in subtler ways. For example, Kevin Ward, who has written a book on the history of global Anglicanism, states,

> The fact that the conflict has focused so fiercely on homo-
> sexuality is itself an indication of the way in which what
> is essentially a conflict within modern western secular
> society has spilled over to the rest of the world, itself
> coming to terms with modernity and the increasing domi-
> nance of secularity and its discontents.[41]

His remarks are problematic because he assumes that the South is lagging behind the West and is only "coming to terms with modernity" in a belated way. His suggestion of a "dominance of secularity" reflects a Western bias, which is not borne out in many societies in the South and the Middle East. Many scholars in the West have talked about a postsecular world, in which religion reenters the realms of politics and public life.

The discussion brings us to the second narrative commonly deployed to explain the Anglican conflict—that of a postcolonial backlash. Mark Chapman, for instance, states that "the global shift in Anglicanism was asserting itself," and describes what happened at Lambeth 1998 as a post-colonial "fight-back," with support from Western conservatives.[42] On the surface, such an analysis has its appeal because polygamy and other sexual practices in Africa had been under scrutiny and attack for more than a hundred years. In the midst of the homosexuality debate, several African bishops have turned the tables and called the American Church an unruly child that needs disciplining. By so doing, they reversed the "civilizing mission" of the West and claimed moral authority in expressing their righteous indignation.

Yet even as the commentators use the term "postcolonial," they have not applied postcolonial theories or insights to examine the postcolonial condition. Postcolonialism is not just about power reversal, but also about an engaged critique of the structures, ideologies, symbols, mentality, and legacy of colonialism. Many seasoned observers question whether colonial and neocolonial domination continues to operate within the Communion. Assessing Lambeth 1998, Ian T. Douglas and Julie Wortman asked whether there is the rise of a truly postcolonial world Anglicanism, in which the Southern Anglicans can participate fully alongside their Northern colleagues, or whether the Communion is still dominated by Northerners, who determine the rules of engagement for Southerners.[43] In her book, Hassett elucidates the material dependence of the Southern churches on the Northern churches and the asymmetry in the transna-tional Anglican alliances. Her conclusion is that "the relative wealth of the Northern churches continues to shape North/South relationships within the Communion. Southern Anglican moral dominance, so eagerly advocated by Northern conservatives, is balanced against, and limited by, continued Northern Anglican material dominance."[44]

Postcolonial theories question the rise of the postcolonial elites and their ascendancy to power after independence. Likewise, we should also question the colonial church structures that have granted so much power to Southern bishops. The bishops do not represent all the voices of the whole Church. One cannot just listen to what the loudest and most vocal bishops have said, without paying attention to other voices and the wide spectrum of perspectives. For example, while some African and other conservative bishops threatened to boycott Lambeth 2008, a group of Anglican women attending a United Nations Conference reiterated their commitment to remaining always "in communion" with and for one another amid deep divisions over sexuality in the Communion. The more than eighty women from thirty-four countries acknowledged global tensions in the Church, but did not "accept that there is any one issue of difference or contention which can, or indeed would, ever cause us to break the unity as represented by our common baptism."[45] Jenny Plane Te Paa from Aotearoa New Zealand, a member of the Commission that produced the Windsor Report, was explicit when she said, "The women of the Communion have, I believe, moved from bewilderment to outrage at the ways in which a small cabal of leaders have continued to insist that the issues exercising them alone over human sexuality are inevitably to preoccupy us as well."[46]

Postcolonial theorists challenge us to listen to the voices of the subaltern, people who are multiply oppressed and situated at the margins of society. African gay and lesbian activists continue to struggle for their human rights, even as some African bishops insist that homosexuality is a Western disease and there are no homosexual persons in their societies. Several gay, lesbian, bisexual, and transgender Anglicans were bold enough to appear in the documentary *Voices of Witness Africa* to share their stories of secrecy, challenges, and hope.[47] Other gay and lesbian activists worked with local and international supporters to protest against Uganda's anti-homosexuality bill and fought to repeal other legislation that criminalizes same-sex relations. In the conservative Anglican Province of Southeast Asia, Leng Lim started *Sanctuary*, the first gay and lesbian Christian fellowship in Singapore in 1992. He has written about his experiences of betrayal and struggle as an Asian gay man and remains active in speaking out against heterosexism after becoming an Episcopal priest.[48]

The controversies surrounding polygamy and homosexuality demonstrate that cultural difference shaped by race, gender, and sexuality has plagued the Anglican Communion from the beginning. From its start as a colonial church that was largely defined by its English character and Victorian understanding of gender roles and marriage, the Anglican Church encountered cultural customs and sexual practices very different from its own. After studying the changing positions of the Anglican Church on polygamy, Jones notes, "The established capacity of the Anglican Communion to tolerate alternative marriage patterns in postcolonial contexts provides a clear challenge to the repression of gay marriage among those living in post-sexual revolution contexts."[49] What he has not mentioned is that the repression is most keenly felt in those postcolonial contexts in which homosexuality can be punishable by death or prison terms. Whether the Anglican Communion will be divided over the issue of homosexuality remains to be seen.

The Future of Anglican Communion

Is the Anglican Communion a colonial relic that is no longer suitable for the postcolonial world? The Anglican Communion is a family of churches of resemblance. The Archbishop of Canterbury enjoys a primacy of honor (*primus inter pares*), but has no legal jurisdiction over other member churches. The resolutions of the Lambeth conferences are seen as advisory rather than legally binding on the autonomous member churches. In the past, some respect was at least shown to the Archbishop as first among equals. But the crisis in the 1990s threatened such bonds. More than a thousand lay and clergy delegates, including more than 291 Anglican bishops, attended the Global Anglican Future Conference in Jerusalem prior to Lambeth 2008. The Conference wanted to organize a new Fellowship of Confessing Anglicans. Its final statement declared, "we do not accept that Anglican identity is determined necessarily through recognition by the Archbishop of Canterbury," and contained "the Jerusalem Declaration," which is intended to form the doctrinal basis for such a new fellowship.[50]

To avoid schism and foster greater unity, the Windsor Report has recommended a pan-Anglican covenant as the way forward and included in the appendix a proposal of such a covenant.[51] Archbishop Williams appointed a Covenant Design Group in 2006 and several drafts were circulated for feedback from the churches.[52] The final version, released in December 2009, was sent for adoption by constituent provinces through appropriate processes.[53] The Anglican Covenant is disappointing in that it is more concerned about resolving conflicts and disciplinary proce-dures than about meeting the challenges of mission in the twenty-first century. Its theology of the Church hearkens back to the past, and shows a curious neglect of liberative impulses in churches across the globe in the second half of the twentieth century.

In the first section on faith commitments, the Covenant weaves together the Chicago-Lambeth Quadrilateral and other widely received documents. It states that the historic formularies of the Church of England "bear authentic witness" to Christian truth (1.1.2). The histor-ical formularies include the Thirty-nine Articles of Religion, the 1662 Book of Common Prayer, and the Ordering of Bishops, Priests, and Deacons. The Thirty-nine Articles have never been adopted by the whole Anglican Communion. The revision of the 1662 Prayer Book took place after Charles II restored the monarchy. The morning and evening prayers included prayers for the English monarch and the royal family. The image of the king was frequently used to describe God in the liturgies. It is regrettable that such patriarchal and historically contingent language is regarded as bearing "authentic" witness to Christian faith.

The Covenant asks the Church to "proclaim a pattern of theological and moral reasoning" based on Scripture and the catholic and apostolic faith. It places the primary responsibility of interpretation of Scripture in the hands of bishops and synods, although the study by lay and ordained scholars should also be taken into account (1.2.4). Instead of recognizing the plurality of ways that Scripture has been interpreted in different cul-tures, the Covenant is cautious about diversity and exhorts the churches to be mindful of the "common councils of the Communion" and the ecu-menical agreements (1.2.1). But as the debates on polygamy and homo-sexuality have clearly demonstrated, there are no easy agreements in the Communion on how Scripture should be interpreted.

Many people have criticized how the Covenant elevates the role and power of bishops, especially Primates, to the neglect of the work and ministry of the laity. "The proposed Anglican covenant says little about the role of the laity," Ruth Meyers notes.[54] She questions how the pro-posed covenant coheres with the emphasis on baptismal ministry in the Episcopal Church in the United States. The Covenant mentions baptism as one of the sacraments, but says little about the baptismal ministry that all who are baptized in Christ are called to do. This reflects a top-down and hierarchical understanding of the Church. Within such an ecclesi-ology, Ellen K. Wondra points out that the bishops are not seen as mem-bers of and a part of the *laos* (people of God). "The issue is that bishops are seen primarily if not entirely in relationship *with each other only*, in isolation from the rest of the Body of Christ," she writes.[55] The importance placed on the bishops as instruments of unity is backward-looking and does not reflect a robust theology of the laity, without which the Church cannot be vitalized.

The Covenant recommends that the Standing Committee of the Anglican Communion, consisting of members of the Primates' Meeting and the Anglican Consultative Council, become the organ to maintain the Covenant and to resolve disputes. Fredrica Harris Thompsett calls this new bureaucratic structure "a concentration of power at the highest levels of the Anglican Communion."[56] It is not clear how the creation of such a centralized body would affect the autonomy of member churches and avoid interference in their polity. As a church historian, she argues that such a development will not solve the present crisis, but acts against Anglican tradition, which understands authority to be dispersed throughout the Communion. Furthermore, the Covenant remains vague on the kind of actions that may provoke controversy and should be adjudicated by the Standing Committee. This opens the door to endless disputes and mutual accusations.

The crisis of the Anglican Communion can mean the danger of schism, but also opportunities for reflection and renewal. The second half of the twentieth century was marked by liberation movements within the Church and society. Formerly oppressed and marginalized groups, such as women, the poor, the youth, the Dalits, the indigenous, racial and ethnic minorities, and gays and lesbians have demanded their voices be heard and changed the ways that theology has been done. The role of laity has been emphasized in waves of renewals of the Church. The basic Christian communities in Latin America have inspired many Christians in the world to find new models of being Church. A leading Brazilian theologian, Leonardo Boff, writes, "Christian life in the basic communities is characterized by the absence of alienating structures, by direct relationships, by reciprocity, by a deep communion, by mutual assistance, by communality of gospel ideals, by equality among its members."[57] He calls this new experience of being Church *Ecclesiogenesis*.

The Anglican Church needs its *Ecclesiogenesis*. The danger of the Anglican Church today is that it will adopt expedient measures to avoid schism and shortchange the process of deep thinking about what the Church can become. Steeped in colonial history, the Anglican Church has much to learn to get rid of its colonial vestiges. This does not mean turning of the tables so that more power is given to the Southern churches over the Northern churches. This means reimagining a Communion that is truly global, multicultural, respecting differences and remaining in conversation and fellowship even when it becomes difficult. It means asking the difficult question of how the Church can come together as "disciples of equals,"[58] given the massive inequity of wealth and power in the world. If the Church can find a way to live out its commitment to mutual responsibility and interdependence, it can offer hope to a broken world and offer a foretaste for God's Kingdom. Many Anglicans would like to see the birth of such a new church: a church that is more concerned about God's mission than policing sexuality. A church that is not afraid of cultural difference, but welcomes diversity as its strength. A church that is not centralized or hierarchal, but celebrates democracy and participation of all who together constitute the Body of Christ.

Notes

1   W. M. Jacob, *The Making of the Anglican Church Worldwide* (London: SPCK, 1997), 151-69.

2   Lambeth Conference 1948, Resolutions 7 and 8, http://www.lambethconference.org/resolutions/downloads/1948.pdf.

3   Miranda K. Hassett, *Anglican Communion in Crisis: How Episcopal Dissidents and Their African Allies are Reshaping Anglicanism* (Princeton, NJ: Princeton University Press, 2007), 71. For Lambeth 2008, invitations were sent to 880 bishops, but only about 650 attended, because of the boycott by bishops who opposed homosexuality.

4   William L. Sachs, *The Transformation of Anglicanism* (Cambridge: Cambridge University Press, 1993); Jacob, *The Making of the Anglican Church Worldwide*; and Kevin Ward, *A History of Global Anglicanism* (Cambridge: Cambridge University Press, 2006).

5   Andrew Wingate, Kevin Ward, Carrie Pemberton, and Wilson Sitshebo, eds., *Anglicanism: A Global Communion* (London: Mowbray, 1998) and Ian T. Douglas and Kwok Pui-lan, eds., *Beyond Colonial Anglicanism: The Anglican Communion in the Twenty-first Century* (New York: Church Publishing, 2001).

6   Rowan Williams, "Why the Covenant Matters," March 5, 2012, http://www.archbishopofcanterbury.org/articles.php/2380/archbishop-why-the-covenant-matters.

7   "The Chicago-Lambeth Quadrilateral," http://anglicansonline.org/basics/Chicago_Lambeth.html.

8   Paul Avis, "Anglican Ecclesiology," in *The Routledge Companion to the Christian Church*, ed. Gerard Mannion and Lewis S. Mudge (New York: Routledge, 2008), 214.

9   Stephen Sykes, *Unashamed Anglicanism* (Nashville, TN: Abingdon, 1995), 125.

10 Avis, "Anglican Ecclesiology," 210-12.

11 Richard Hooker, *Of the Laws of Ecclesiastical Polity*, 2 vols. (London: G. M. Bent and Co., 1907).

12 Mark Chapman, *Anglicanism: A Very Short Introduction* (Oxford: Oxford University Press, 2006), 126.

13 Church of the Province of New Zealand, *A New Zealand Prayer Book* (Auckland: Collins, 1989).

14 Episcopal Church, *The Book of Common Prayer* (New York: Church Hymnal Corp., 1979).

15 "Eucharistic Food and Drink: A Report of the Inter-Anglican Liturgical Commission to the Anglican Consultative Council," http://www.anglicancommunion.org/resources/liturgy/docs/ialcreport.cfm.

16 Sachs, *The Transformation of Anglicanism*, 336.

17 Ian T. Douglas, "Authority, Unity, and Mission in the Windsor Report," *Anglican Theological Studies* 87 (2005): 573.

18 Ibid. This "mutual responsibility and interdependence in the body of Christ" was heralded in the 1963 Anglican Congress. See Stephen Fielding Bayne, *Mutual Responsibility and Interdependence in the Body of Christ* (New York: Seabury Press, 1963).

19 R. S. Sugirtharajah, *The Bible in the Third World: Precolonial, Colonial, and Postcolonial Encounters* (Cambridge: Cambridge University Press, 2001), 120-21.

20 Timothy Willem Jones, "The Missionaries' Position: Polygamy and Divorce in the Anglican Communion, 1888-1988," *Journal of Religious History* 35, no. 3 (2011): 395.

21 Ward, *A History of Global Anglicanism*, 139.

22 Lambeth Conference 1888, Resolution 5, http://www.lambethconference.org/resolutions/1888/1888-5.cfm.

23 Jones, "The Missionaries' Position," 401.

24 Lambeth Conference 1958, Resolution 120, http://www.lambethconference.org/resolutions/1958/1958-120.cfm.

25 Lambeth Conference 1968, Resolution 23, http://www.lambethconference.org/resolutions/1968/1968-23.cfm.

26 Esther Mombo, "The Bible and Polygamy: A Mothers' Union Perspective," *AICMAR Bulletin* 1 (2002): 35-41.

27 Felix K. Ekechi, "African Polygamy and Western Christian Ethnocentrism," *Journal of African Studies* 3, no. 3 (1976): 349, quoted in Jones, "The Missionaries' Position," 406.

28 A. O. Nkwoka, "The Church and Polygamy in Africa: The 1988 Lambeth Conference Resolution," *African Theological Journal* 19, no. 2 (1990): 140.

29 Mombo, "The Bible and Polygamy," 44.

30 Musimbi R. A. Kanyoro, "Engendered Communal Theology: African Women's Contribution to Theology in the Twenty-first Century," in *Hope Abundant: Third World and Indigenous Women's Theology*, ed. Kwok Pui-lan (Maryknoll, NY: Orbis Books, 2010), 30.

31 Vinay Samuel and Christopher Sugden, *Lambeth: A View from the Two Thirds World* (London: SPCK, 1988), 4.

32 Lambeth Conference 1988, Resolution 26, http://www.lambethconference.org/resolutions/1988/1988-26.cfm.

33 Jones, "The Missionaries' Position," 408.

34 Lambeth Conference 1988, Resolution 64, http://www.lambethconference.org/resolutions/1988/1988-64.cfm.

35 Hassett, *Anglican Communion*, 47-70.

36 Andrew Carey, "African Christians? They're Just a Step up from Witchcraft," *Church of England Newspaper*, July 10, 1998, quoted in ibid., 72.

37 James E. Solheim, *Diversity or Disunity: Reflections on Lambeth 1998* (New York: Church Publishing, 1999), 65.

38 Lambeth Conference 1998, Resolution 1.10, http://www.lambethconference.org/resolutions/1998/1998-1-10.cfm.

39 Philip Jenkins, *The Next Christendom: The Coming of Global Christianity*, rev. ed. (New York: Oxford University Press, 2007).

40 Peter C. Phan, "A New Christianity, But What Kind?" *Mission Studies* 21, no. 1 (2005): 75.

41 Ward, *A History of Global Anglicanism*, 315.

42 Chapman, *Anglicanism*, 139.

43 Ian T. Douglas and Julie Wortman, "Lambeth 1998: A Call to Awareness," *Witness*, September-October 1998, 24-25.

44 Hassett, *Anglican Communion*, 241.

45 "Solidarity Statement," Anglican Women's Empowerment, http://anglicanwomensempowerment. org/?page_id=46.

46 "Anglican Women Pledge Solidarity at UN Meeting," April 1, 2007, *Anglican Journal*, http://www. anglicanjournal.com/nc/other/news-items/archive/2007/04/article/anglican-women-pledge-solidarity-at-un-meeting-7237//abp/167.html.

47 Episodes of the documentary can be found on the *Voices of Witness* website, http://www. voicesofwitness.org/.

48 You-Leng Leroy Lim, "Webs of Betrayal, Webs of Blessings," in *Q & A: Queer in Asian America*, ed. David L. Eng and Alice Y. Hom (Philadelphia: Temple University Press, 1998), 323–34. See also, Leng Lim, Kim-Hao Yap and Tuck-Leong Lee, "The Mythic-Literalists in the Province of Southeast Asia," in *Other Voices, Other Worlds: The Global Church Speaks Out on Homosexuality*, ed. Terry Brown (New York: Church Publishing, 2006), 58-76.

49 Jones, "The Missionaries' Position," 408.

50 "Statement on the Global Anglican Future," June 28, 2008, GAFCON, http://gafcon.org/news/gafcon_final_statement.

51 Lambeth Comission on Communion, "The Windsor Report 2004, Appendix Two," http://www. anglicancommunion.org/windsor2004/appendix/p2.cfm.

52 Marilyn McCord Adams provides an astute analysis of the first two drafts of the Covenant. See "Unfit for Purpose: or, Why a Pan-Anglican Covenant at This Time Is a Very Bad Idea!" *Modern Believing* 49, no. 4 (2008): 23-45.

53 "The Anglican Communion Covenant," http://www.anglicancommunion.org/commission/covenant/final/text.cfm.

54 Ruth Meyers, "The Baptismal Covenant and the Proposed Anglican Covenant," in *The Genius of Anglicanism: Perspectives on the Proposed Anglican Covenant*, ed. Jim Naughton (Chicago: The Chicago Consultation, 2011), 13. http://www.chicagoconsultation.org/site/1/docs/Genius_of_Anglicanism_final. pdf.

55 Ellen K. Wondra, "Problems with Authority in the Anglican Communion," chapter 2 in this volume, #23.

56 Fredrica Harris Thompsett, "Inquiring Minds Want to Know: A Layperson's Perspective on the Proposed Anglican Covenant," in Naughton, *The Genius of Anglicanism*, 30.

57 Leonardo Boff, *Ecclesiogenesis: The Base Communities Reinvent the Church*, trans. Robert R. Barr (Maryknoll, NY: Orbis Books, 1986), 4.

58 Elisabeth Schüssler Fiorenza, *In Memory of Her: A Feminist Theological Reconstruction of Christian Origins*, tenth anniversary ed. (New York: Crossroad, 1994), 140, 150.

2

PROBLEMS WITH AUTHORITY IN THE ANGLICAN COMMUNION

Ellen K. Wondra

Much of the conflict and dis-ease in the Anglican Communion over the last fifty years has been prompted by quite explicit issues of gender, sexuality, race and ethnicity, and continuing colonialism. These disputes have made it clear that there are a number of other issues at work as well: the interpretation of Scripture, what constitutes communion in a global Church in the twenty-first century, the nature and exercise of authority in the Church, and so on. Many of the official reports addressing the current conflicts focus on these latter issues. And they are important, no doubt about that. But often discussions of Scripture, communion, and authority address these matters as if social location does not matter. That is, from these reports it appears that these pressing ecclesiological questions can be worked out without more than an occasional reference to the concrete realities of difference, which is to say, the concrete, real, lived differences in power and authority found in everyday life in and out of the Church.[1]

To put it simply: difference matters. Gender matters. Race, ethnicity, sexual identity, social and historical location relative to social structures including colonialism—all these matter. Yet little attention is paid to any of these, let alone to their central role in forming the very traditions of theology and practice that are at the Church's foundations.[2] The critical inquiries, insights, and constructive projects of feminist and postcolonial theologians and their allies consistently press the question beyond the observable and official role of women in the Church and the anthropological language of the Book of Common Prayer. But their work is resisted: officially commissioned church reports, resolutions, and actions reiterate the conviction that the Church as it is, is justified and sanctified by its founding traditions, themselves cast as the revelation and inspiration by God for the Church's good. Beyond that, the response has often been to incorporate a few persons into dominant forms that change little, thereby in large measure denying that difference is of much real importance at all. That is, reports consistently adopt the familiar rhetorical strategy of identifying a particular strand of Scripture, such as *koinonia* or communion, along with particular Scriptural passages related to the strand in a particular way, in order to ground a specific theological and ecclesiological point of view that then has (ostensibly) clear outworkings in ecclesial structures and practices.

To be clear: there is nothing wrong with this strategy *as such*, and it demonstrates that what many consider a properly Anglican argument is being made in that it uses Scripture as the primary source, supported and elaborated by widely held and widely recognized traditions and by forms of reason that are recognizable in their form and their content. Further, these reports contribute crucial concepts and insights that have helped Anglicans deal with difference among themselves and in relation to other Christians. The most significant of these is the notion of Church as communion, an interrelationship among churches and with God in which particular identities, practices, cultures, and so on contribute to a unity that is the human, historical image of the interdependent and mutual relations of the Persons of the Holy Trinity.[3] Communion (or *koinonia* or *communio*) ecclesiology has proven crucial in moving past certain ecumenical impasses and, as The Virginia Report (1997) of the Inter-Anglican Theological and Doctrinal Commission (IATDC) suggests, it has great promise for providing a theological framework for understanding diversity.[4] The same must be said for the concepts of distributed or dispersed authority,[5] synodality,[6] and subsidiarity[7]—concepts that are required to make current crises bearable and to resolve them.

At the same time, in many of these reports, there is little or no evidence that adequate study has been made of how the particular theme (such as communion) is understood in the context of the rest of Scripture, or in the sociohistorical contexts of Scripture and interpretation, down through the ages. Similarly, there is little or no evidence that the historical traditions and contemporary corollaries adduced have been examined critically in light of their origins and contexts or their history of interpretations and effects. What evidence is adduced often comes from well-known theologians and from other church documents, which, regardless of their formal status—or lack thereof—gain authority from this use.[8] Critical commentary and response seems largely ignored, indicated in part by the fact that each successive document is often criticized for the same omissions, preferences, and methodological inadequacies as its predecessors.

The Eclipse of the Laity

To give but one example: a major criticism has often been that these reports ignore the role of the laity in the Church[9]—the largest and most foundational "order" in the Church,[10] and the only one where the majority are women, and where women's existing ministries and missional orientation are the most evident. The reports also see deacons and priests in light of their relationship to bishops rather than the company of the baptized overall, or their importance in the mission of reconciliation that the Church has in the world. Instead, these reports almost inevitably focus on the office and authority of the ordained episcopate—the bishops—and on the inter-relationship—the collegiality—of bishops as being of primary importance to the unity and mission of the Church.[11]

To put it another way, these reports do not focus on bishops as members of and participants in the overall *laos*, nor on the specific responsibility for communion and continuity that bishops hold within that *laos*, a responsibility they do not exercise alone either within or beyond their dioceses. Rather, the issue is that bishops are seen primarily if not entirely in relationship *with each other only*, in isolation from the rest of the Body of Christ. Obviously, bishops form an elite, and, with a very few exceptions, they are privileged males—privileged in Church, privileged in society.

Official and quasi-official responses to this criticism are familiar as well. There have been bishops from earliest—though perhaps not Scriptural—times.[12] The fact that most Christian bodies over time and space have affirmed and supported the leadership of bishops *may* be a sign of divine providence,[13] so that one might reasonably conclude that bishops are of the *bene esse* (the benefit of the Church) though not necessarily the *esse* (necessary essence) of the Church. And there is broad ecumenical agreement at the highest levels that the coming, united Church for which Christ prayed will maintain the historic episcopate and its centrality in sacramental life, in teaching and governance, and so on. None of this is what is being criticized, however. Rather, what is problematic is the often-reiterated official view that the prelates of the Church are leaders who together determine the shape of the Church and its mission, but are not equivalently or reciprocally authorized, influenced, or even directed by the day to day life of the Church and its members in the midst of quite concrete sociocultural realities—a life in which the majority of participants are not elites (at least in church terms) and are not men.

Again, the problem is not bishops as such. Neither is it leadership, nor even hierarchical structure as such. Rather it is that leadership is portrayed as legitimately, even desirably, exercised outside of relationship with the larger body of the Church, and outside of relationship with the concrete, historical contexts in and through which all human life— including the lives of leaders—is lived. This ecclesiology is connected to actual ecclesial practice as an ideal that should shape the practical, but should not be shaped by it.

The bases of this ideal are clearly patriarchal or, better, kyriarchal, in origin.[14] That is, this notion of the ideal in a one-way relationship with the practical or real springs from and reflects a context in which society is structured with the many, male and female, subordinate to the few (generally males of the ruling group), and with that subordination seen as natural (i.e., given by nature and/or the divine) and necessary, in that the subordinate groups lack characteristics essential to full humanity, a full humanity that is evident in the dominant group. Whatever the teachings of Jesus and the impulses of at least some early Christian groups,[15] it did not take long for nascent Christianity to adopt and adapt the dominant social arrangements of the Greco-Roman world and the Roman Empire.

No doubt, these social arrangements and cultural forms captured something of the encounter with the divine; but that is not all they have done. They also give legitimation to the very kyriarchal images and structures they have borrowed, images and structures that continue today, even as they have been and are contested by past and present alternatives, by critical examination, and by imaginations of a different future. At the same time, what legitimates also subverts: portraying God in the image of rulers not only gives shape to the experience of God and legitimacy to rulers; it also suggests that rulers and the dominant system are themselves subject to something that transcends, undermines, or surpasses them.

In fact, this is one of the factors prompting the continuing conflicts and dis-ease in the Anglican Communion: dominant systems no longer have the legitimacy they once had. Scripture is no longer read only as commanding obedience to earthly rulers whose legitimacy derives from God (the customary reading of Rom. 13); it also narrates resistance to oppressive structures and liberation based on fidelity to God first and foremost. Tradition not only portrays a largely harmonious, steady development of a church faithful to the Gospel; it also provides contested alternatives that have destabilized the familiar and redefined fidelity again and again and again. Theology is not merely a set of propositions the faithful are to accept on faith; it is also a reaching toward mystery, a poetic construction, an account of how the divine interrupts all human plans. Reason is shown to include the affective, the unconscious, the experiential, the political. Scripture, tradition, theology, and reason: these are the fundamentals of ecclesiology, and as understanding of them changes, so must ecclesiology. Otherwise, it will lose its capacity to spark imagination and vision of what Christian communities of faith might be like.

So, yes, the Anglican Communion is facing a crisis of authority, and a pervasive one at that. And yes, that crisis is prompted by the insistence of women and men of all races, ethnicities, ages, and sexual identities that they be treated as who they are: baptized members of the Body of Christ, created, redeemed, loved, and empowered by God. Anglicans are having a crisis of authority not because certain people are rebellious, misguided, or ignorant. We are having a crisis because customary forms and instruments of authority are losing their legitimacy precisely because they are no longer able to provide what they promise: communion and effective modes of mission for those who have seen Jesus.

The Anglican Covenant cannot ease this crisis. Even though it now includes the Marks of Mission,[16] it can only exacerbate the situation. The same must be said of the other reports of the last several years, including the IATDC's *Communion, Conflict, and Hope*[17] (which at least acknowledges that difference and conflict are signs of life and hope rather than inevitable decay and disaster). These and reports like them will not be satisfactory or helpful until they overcome the split between ecclesiology and ecclesial life and practice so that ecclesiology not only shapes but is shaped by the lives and witness of ordinary Christians who are gendered, sexual, postcolonial subjects whose races and ethnicities are integral to who they are and how they live. Only when ecclesiology is explicitly shaped by actual ecclesial life with all its difference can it serve its purpose of informing reflection and stimulating imagination and vision of what it means to be a faithful community following Christ.

A crucial aspect of this needed reform of ecclesiological method, I think, is a more adequate description of how authority actually operates in the Church—of how authority is constituted, legitimated, and conferred, and how it is exercised and by whom. Most ecclesiological accounts of authority and of processes of legitimation are paltry, unhelpfully scant, and thin.[18] They tend to focus on the decision-making powers of the hierarchically highest group in the Church—for Anglicans, the bishops.

Thereby they obscure the complexity and importance of the exercise of authority in three dimensions: what kind of authority is exercised, in what areas of the Church's life and mission authority is exercised, and who legitimately exercises it. The effect of these minimalist accounts in ecclesiology is two-fold. At first and even second reading, they convey a degree of apparent commonality, agreement, and consensus, common ground on the basis of which unity can be established and maintained within "the appropriate range of diversity"[19] and the prospect of greater harmony and less conflict. But at the same time, these accounts obscure, ignore, and suppress the actual differences that exist, as if all difference is only divisive and not potentially enriching. This renders these accounts unreal and non-credible, aggravating misunderstanding, dis-ease, and conflict rather than contributing to creative and constructive resolution.

Authority in the Anglican Communion

In the rest of this chapter, then, I want to sketch the general outlines of a more adequate description of authority in the Anglican Communion. I do so as a white woman who is a member, priest, and teaching theologian of the Episcopal Church in the United States, fully mindful that my knowledge and experience are both privileged and limited. I have had the opportunity to ponder these matters deeply and discuss them with others as a participant in a number of ecumenical dialogues. My most profound experience has been as a long-time member of the Anglican-Roman Catholic Consultation in the United States (ARC-USA), where as an ordained woman I have been the embodied presence of a reality others in the dialogue have found impossible to conceive. I claim anything but objective and universal knowledge and understanding here.

In the Church, human authority is understood as originating first and foremost in God: all authority derives from God's authority, the clearest sense of which comes from Scripture and, for human authority, preeminently from the life and ministry of Jesus. So human authority is properly used only in service of the mission and purposes of God: reconciliation, service, teaching, and increasing the well-being of all God's creatures. Authority is exercised for the good of creation, not for coercion or the maintenance of injustice, dehumanization, and degradation. Of course this view of authority is both an ideal and an eschatological hope, and it is treated as such in the various reports upon which I have drawn. This view of authority, drawn from Scripture, from theological and ecclesial traditions over centuries, and from reason coupled with conventional experience, then legitimates the actual exercise of authority within the Church.

Authority is also granted, conferred, or recognized. It cannot simply be claimed or asserted. Whatever authority is claimed for an office is only effective insofar as the exercise of authority by that office is seen by those who receive it as legitimate, credible, and pertinent to some desired good or purpose. Authority requires compliance; legitimacy requires recognition. Without these, authority does not exist.

From earliest times, baptism has been what incorporates women and men into the Body of Christ and legitimates their participation within the scope of their ecclesial status or "order." They are called to be faithful followers of Christ and witnesses to God's saving work in the world. A major component of this has been obedience, first and foremost to God, and also to God's legitimate representatives within the Church, the ordained who exercise *episcope* or oversight—generally though not only bishops (*episcopoi*)—and those to whom some measure of *episcope* has been delegated, such as priests, deacons, and secular rulers at various levels. Priests' and deacons' faculties and authorities derive from those of the bishops, who alone can convey and legitimate this authority. Among bishops there is a hierarchy as well, of course, initially based on the importance of the see city, conveyed perhaps by its association with particular apostles and martyrs, perhaps by its importance as a center of trade and secular power. With the Protestant and Catholic Reformations and later reforms associated with the twentieth-century ecumenical movement and the Vatican Council II, these hierarchies have been softened and to some extent flattened, and various modes of accountability to those "below" as well as those "above" have been added. Yet the notion that this ordering is established by God, either directly or through the workings of providence over time, is still maintained, particularly among the more hierarchically ordered churches, such as those of the Anglican Communion. While the ministers of the Church may be "the baptized, bishops, priests, and deacons,"[20] the scope, limitations, and responsibilities of each order vary, and are arranged in a hierarchy of authority and accountability.

Or so it would appear. The ecclesiological descriptions and definitions of authority within these arrangements do not reflect how authority is actually exercised. And in part this is because these accounts do not tend to the relationships between the various orders other than in a "top down" manner. Nor do they differentiate between degrees of authority, or between the various areas of church life where authority is in fact exercised.

Generally in ecclesiology, authority is taken, first, to be conferred and legitimated by God through sacramental means such as baptism and ordination, and second, to involve the making of various types of decisions and judgments that conduce to harmonious order. Thus, those with a high degree of authority have responsibility for governance and discipline and for teaching (both doctrine and morals), as well as for the Church's sacramental life, and in these areas they are empowered to make legitimate and legitimating decisions that, it is expected, will command respect and compliance if not obedience.

But decision making, as important as it is, is not the only degree or type of authority there is in practice. In the process of decision making, other authority-laden activities are often involved. Decision-making persons or bodies may be required to consult with others, individuals and groups; and their counsel must be seen to be taken into account. Otherwise, decisions may be illegitimate or invalid. So consultants have a degree of authority short of decision making. The same may be true of advisors or advisory bodies, consultation with whom is not formally required, but is expected as a matter of wisdom and prudence; advisors too have a degree of authority. Further, decisions must be implemented, so that those with the ability and responsibility to carry out decisions—or to fail or refuse to do so—also have a degree of authority. A similar analysis of areas of church life is instructive as well, and the fact that bishops have a high degree of authority in the Church's sacramental life and in its governance does not inevitably mean that they have the same degree of authority in management, financial, pastoral, and other matters.

Church constitutions, canon law, by-laws, and the like may spell this out formally, but beyond these official statements there is the informal exercise of authority, based on relationships that are given as well as those that are chosen. That is, whether a bishop chooses her or his own financial advisors or inherits them upon consecration, the bishop cannot effectively lead the diocese without at least a functioning relationship with them. And by definition, that means that the advisors exercise some degree of authority in this area of the church's life.

This thicker description of the distribution or dispersal of authority brings into view the likelihood that even the most formal of decisions by the individual or body placed highest in the hierarchy of authority is in fact the construction of a range of people and groups other than the stipulated decision maker(s). And any decision generally requires persons other than the decision maker(s) to carry it out.

Looked at in this way, it is clear that while a certain degree and scope of formal authority may be conferred on bishops alone, how they are able to exercise that authority relies on the participation of others—often lay people as well as priests and deacons. In some cases, this shared authority may be specified in formal statements such as canon law. But even when it is not, *informal* authority is almost always a factor: decision making involves relationships beyond those that may be officially or formally prescribed. These relationships likely involve influence and persuasion and they are more or less likely to make effecting a decision easier or more difficult. It is also at the informal level that the effectiveness of any attempt to exercise authority is negotiated, in that authority is not just claimed but also granted. What this means quite concretely is that women and men of many different ecclesial and social locations are integral to the exercise of authority.

This fact, though, is obscured by two things. First, it is extremely difficult to give an adequate account of how informal authority operates over time in a given location or area of the Church's life. Too many people and too many variable factors are involved. As I have indicated earlier there are multiple overlapping areas in which authority is exercised—for example, worship (including preaching and sacraments), pastoral oversight, formal governance, financial planning and management. And there are multiple degrees or types of authority—modes or processes of decision making, consultation, advising, implementation. Authority is exercised by a wide range of people with different roles and offices, only some of which are formally or officially described. And, second and most crucially, how individuals and groups exercise authority is always—*always*—influenced though not determined by social location, cultural history, expectations and fears for the future, and the like, even when these have no explicit or overt relationship to the ecclesial matters at hand.

The preferred mode of dealing with this complexity has been to focus accounts of authority primarily on the most powerful and prominent offices and individuals involved, as is the case in ecclesiological statements with their emphases on bishops and their relative silence on the majority of the baptized.[21] This does not render these accounts useless. To the contrary, they serve as generally helpful overviews of how authority works, and they provide aspirational visions of how authority *ought* more nearly to work not only in an ideal church but in the actual, historical ones being studied. However, it is vital to remember three things about these accounts.

First, these accounts are ultimately constructive or prescriptive rather than merely descriptive. That is, they are constructed to move present practices, realities, and understandings in a particular direction, one of greater theological and ecclesial coherence, consistency, and unity in which conflicts are rendered bearable if not resolved.

Second, these accounts are produced by individuals and groups who are presenting these accounts on behalf of a particular church in order to further particular purposes, such as greater communion or unity within the worldwide Anglican Communion[22] or a greater degree of understanding and cooperation between Episcopalians and Roman Catholics in the United States.[23]

Third, and often overlooked, these accounts are thin or minimalist descriptions of a thicker reality, and as such their sufficiency is questionable. As social scientist Michael Walzer writes, moral and other arguments one group presents to another are thin or minimalist in the sense that they reiterate particular features of a larger reality whose full (thick or maximalist) descriptions are characterized by "qualification, compromise, complexity, and disagreement."[24] Thin descriptions cannot be used alone to ground or warrant universal claims. Thin descriptions, properly understood, are "close to the bone."[25] "[M]inimalism provides a critical perspective."[26] But Walzer says, "I want to stress again that the moral minimum is not a free-standing morality. It simply designates some reiterated features of particular thick or maximal moralities."[27] He writes:

> Minimalism makes for a certain limited, though important and heartening, solidarity. It doesn't make for a full-blooded universal doctrine . . . It explains how it is that we come together; it warrants our separation. By its very thinness, it justifies us in returning to the thickness that is our own. The morality in which the moral minimum is embedded, and from which it can only temporarily be abstracted, is the only full-blooded morality we can ever have.[28]

Thin descriptions articulate insights that conduce to solidarity across groups, solidarity that is at risk because of some sort of social (here, ecclesial) crisis. But a thin description cannot do so effectively unless it is truly "close to the bone," that is, unless it "designates some reiterated features of particular thick or maximal moralities" and other accounts.[29]

The accounts of authority I have been referring to in this chapter fall short of this criterion in that they omit key moral and social realities related to the distribution and use of various modalities of power, access to resources, and capacity to speak and be heard—which is to say that they are not sufficiently "close to the bone" to promote solidarity across difference. Rather, through their omissions they claim a kind of universality that negates the real import of difference.[30] And in any event, as thin descriptions they must be seen and used in light of much thicker and more accurate descriptions of the diverse realities from which they are abstracted.

In my discussion of official accounts of authority in the Church, I have suggested three things that guide my proposals for an account of authority that takes into account social location and sociocultural and historical locations and practices.

First, official accounts of ecclesiology and so of authority do not adequately reflect the actual practices of the Church relative to worship, missional and pastoral life, governance, and daily life. Ecclesiology focuses on a thin description of the Church; it is oriented toward an ideal that is often universalized; and its explicit attention to actual ecclesial practice often takes the form of critique of particular practices (such as the ordination of women or of LGBT persons) that are viewed as in need of significant reform.

Second, official accounts of authority continue to be patterned on patriarchal or kyriarchal and imperial theology, without adequate critique of this pattern. This is apparent, for example, in official documents' accounts of contemporary struggles relative to gender and sexuality as compared to the accounts rendered by those most directly involved or affected.[31]

Third, these accounts fail to recognize that social location matters. *All* persons are gendered, not just women; *all* persons are formed and influenced within culturally various notions of race and ethnicity, of sexuality, of class and status, of location relative to culture and economic centers and margins. Furthermore, ideas and norms (including theology and doctrine), organizations, structures, and institutions as well as polity and practice are deeply influenced by and influence the gender, racial/ethnic, sexual, class, and other characteristics associated with particular persons and groups. Social location always matters. It is not an accidental characteristic of an essential universal human.[32] Social location is an inevitable aspect of what it means to be human persons, human groups.

Any discussion of authority that might be adequate to the needs of contemporary communities of faith, Anglican and otherwise, must take these things into account. To put it another way, adequate discussions of authority will be based in thick descriptions of actual human relationships, formal (official, structural) and informal, group and individual. For views of the nature and exercise of authority are theorized from experience within and over against cultural norms and frameworks.

Contemporary Account of Authority

Any relatively adequate, contemporary account of authority must be grounded in a description and analysis of social structures and characteristics such as gender, race/ethnicity, and class in the concrete locations considered. Actual practices and enactments of authority must be looked at closely, and in relation to larger aspects of daily life in and outside the Church. These analyses need to use theories of power, organization, culture, personal and cultural development, and so on that themselves recognize not just diversity but difference, that recognize that various material and cultural resources are distributed and used differently on the basis of deep-seated, culturally embedded notions of gender, race, class, and so on. In practice, this means deliberate, thorough attention to the experience and analysis, to the practices and reflections of those who are marginalized and silenced but who nonetheless are human agents who are always involved in the making of their own lives, however much their agency may be curtailed.[33]

Second, contemporary accounts of authority must look closely and critically at the theological and cultural assumptions that are embedded in how questions and topics are phrased, what resources are considered useful, adequate, and authoritative, and how analyses and constructive positions are shaped relative to presumptive audience. There is no question that theology, ecclesiology, and Christian practices of various sorts have deep, complex roots in kyriarchal and imperial modes of thought and practice. Certainly, these are not their only roots. But this sociohistorical reality cannot be bracketed, ignored, or suppressed. The demonstrable inability of official documents to help resolve current disputes is sufficient evidence of this claim, as I have argued previously.

Third, contemporary accounts of authority must attend to the full range of ecclesial life as well as ecclesiological accounts of what we hope the Church might become by the grace of God, or what the Church ought to be if only everyone shared a right understanding. Official statements, the work of well-known theologians, historical precedents, and the history of doctrine are not in themselves enough. Anglicans are fond of saying that praying shapes believing (*lex orandi, lex credendi*), so it would be "natural" to turn as well to liturgies (including rubrics, ceremonials, hymnals, collects, and the like), sermons, spiritual and moral guides, and so on. Also important are various narrative and analytic accounts of church practices as well as qualitative research with participants in church life. In other words, theological scholars interested in ecclesiology and the theology and practice of authority must broaden their own use of sources and their skills in research and analysis, working in a way that is consistently more interdisciplinary, multicultural, and grounded in practices of daily life.

Studies of this sort are likely to reveal, for example, that in churches where women's formal participation in ordained ministry or high-level church councils is minimal, individual women and women's groups such as the Mothers' Union are major actors in actually implementing decisions and programs, particularly those having to do with daily life and fundamental human survival and thriving, which is to say to the Church's mission in the world. How women carry out these programs, how they use human and material resources, what they say and do not say and to whom—all of this is exercising authority, even though it may not be officially provided for in, for example, the canon law or diocesan by-laws of a particular church.

In turn, this produces a very different ecclesiology of the role of laity relative to bishops than is found in ARCIC's *Gift of Authority* and/or any version of the Anglican Covenant. On the view I am presenting here, lay people's reception of church teaching and programs is not only quite active,[34] it is a key component in the Church's capacity to embody the Gospel in outward and visible ways in particular contexts. To continue with the example earlier: official church bodies and leaders may mandate teachings and programs about sexual activity as it relates to HIV/AIDS, but teachings do not become effective as part of the life of persons and communities of faith unless and until they are embraced in practice by women in local communities. From a different angle, on the view presented here, church theological and moral teachings on environmental and economic sustainability ought to grow out of careful theological reflection on how sustainability is being practiced in particular locations, reflections that involve those engaged in sustainable practices. When this is the approach taken, it is more likely that such teachings will be granted a much greater degree of authority than some of them currently receive, precisely because they acknowledge the ways in which the Gospel is being faithfully incarnated in the daily lives of the members of the Body of Christ.

None of this is to suggest that contemporary accounts of authority coming from formally constituted bodies have nothing to offer. To the contrary. Some of the most important concepts in current ecclesiology— Church as communion, synodality, subsidiarity, reception, and more— already point in the direction I have sketched here.

But more is needed. Those who study and think and speak and write about authority and about the Church need a larger methodological imagination than they have found it necessary to use. After all, members of marginalized and suppressed groups have been resisting and proposing alternatives to prevailing views throughout history. In an era of mass communication such as we have lived in for at least half a century, there is no credible reason that these "different voices" are not being heard. This means that beyond methodological imagination there is also a need for greater moral courage to risk listening to the different voices who so eagerly offer their practice and wisdom to the Church of the God they follow. When such listening begins to be evident in official reports and discussions of authority, they will have greater credibility. They will begin to make a real difference. Short of this, though, Anglicans will continue to have deep-seated, pervasive, and persistent problems with authority.

Notes

1 Postcolonial theorists Homi Bhabha and Kwok Pui-lan make an important distinction between "difference" and "diversity," which I am following here. In common discourse, "diversity" refers to "different cultures as mutually interacting and competing on the same footing in the public square." By contrast, "the term 'cultural difference'. . . underscore[s] the interaction of cultures in the postcolonial world is always imbued with power and authority." See Kwok Pui-lan, *Postcolonial Imagination and Feminist Theology* (Louisville, KY: Westminster John Knox Press, 2005), 42-43.

2 For example, the 1986 report by the Inter-Anglican Theological and Doctrinal Commission (IATDC), *For the Sake of the Kingdom*, whose purpose was "an exploration of the complex relations between the Gospel and social or cultural forms in the light of the central assertion of the Gospel itself—that the Kingdom of God is at hand" (paragraph 4), does not use the words women or gender at all, whereas it refers to race only twice and colonialism only eleven times. http://www.anglicancommunion.org/ministry/theological/iatdc/docs/for_the_sake_of_the_kingdom_1986.pdf.

3 The literature on this is vast and continues to grow. See particularly Jean-Marie Tillard, *Eglise d'Eglises: L'ecclesiologie de communion* (Paris: Cerf, 1987); John D. Zizioulas, *Being as Communion: Studies in Personhood and the Church* (Crestwood, NY: St. Vladimir's Seminary Press, 1985); and John D. Zizioulas, *Communion as Otherness: Further Studies in Personhood and the Church* (London: T & T Clark, 2006). IATDC's Virginia Report gives a basic Anglican reading, http://www.lambethconference.org/1998/documents/report-1.pdf

4 IATDC, Virginia Report, ch. 5.

5 The concept that Anglicans disperse authority is articulated in The Lambeth Conference 1948, Report No. IV, "The Anglican Communion," 84-85 quoted in Stephen Sykes, "Authority in the Church of England," in Stephen Sykes, *Unashamed Anglicanism* (Nashville, TN: Abingdon Press, 1995), 168-69.

6   Synodality refers to structures and decision-making processes in which bishops, other clergy, and laity work together formally and informally to provide for the oversight and guidance of the church. Synodality is structured into the Anglican Communion's instruments of communion, most obviously in the Anglican Consultative Council, whose formal membership includes laity and clergy in equal numbers with bishops.

7   Subsidiarity is the idea that ecclesial decisions and tasks of many sorts ought to be performed at the most immediate or local level possible—but in a way that continuity and consistency can be maintained. See Virginia Report, 4.8-4.18.

8   This has certainly been the case with the 1997 Virginia Report. Prepared at the request of the 1988 Lambeth Conference of Anglican bishops, the 1998 Lambeth Conference quite simply "welcome[d]" the report "as a helpful statement of the characteristics of our Communion"; it did not approve it or deem it authoritative. However, The Virginia Report is used as an authoritative source in the 2004 Windsor Report, IATDC's 2008 *Communion, Conflict, and Hope*, the various drafts of the Anglican Covenant, and a number of agreed statements from officially constituted international ecumenical dialogues. In the order of reference: IATDC, The Virginia Report. Lambeth Conference 1998, Resolution III.8; http://www.lambethconference.org/resolutions/1998/1998-3-8.cfm. Lambeth Commission on Communion, The Windsor Report 2004, http://www.anglicancommunion.org/windsor2004. IATDC, *Communion, Conflict, and Hope* (London: Anglican Communion Office, 2008), http://www.aco.org/ministry/theological/iatdc/docs/communion_conflict_&_hope.pdf. Material on the Anglican Covenant, including all drafts and some supporting material, is available at http://www.anglicancommunion.org/commission/covenant/index.cfm.

9   See, for example, the 2003 "Response of the Anglican-Roman Catholic Consultation in the USA to the Anglican-Roman Catholic International Commission's *The Gift of Authority*," http://old.usccb.org/comm/archives/2003/03-075.shtml#1; and the 2012 "Executive Council D020 Task Force on the Response to the Anglican Covenant" (The Office of the General Convention of the Episcopal Church, *Report to the 77th General Convention Otherwise Known as The Blue Book*. Reports of the Committees, Commissions, Agencies, and Boards of The General Convention of the Episcopal Church, 2012, 633-37), http://generalconvention.org/gc/prepare.

10 According to the Catechism in the 1979 Book of Common Prayer of the Episcopal Church (BCP), "The ministers of the Church are lay persons, bishops, priests, and deacons." (*The Book of Common Prayer* [New York: Oxford University Press, 1979], 855.)

11 In addition to the reports already cited, see *Report of the Archbishop of Canterbury's Commission on Communion and Women in the Episcopate* (London: Church House Publishing, for the Anglican Consultative Council, 1989); IATDC, *For the Sake of the Kingdom: God's Church and the New Creation* (London: Published for the Anglican Consultative Council by Church House Publishing, 1986), http://www.anglicancommunion.org/ministry/theological/iatdc/docs/for_the_sake_of_the_kingdom_1986.pdf; Anglican-Roman Catholic International Commission (ARCIC), *Authority in the Church I* 1977, http://www.pro.urbe.it/dia-int/arcic/doc/e_arcic_authority1.html; ARCIC, *Authority in the Church II* 1981, http://www.pro.urbe.it/dia-int/arcic/doc/e_arcic_authority2.html; and ARCIC, *The Gift of Authority: Authority in the Church III* 1998, http://www.pro.urbe.it/dia-int/arcic/doc/e_arcicII_05.html.

12 For example, ARCIC, *Ministry and Ordination* 1973, Introduction 6, http://www.pro.urbe.it/dia-int/arcic/doc/e_arcic_ministry.html.

13 Lutheran Episcopal Coordinating Committee, *Commentary on "Called to Common Mission,"* 2002, esp. the section "Agreements in Ministry" and comments thereupon, http://www.elca.org/Who-We-Are/Our-Three-Expressions/Churchwide-Organization/Office-of-the-Presiding-Bishop/Ecumenical-and-Inter-Religious-Relations/Resources/All-Resources/LuthEpiscopal-Resources.aspx.

14 Elisabeth Schüssler Fiorenza uses the term "kyriarchy" to refer to "the rule of the emperor/master/lord/father/husband over his subordinates," see, *Jesus: Miriam's Child, Sophia's Prophet* (New York: Continuum, 1994), 14.

15 Elisabeth Schüssler Fiorenza, *In Memory of Her: A Feminist Theological Reconstruction of Christian Origins* (New York: Crossroad, 1983), and *Discipleship of Equals: A Critical Feminist Ekklesialogy of Liberation* (New York: Crossroad, 1993), and throughout her work.

16 Covenant Design Group, *The Anglican Communion Covenant* 2009, 2.2.2, http://www.anglicancommunion.org/commission/covenant/final/text.cfm.

17 IATDC, *Communion, Conflict, and Hope.*

18 Michael Walzer, *Thick and Thin: Moral Argument at Home and Abroad* (Notre Dame: University of Notre Dame Press, 1994). See the discussion of thick and thin arguments in the next section.

19 Lambeth Commission on Communion, Windsor Report, 5.

20 BCP, "Catechism," 95.

21 The reason given for this is often that it is this level of authority that is the most contested. However, when authority is viewed relationally, this reason is not convincing.

22 For example, the various documents of the IATDC referred to in this chapter.

23 For example, the documents of international and national Anglican-Roman Catholic dialogues published in Joseph W. Witmer and J. Robert Wright , eds., *Called to Full Unity* (Washington: USCCB, 1986); and Jeffrey Gros et al., eds., *Common Witness to the Gospel: Documents on Anglican-Roman Catholic Relations, 1983-1995* (Washington: United States Catholic Conference, 1997).

24 Walzer, *Thick and Thin*, 3-6.

25 Ibid., 6.

26 Ibid., 10.

27 Ibid.

28 Ibid., 11.

29 Ibid., 10.

30 Walzer writes: "Societies are necessarily particular because they have members and memories, members with memories not only of their own but also of their common life. Humanity, by contrast, has members but no memory, and so it has no history and no culture, no customary practices, no familiar life-ways, no festivals, no shared understanding of social goods. It is human to have such things, but there is no singular human way of having them. At the same time, the members of all the different societies, because they are human, can acknowledge each other's different ways, respond to each other's cries for help, learn from each other, and march (sometimes) in each other's parades." Ibid., 8.

31 See, for example, the quite different accounts of the movement for the ordination of women in the Episcopal Church and Anglican Communion in IATDC, Virginia Report, 4.15ff., and Lambeth Commission on Communion, Windsor Report, 12ff., on the one hand, and on the other, Heather Ann Huyck, *To Celebrate a Whole Priesthood:The History of Women's Ordination in the Episcopal Church* (PhD diss., University of Minnesota, 1981); and Pamela W. Darling, *New Wineskins: The Story of Women Transforming Power and Leadership in the Episcopal Church* (Boston: Cowley, 1994).

32 See Walzer, *Thick and Thin*, 8.

33 Sharon D. Welch, *A Feminist Ethic of Risk*, rev. ed. (Philadelphia: Fortress Press, 1990).

34 Over against, for example, the claim in ARCIC, *Gift of Authority*, 43.

3

BONDS OF AFFECTION?
DEBATES ON SEXUALITY

Jane Shaw

The Lambeth Conference—that once-a-decade gathering of worldwide Anglican bishops that first met in 1867—has been debating sex and sexuality since its third meeting in 1888. It was at that meeting that it first addressed the question of polygamy among converts, an issue that would return for discussion exactly a hundred years later in 1988. The 1888 Lambeth Conference also discussed divorce and "sexual purity," and how to regard divorcees in church, a topic that recurred repeatedly in the twentieth century. The conference spoke about "Problems of Marriage and Sexuality Morality" at its 1920 meeting, but this time the discussion was focused on birth control, and was continued at its 1930 meeting. Homosexuality was first discussed in 1978, and has been discussed at every Lambeth Conference since.

Lambeth Conference resolutions are not binding on the individual provinces of the Communion. Furthermore, the debates and the resolutions do not necessarily tell us the Church's "mind" on a given topic at a given moment; rather, they tell us what a group of male (and recently a few female) bishops, and their advisers, think about that issue in that year. Nevertheless, these resolutions, and the debates that precede them, do helpfully indicate the issues within society that the Church regarded—and continues to regard—it necessary to tackle. They also show the recurring nature of debates about sex and sexuality, and reveal how and when the Church has made new decisions, as well as reversals of thought about these questions, changing the Tradition or moving it in new directions.

Marriage is always going to be defended by the Church because of its sacramentality. The nature of family is always going to be debated because what family is, and what it means, varies so widely among the 85 million Anglicans across the world. The question of reproduction will always be an issue because it touches on the status of women and relates to demographical questions. Homosexuality has become the touchstone for all these issues—and many more, not least postcolonialism—in the last two decades, leading to fierce debates across the Anglican Communion that have yet to be resolved.

The Anglican churches, including the bishops in conference at Lambeth, clearly debated many questions about sex and sexuality before they began to talk about homosexuality, and we will be returning to some of those discussions later in this chapter. But it is the ferocity of recent debates, ostensibly at least about the ordination of openly gay men and lesbians as priests—and, in particular, as bishops—and the blessing of same-sex unions, that led many to declare the Communion to be in such crisis that it might split. Mary-Jane Rubenstein was not alone in expressing in 2008 (the year of a Lambeth Conference) that "the current quality of internecine rancour might ultimately prove too much for the Communion to bear."[1] Four years later, as I write this article in 2012, the proposed Anglican Covenant—designed to hold the Communion together by encouraging provinces to covenant together while at the same time making some churches "second rank" if they strayed too far from a general consensus on issues such as homosexuality—has been rejected by a range of Anglican provinces, including the Church of England. Despite threats from some parties, the Anglican Communion has not split, though there are splinter groups that have left. Rather, national churches are looking for ways to bind themselves together, join with other provinces, remain true to their cultural identities, and yet retain the bonds of affection that allow cross-provincial cooperation and friendship. We need a new model for retaining these bonds of affection.

Homosexuality and the Anglican Communion

The 1978 Lambeth Conference passed a resolution that opened up a wider discussion of homosexuality in the Church. It was the first of many calls for learning and listening. "While we reaffirm heterosexuality as the scriptural norm, we recognise the need for deep and dispassionate study of the question of homosexuality, which would take seriously both the teaching of Scripture and the results of scientific and medical research. The Church, recognizing the need for pastoral concern for those who are homosexual, encourages dialogue with them. (We note with satisfaction that such studies are now proceeding in some member Churches of the Anglican Communion.)"[2] The 1988 Lambeth Conference reaffirmed this 1978 resolution and its call for "dispassionate study of the question of homosexuality," and also asked "each province to reassess, in the light of such study and because of our concern for human rights, its care for and attitude towards persons of homosexual orientation."[3]

By the time the 1998 Lambeth Conference met, some provinces in the Communion, most notably the Episcopal Church of the United States, the Anglican Church of Canada, and the Church of England, had been studying the subject of homosexuality, as urged by the 1978 and 1988 meetings. The Episcopal Church had gone beyond study and had begun to ordain openly gay men and lesbians as priests. In 1977, Bishop Paul Moore of New York ordained Ellen Barrett, the first openly lesbian priest. In 1994, the Episcopal Church's General Convention had passed a resolution stating: "No one shall be denied access to the selection process for ordination in this Church because of race, color, ethnic origin, age, national origin, marital status, sexual orientation, disabilities or age, except as otherwise specified by these Canons." Nevertheless, it clarified, "No right to ordination is hereby established."[4] This did not settle the matter in the Episcopal Church by any means. In 1995, a group of conservative bishops filed heresy charges against retired Bishop Walter Righter on the grounds that he had ordained an openly gay man as a deacon, in the Diocese of New Jersey where he was an assisting bishop. The ecclesiastical court dismissed the charges, by a vote of 7 to 1, stating that the Episcopal Church "has no doctrine prohibiting the ordination of homosexuals, and that Bishop Righter did not contradict the 'core doctrine' of the Church."[5]

In England, the Lesbian and Gay Christian Movement (LGCM) had been founded in 1976, and celebrated its twentieth anniversary with a service in Southwark Cathedral in 1996. Official reports had assessed the subject, such as the 1979 document, *Homosexual Relationships: A Contribution to Discussion.*[6] This was considered too liberal, however, so in 1986, a standing committee of the Church of England House of Bishops asked the Board for Social Responsibility to form a working party that would advise the House of Bishops on homosexuality and lesbianism. The Reverend June Osborne (then team vicar of the Old Ford parishes in Tower Hamlets, London, now dean of Salisbury) chaired the working party, and the result was the Osborne Report of 1989, which drew on the direct testimony of gay and lesbian Christians. The working party did precisely what the Lambeth resolutions had asked national churches to do: it set out to report the "experiential facts" as well as the choices that gay Christians made about their lives, so that any discussion faced up to "what actually happens." As a result of this listening, the working party suggested that the Church of England should be more welcoming to gays and lesbians, and should actually listen to them. "Homosexuality is about homosexual people. We should never lose sight of the painful and stressful journey many homosexual people have to make in the church and in society—with little understanding from either." The report also called upon bishops

> to affirm the catholicity and inclusiveness of the Church.
> The bishops have an important role in helping the Church
> live with unresolved issues. The way to resolve the conflict
> and tensions between groups is not by the exclusion of one
> or more minority groups. We have been very conscious of
> the poor experience of the Church encountered by many
> homosexual people [...] The Bishops, as the chief pastors
> of the Church, have a particular responsibility to set a tone
> of welcome, and acceptance in these matters.[7]

The Osborne Report was also considered too liberal, with its response to the Lambeth Conference call for all voices to be heard, and it was never published. Over twenty years later, in 2012, as the Church of England was responding to the British government's proposals for gay marriage, the *Church Times* decided to publish it on its website, indicating its enduring importance for discussion.[8]

One reason that the Osborne Report had not been published was the eruption of a fierce debate in the Church of England General Synod in 1987, a year after the Osborne Report was commissioned, and two years before it was completed. The conservative resolution that emerged from that bitter debate led the bishops to publish their own document in 1991, *Issues in Human Sexuality*, which also called for further dialogue and discussion. As George Carey, then Archbishop of Canterbury, put it, "we do not pretend [this] to be the last word on the subject."[9] Crucially, this report drew a distinction between ordained and lay, saying that gay priests needed to remain celibate, while considering it permissible (though not ideal) for gay and lesbian laypeople to enter into same-sex monogamous relationships.

Meanwhile, official reports and debates aside, in both the Church of England and the Episcopal Church, the blessing of such same-sex unions had been happening unofficially for some time. The LGCM in England had a confidential list of forty clergy willing to officiate at such services and, by the late 1990s, was getting about five hundred inquiries a year about such blessings. In 1997, the year before the Lambeth Conference was to meet again, the House of Deputies at the Episcopal Church's General Convention debated a resolution to prepare liturgical materials for blessing same-sex partnerships, and that failed by just one vote. For some people, as Stephen Bates puts it, "The gays seemed to be winning the argument. And then came the 1998 Lambeth Conference."[10]

The 1998 Lambeth Conference was a turning point on the subject of homosexuality. The tenor of the event is perhaps caught in one single image: the sight of Bishop Emmanual Chuckwuma of Enugu, Nigeria—outside the conference halls—attempting to exorcize the homosexual demons out of Richard Kirker, the coordinator of the LGCM in England, after telling him that Leviticus demanded the death penalty for homosexuality.[11] The 1998 Lambeth Conference did not set the tone or provide the environment for a respectful discussion across the divides. The bishops failed to meet formally (or, in most cases, informally) with gay and lesbian Christians to hear their experiences, despite requests for them to do so. It was as if all the calls for careful listening and greater education over the past three decades had been for naught. Resolution 1.10 on homosexuality was far more conservative than the 1978 and 1988 resolutions. It called for further education and dialogue as those previous resolutions had, and yet at the same time undermined that call by rejecting "homosexual practice as incompatible with Scripture" and declaring that it could "not *advise* the legitimizing or blessing of same sex unions nor ordaining those involved in same gender unions." [my italics] The word "advise" is significant, because Lambeth resolutions are not, and never have been, binding on individual provinces, though many conservatives would go on to evoke Resolution 1.10 as if it were "holy writ" (as Bates put it)[12] in the years following, as openly gay, partnered bishops were proposed in the United States and England, the first by election, the second by appointment.

Much has been written about the consequences of Gene Robinson's election as diocesan bishop of New Hampshire in June 2003, his ratification as bishop at the 2003 General Convention, and the moratorium on gay bishops and same-sex blessings passed at that Convention. The details do not need to be rehearsed once again here.[13] Robinson entered office as bishop of New Hampshire in 2004. The Archbishop of Canterbury, Rowan Williams, did not invite him to the 2008 Lambeth Conference. That

Conference steered clear of any votes, sticking to its remit of conversation. A group of about two hundred conservative bishops chose not to go, and had an alternative conference (in a group known as Global Anglican Future Conference, GAFCON). In 2009, the General Convention of the Episcopal Church lifted the moratorium on gay bishops; Mary Glasspool, an openly lesbian priest with a partner, was elected suffragan bishop of Los Angeles later that year, and consecrated in the spring of 2010. That convention also mandated its liturgy group to draw up a draft of a same-sex blessing covenant.

While the Episcopal Church of the United States forged ahead, the Church of England—or at least Rowan Williams, the Archbishop of Canterbury—backed down. When Richard Harries, bishop of Oxford, appointed Jeffrey John as his suffragan bishop of Reading in 2003, he cleared it first with the Archbishop, because John was an openly gay man with a partner, though he affirmed that they had a celibate relationship, in accordance with the 1991 document, *Issues in Human Sexuality*. But that document had itself become "holy writ" rather than the discussion document it was intended to be and when it looked as if John might be consecrated a bishop, the conservatives swung into action, using as a weapon an article that Jeffrey John had written in favor of same-sex relationships. The opposition became bitter; the Archbishop of Canterbury backed down and put pressure on John to resign and—unlike the Episcopal Church—England was not to have an openly gay, partnered bishop after all.

Battle lines had drawn by the 1998 Lambeth Conference, and the conservatives, having triumphed in 1998, were ready to go into action when Gene Robinson was elected bishop of New Hampshire, and when Jeffrey John was appointed bishop of Reading in England. The differences of opinion about homosexuality are often rather crudely drawn in the press: as being between conservatives and liberals, the Global South and the West. But none of these groups spoke with one voice. Once Gene Robinson's election was announced, conservatives in the West—especially North America—certainly harnessed the conservative voices of the Global South, especially in Africa, in their opposition to Robinson. The Global South is not united in its views on homosexuality.

Meanwhile in the United States, a group of nineteen American bishops, led by Robert Duncan of Pittsburgh, made a statement warning the Church of a possible schism between the Episcopal Church and the Anglican Communion; five years later, Duncan himself left the Episcopal Church to head up a small splinter church (Anglican Church in North

America, known by its acronym ACNA), taking some parishes from the Diocese of Pittsburgh with him.

These often bitter arguments about homosexuality were about many issues, not least central control versus provincial autonomy and the interpretation of Scripture, but in many ways they were about who would ultimately "own" the "Anglican franchise." This debate was shot through with questions about identity, colonialism and postcolonialism, and gender, just as other debates about sexuality had been.

Reversals: Polygamy, Divorce, Birth Control

In the debates about homosexuality, conservatives set up a false dichotomy between "traditionalists" and "revisionists," regarding Scripture and tradition as having spoken with a unitary, unchanging, and timeless voice on that subject. However, even a cursory look at the Anglican Church's thinking and decisions shows reversals about other aspects of sexuality over the twentieth century, indicating that tradition is dynamic, never static, and Scripture is always necessarily interpreted in relationship to the context in which it is read. And in the cases of polygamy and divorce, it is clear that, until very recently, the principle of provincial autonomy was clearly held.

Polygamy

The 1988 Lambeth Conference not only addressed the issue of polygamy; it reversed its previous resolution, passed in 1888, on the subject. Nineteenth-century missionaries encountered polygamy in many of the societies they traveled to, and faced the problem of what to do about this practice, so clearly rejected by Christian tradition. It proved a particularly tough issue in parts of Africa. Incentives to give up polygamous households—such as hut taxes—were introduced by the colonial administration, but the issue remained, especially in parts of Southern Africa. By the 1860s, missionaries were writing back to the Church of England for advice on what to do. As Timothy Willem Jones writes:

> For the missionaries in the field and church policy makers at home, polygamy proved to be an almost impossible problem. Polygamy was seen to be in absolute conflict with Christianity. A Christian who entered a polygamous relationship would be excommunicated, and it was generally thought impossible for someone in a pre-existing polygamous relationship to convert whilst remaining in the

plural marriage; in order to convert to Christianity they would have to renounce their sinful lifestyle.[14]

There were those who argued for a more lenient approach, especially Bishop John Colenso of Natal, who had liberal views about a number of doctrines, as well as the question of Christian inculturation. He wrote an open letter to the Archbishop of Canterbury in 1861, saying that to require a man to put away all his wives was not warranted by Scripture, was opposed to the practice of the apostles, condemned by common reason, and not justifiable. He did not wish to promote polygamy, nor did he regard it as a Christian practice, and he hoped it would eventually phase out, but he did think that all a man's marriages were permanent, and believed that a polygamous man could be admitted to the Church.

Colenso's more open view did not prevail. But by the 1880s it was clear that the Church's position on polygamy seriously hampered mission. Thus the issue came to the Lambeth Conference of 1888. The resolution on polygamy issued by that meeting stated that polygamy was "inconsistent with the law of Christ respecting marriage." Polygamous men could not, therefore, be baptized, though they could be admitted as candidates for baptism "until such time as they shall be in a position to accept the law of Christ." The wives of polygamists were, in some cases, to be admitted to baptism on the grounds that they were faithful to one husband, and usually had "no personal freedom to contract or dissolve a matrimonial alliance."[15]

As Jones points out, this was not the end of the matter. Other churches in the region, such as the Yoruba Independent African Church (founded 1882) were happy to baptize polygamous men if it meant more converts. On the ground, some missionaries baptized polygamous men: evangelical Church Missionary Society missionaries began the practice in 1909 and seem to have continued it throughout the twentieth century. Polygamy was discussed, albeit not at length, at several twentieth-century Lambeth Conferences—1920, 1958, and 1968—but the bishops' position remained consistent until 1988 when they made a reversal. For example, resolution 23 on "Marriage Discipline," passed in 1968, was very clearly opposed to making any concessions to those in polygamous marriages:

> The Conference recognizes that polygamy poses one of the sharpest conflicts between the faith and particular cultures.
>
> The Church seeks to proclaim the will of God in setting out the clear implications of our Lord's teaching about

marriage. Hence it bears witness to monogamous life-long marriage as God's will for mankind.

The Conference believes that such marriage alone bears adequate witness to the equal sanctity of all human beings which lies at the heart of the Christian revelation; yet recognises that in every place many problems concerning marriage confront the Church.

The Conference therefore asks each province to re-examine its discipline in such problems in full consideration with other provinces in a similar situation.[16]

The cultural conflict inherent in these deliberations did not go away. In African countries with large Muslim populations, the question repeatedly occurs when a Muslim man is converted to Christianity: if he is polygamous, should he give up all but one of his wives when baptized? If he does, he knows that those women will be rejected by his tribe (into which they have married) and by their tribe of birth, and therefore will have few means of financially supporting themselves, the most obvious being prostitution. So it can be argued that it is a matter of compassion to allow the polygamous man to retain all his wives after he has been baptized Christian, even though this has been clearly rejected by Christianity. It also takes into account the woman's perspective and experience, which is rare in most Christian conversations about sexuality.

In 1972, the Anglican archbishops in Africa asked the Roman Catholic priest and academic historian, Adrian Hastings, to research Christian marriage in Africa and produce a report. As Jones points out, Hastings was an outspoken critic of colonialism, and, while holding monogamy as the ideal of Christian marriage, he recommended: "while Christians should not feel free to take on a second wife, people within a polygamous marriage should, if otherwise suitably disposed, be received to baptism and communion." Hastings's report came out at just the moment that some African writers, such as Felix Ekechi, were arguing for the full acceptance of polygamy as a legitimate form of Christian marriage. Ekechi wrote: "the espousal of monogamy as the only ideal Christian family life is now being interpreted as merely reflecting European values, which invariably, conform with the Western nuclear family structure as opposed to the African extended family system."[17]

The Anglican Consultative Council (one of the four instruments of Communion) commended Hastings's report in 1973, and in 1984 asked the African provinces to prepare a proposal to bring to the next Lambeth

Conference. In 1988, a Kenyan bishop brought forward a motion at Lambeth that the matter of polygamy was a local African matter, and the African bishops should be given the discretion to address it in their own way. The Western bishops at the 1988 Conference, while disagreeing with polygamy and regarding it as un-Christian, understood this argument, and decided to see this as a local African issue, trusting their colleagues to deal with it in a sensitive way. Resolution 26 upheld "monogamy as God's plan" and yet said that a polygamous man may be baptized and confirmed providing: "(1) that the polygamist shall promise not to marry again as long as any of his wives at the time of his conversion are alive; (2) that the receiving of such a polygamist has the consent of the local Anglican community; (3) that such a polygamist shall not be compelled to put away any of his wives, on account of the social deprivation they would suffer."[18] The decision of 1888 had, just a hundred years later, been reversed.

Divorce

As Jones points out, the nineteenth-century debates about polygamy were entwined with considerations of the possibility of divorce. Civil divorce was only established in England in 1857. The Matrimonial Causes Act, which made divorce possible, automatically permitted remarriage; this caused controversy in the Church, which was, for the most part, vehemently opposed to remarriage because of Jesus' teaching that anyone who divorced and remarried committed adultery against their spouse. Jesus' words in Matt. 5:32 and 19:9 allow divorce and remarriage on the grounds of adultery; this "Matthean exception" as Jones points out, was, at the end of the nineteenth century, interpreted primarily to mean that the Church would accept divorce only for adultery but would not permit remarriage during the lifetime of the other spouse. Those who remarried could face excommunication, depending on their bishop's attitude. This was essentially the position of the 1888 Lambeth Conference.

Throughout the twentieth century, the bishops at Lambeth reasserted lifelong monogamy as the ideal Christian model for marriage, but as divorce rates increased, there was pressure for the Christian churches to rethink their long-standing position on divorce. Within Anglicanism, this was done piecemeal, reflecting provincial autonomy. Indeed, as early as 1920, the Lambeth Conference had produced a resolution (resolution 67) that allowed for provinces to act as they believed fit on this matter:

> The conference affirms as our Lord's principle and stan-
> dard of marriage a life-long and indissoluble union, for
> better or worse, of one man with one woman, to the

exclusion of all others on either side, and calls on all Christian people to maintain and bear witness to this standard.

Nevertheless, the Conference admits the right of a national or regional church within our Communion to deal with cases which fall within the exception mentioned in the record of our Lord's words in St Matthew's Gospel, under provisions which such Church may lay down.[19]

Knowing that it could not infringe on the autonomy of the national churches, the Lambeth Conference of 1930 followed up its 1920 resolution with a cautiously worded statement against the remarriage of divorced persons while a former spouse was alive:

The Conference while passing no judgment on the practice of regional or national Churches within our Communion, recommends that the marriage of one, whose former partner is still living, should not be celebrated according to the rites of the Church.[20]

In many places, change happened on the ground and the Canons of the Church caught up with the reality later. In the Episcopal Church for example, different dioceses had their own canons, and the remarriage of divorcees was allowed in certain circumstances even before World War II; it was in 1973 that the Episcopal Church's General Convention passed a Canon that allowed the remarriage of those divorced in circumstances other than those traditionally allowed by Scripture. In the Anglican Church in Australia, a canon of 1981 reaffirmed that the remarriage of divorcees in church could only occur in accordance with Scripture and with the permission of the diocesan bishop; in 2007, these conditions were modified.[21] In 2002 the Church of England agreed that divorced people could remarry in church in certain circumstances, according to the discretion of the priest. These brief examples illustrate the ways in which individual provinces, particularly in countries where the issue was a live one, dealt with it in their own time and governance structures, while the Lambeth Conference resolutions continued to affirm the monogamous, lifelong nature of Christian marriage.

Birth Control

The Anglican churches adhered to the three goods of marriage, as outlined by Augustine in the early fifth century, in his *De Bono Coniugali*: offspring, fidelity, and the sacramental bond. The emphasis on procreation—a marriage should produce children—meant that as more reliable forms of contraception began to be developed in the early twentieth century, the churches did not consider them suitable for use by Christians. From the nineteenth century, some radical and feminist writers and activists were making the case that women should have control over their own fertility.[22] Simultaneously, the eugenics movement was gaining ground across the political spectrum. The supposed science of making "better" people and controlling population growth appealed to Progressives and Imperialists alike. These different streams of thought all converged in the arguments for and against birth control and better sex education.

At the 1908 Lambeth Conference, the bishops pronounced on the use of birth control and held to the line generally professed by the medical and intellectual establishment:

> The conference regards with alarm the growing practice of the artificial restrictions of the family, and earnestly calls upon all Christian people to discountenance the use of all artificial means of restriction as demoralizing to character and hostile to national welfare.[23]

Eugenicist fears were playing their part in the background. The Lambeth Conference committee that considered Marriage Problems (defined as divorce, prohibited degrees, and population restriction) began its report with the concern that "in every Western country there has been a decline in the birth-rate; but this decline has been most marked among the English-speaking people, once the most fertile of races." Noting that population declined not only in England and Wales, but also Australia, New Zealand, Canada, and America, the committee concluded that "the decline appears to be chiefly among the old English-speaking stocks."[24]

In 1914, in the United States, Margaret Sanger began her magazine, *Woman Rebel*, and coined the term "birth control" in her June issue, following that up with her pamphlet, *Family Limitation*. In England, Marie Stopes produced a number of popular texts, including *Married Love* (1916) and *Wise Parenthood* (1918).[25] In 1920, she circulated at the Lambeth Conference her *New Gospel: A Revelation of God Uniting Physiology and the Religion of Man*,[26] but the bishops were not moved, and they passed another resolution affirming their position of 1908. Resolution 68 regarded "with grave concern the spread in modern society of theories and practices hostile to the family." Its injunction against birth control appealed to the traditional good of procreation in marriage and eugeni-cist fears:

> We utter an emphatic warning against the use of unnatural means for the avoidance of conception, together with the grave dangers—physical, moral and religious—thereby incurred, and against the evils with which the extension of such use threatens the race. In opposition to the teaching which, under the name of science and religion, encourages married people in the deliberate cultivation of sexual union as an end in itself, we steadfastly uphold what must always be regarded as the governing considerations of Christian marriage. One is the primary purpose for which marriage exists, namely the continuation of the race through the gift and heritage of children; the other is the paramount importance in married life of deliberate and thoughtful self-control.[27]

The 1920s saw a number of changes. Marie Stopes opened her Mothers Clinic, to educate and distribute contraception to working-class women, in London in 1921. Medical opinion on the subject began to change. For example, in that same year, 1921, the King's personal physician, Lord Dawson, spoke to the Church Congress of the Church of England meeting in Birmingham, in favor of birth control. Opinion remained divided but, as the use of birth control became more widespread and accepted in various circles, the Church had to wrestle with what to do.

Remarkably, in 1930, the Lambeth Conference made a 180-degree turn and agreed to the use of birth control in certain circumstances. It was the first major church to do so. While Resolution 13 noted that "the primary purpose for which marriage exists is the procreation of children," it also noted "that intercourse between husband and wife as the consummation of marriage has a value of its own within that sacrament, and that thereby married love is enhanced and its character strengthened." Resolution 15 stated: "Where there is a clearly felt moral obligation to limit or avoid parenthood, the method must be decided on Christian principles." The preferred method was abstinence. "Nevertheless in those cases where there is such a clearly-felt moral obligation to limit or avoid parenthood, and where there is a morally sound reason for avoiding complete abstinence, the Conference agrees that other methods may be used, provided that is done in the light of the same Christian principles." In the report from the committee looking at marriage and sex, it was clear that medical and scientific authority had affected the bishops' decision. The Church was following expert advice and the flow of society. This resolution was passed by 193 to 67 votes. But the bishops made it clear in Resolution 18 that the use of contraceptives did not remove the sin of sex outside marriage, and pressed for legislation forbidding the unrestricted advertisement of contraceptives and for restrictions on their purchase.[28]

While there were various conditions and limits attached to the bishops' approval of the use of birth control, nevertheless an extraordinary sea change occurred in 1930, which had far-reaching effects, not only for heterosexual but also for homosexual relationships. One of the three "goods" of marriage—children—was potentially omitted. Once this occurred, and the bishops admitted that "the consummation of marriage has a value of its own," then the prohibition of sexual activity between two adults where such sexual activity was clearly for the purpose of companionship, and yet where procreation was impossible—namely, between two men or between two women—became much more difficult to sustain.

Marriage as a lifelong, monogamous relationship between two people of the opposite sex, primarily intended for reproduction, has been challenged in various ways in the modern history of the Church, as these brief examples illustrate. My point is not that polygamy, divorce, and birth control are all on equal ethical footing, but rather, that the history of Anglican deliberations and Lambeth Conference resolutions on these topics highlights that a so-called "traditional" position on sexuality and marriage has been far more diverse and contested than is usually admitted. We could too—but lack of space does not permit it here—look at the ways in which that ideal of marriage is largely a modern, Western, and middle-class ideal, thereby putting it into a longer historical sweep, which saw celibacy as the greater good for more than a thousand years of Christian history.[29] These examples also illustrate three important things that the bishops at Lambeth realized, but which are are often overlooked. First, many issues are local and need to be treated as such (most obviously polygamy)—many are, too, unavoidably shot through with colonialism; second, Conference resolutions could never be binding, provincial autonomy being a central principle of communion among Anglicans (divorce being an illustration of this); and third, there is an appropriate time and place for taking medical scientific authority seriously (birth control). Anglican moral theology has always engaged with particular circumstances and taken expert advice in this way, while reading with seriousness of purpose Scripture and the wisdom of those who have gone before, making tradition genuinely dynamic.

Going Forward

When homosexuality has been discussed in global Anglican contexts, many of these principles have been lost or forgotten or ignored. The particular context in which North American, and to some extent British, churches wished to be able to include gay and lesbian people in the ordained ministry, and provide blessings for same-sex unions, was not taken seriously by other Anglicans, in the ways that the particular context that gave rise to a new decision on polygamy was in 1988.

At Lambeth 1988, polygamy was treated as a local issue, and the Anglican provinces for which this was a live issue were given the freedom and autonomy to address it as they saw fit. It may have been something of a shock to other bishops, especially many of the North Americans, expecting the same courtesy from fellow bishops with regard to their own live issue, namely homosexuality, that it was debated with such acrimony and bitterness ten years later in 1998. But by then, the longstanding ideal of local autonomy was being largely jettisoned.

The Windsor Report and the proposed Anglican Covenant that emerged from the Windsor process, set up by Archbishop Williams after Gene Robinson was consecrated a bishop in November 2003, sought to address the debates and arguments by imposing uniformity. There was a new desire to impose like-mindedness. There were also many new alignments across national and provincial boundaries, which were largely confessional, and in opposition to a wider sense of communion. The Windsor Report and the proposed covenant seemed to interpret Communion as being of one (or common) mind. Mary-Jane Rubenstein, in her article, "Anglicans in the Postcolony," reminds us that genuine community consists of constant, mutual interruption. In fact she goes so far as to call that *contamination*: "when bodies exist in community with one another, the integrity of each is constantly undermined and contaminated by otherness." She suggests that the choice is between a "communal" model of relationship which operates "on the principle of subsuming differences under one essence" or a "community" model of relationship which embraces differences and finds ways of living with those differences—as in the Eucharist for example.[30] Winnie Varghese's description of communion "across borders we might not otherwise cross," and the narrative of her meeting with the bishop of Madras of the Church of South India one day in New York, including the conversations they had across their differences, is such an example of the community model. If we are to have a covenant, then it should be one that encourages the unrealized potential in transformative encounters of that sort. "It would be quite something," she writes, "if we generated a document that strengthened or organized some of that potential, but I don't think we've seen that document yet."[31]

With the failure of the proposed Anglican Covenant, with its communal model of like-mindedness, we have the opportunity to devise a new form of genuine community in the Anglican Communion, across differences. Such a community would recognize that differences exist not only across cultures and geography, but also across time, rendering the distinction between traditionalists and revisionists null and void, and remembering that our Anglican tradition is always dynamic.

Notes

1 Mary-Jane Rubenstein, "Anglicans in the Postcolony: On Sex and the Limits of Communion," *Telos* 143 (Summer 2008): 134. For extended discussions of the Anglican Communion in crisis theme, see also Miranda K. Hasset, *Anglican Communion in Crisis: How Episcopal Dissidents and their African Allies are Reshaping Anglicanism* (Princeton: Princeton University Press, 2007) and Stephen Bates, *A Church at War: Anglicans and Homosexuality* (London: I. B. Tauris, 2004).

2 Lambeth Conference 1978, Resolution 10, http://www.lambethconference.org/resolutions/1978/1978-10.cfm.

3 Lambeth Conference 1988, Resolution 64, http://www.lambethconference.org/resolutions/1988/1988-64.cfm.

4 "General Convention of the Episcopal Church 2012 Archives' Research Report," http://www.episcopalarchives.org/gc2012/14_min/2012-D019.pdf.

5 For Righter's own account of these events, see Walter C. Righter, *A Pilgrim's Way* (New York: Knopf, 1998).

6 *Homosexual Relationships: A Contribution to Discussion* (London: CIO Publishing for the General Synod Board for Social Responsibility, 1979).

7 *The Osborne Report*, unpublished manuscript, 1989, 34, 33, 132, quoted by permission of the Very Reverend June Osborne.

8 *Church Times*, January 20, 2012.

9 George Carey, "Introduction," in *Issues in Human Sexuality* (London: Church House Publishing, 1991), vii.

10 Bates, *A Church at War*, 124.

11 Ibid., 125-41.

12 Ibid., 140.

13 See, for example, Gene Robinson's own account, *In the Eye of the Storm: Swept to the Center by God* (New York: Seabury, 2008) and the 2012 documentary, *Love Free or Die*.

14 Timothy Willem Jones, "The Missionaries' Position: Polygamy and Divorce in the Anglican Communion, 1888-1988" *Journal of Religious History* 35, no. 3 (2011): 396.

15 Resolution No. 4 in "Report of the Committee Appointed to Consider the Subject of Polygamy of

Heathen Converts," in *The Six Lambeth Conferences 1867-1920*, ed. Randall Thomas Davidson (London: SPCK, 1920), Part II, 133-35.

16 http://www.lambethconference.org/resolutions/1968/1968-23.cfm.

17 Both Hastings and Ekechi are quoted in Jones, "Missionaries' Position," 406.

18 http://www.lambethconference.org/resolutions/1988/1988-26.cfm.

19 "Lambeth Conference of 1920," in *The Six Lambeth Conferences*, 44.

20 Resolution 11, *The Lambeth Conference 1930* (London: SPCK, 1930), 42.

21 "Marriage of Divorced Persons Canon 1981," http://www.anglican.org.au/docs/canons/Canon%20 1985-07%20Divorced%20persons.pdf, and "Solemnization of Matromony Canon 1981," https:// sn2prd0710.outlook.com/owa/?exsvurl=1&realm=eds.edu&wa=wsignin1.0.

22 See Sheila Rowbotham, *Dreamers of a New Day: Women Who Invented the Twentieth Century* (London: Verso, 2010), chapter 4.

23 Lambeth Conference 1908, Resolution 41, http://www.lambethconference.org/ resolutions/1908/1908-41.cfm.

24 "Lambeth Conference of 1908," in *The Six Lambeth Conferences*, Part II, 399-400.

25 Marie Carmichael Stopes, *Married Love*, 7th ed. (London: G. P. Putnam's Sons, 1919), and *Wise Parenthood*, 5th ed. (London: G. P. Putnam's Sons, 1919).

26 Revised and published later as Marie Carmichael Stopes, *A New Gospel to All Peoples*, rev. ed. (London: The Mothers Clinic, 1922).

27 "Lambeth Conference of 1920," in *The Six Lambeth Conferences*, 44-45.

28 *Lambeth Conference 1930*, 43-44, 91, 44.

29 See Jane Shaw, "Marriage, Sexuality and the Christian Tradition," in *The Bible, Homosexuality and the Church*, ed. Nicholas Coulton (London: Darton, Longman and Todd, 2005), 49-79.

30 Rubenstein, "Anglicans in the Postcolony," 152, 159-60.

31 Winnie Varghese, "The Covenant We Have Been Offered Is Not the Covenant We Need," in *The Genius of Anglicanism: Perspectives on the Proposed Anglican Covenant*, ed. Jim Naughton (Chicago: Chicago Consultation, 2011), 54.

4

THERE FOR THE BURIALS; THERE FOR THE BIRTHS: WOMEN IN LEADERSHIP IN THE ANGLICAN COMMUNION

Wendy Fletcher

When I was a seminarian almost thirty years ago, for the first time women were appearing in seminary classrooms in some number. That is to say, there was more than one. I was in a class with three older women, all of whom were more fully developed in their capacity to engage in gender analysis than I was at that point. One day, after a particularly complicated class in which there had been notable conflict, one of the women turned to me and said, "You understand why women are being called to leadership in the church in this generation, don't you?"

"Why?" I responded.

"Because in every culture women are there for the burials and the births."

Historically, institutions have not been known for their flexibility. Especially with reference to institutions such as the Church, which have served a hegemonizing function in social discourse, change is a complex matter. Seen through one hermeneutical lens, from the first installation of a woman deaconess within the Anglican Communion in the Diocese of London in 1861, nothing short of a leadership revolution has been unfolding within the Anglican world. Seen through another, there is nothing new under heaven. It is to an exploration of the paradox of change and stability, of revolution and persistence in Anglican leadership forms, with particular reference to the matter of gender, that we now turn.

Much of what frames the Anglican story happens at the local level. Dioceses (regional ecclesiastical areas) under the leadership of a diocesan bishop are where power at the micro level resides. However, the micronarratives of local history for Anglicans are part of a much larger story, which frames the macronarrative of the Anglican Communion. Formulating the discourse between the micro- and the macronarrative has been a project that has grown increasingly complex as the Communion itself has grown, along with the diversity inherent in local stories. We will attempt here to construct the macronarrative of the shifting place of women's leadership within Anglicanism, with particular but not exclusive reference to the question of ordained leadership (given the predominantly clerical ethos of the Anglican orientation in decision making historically). We will, as well, explore the micronarrative of the Canadian church's story, as an opportunity for more nuanced analysis of how change happens in an institution that has heretofore served as a pillar of continuity within the social fabric of Euro-descent Western culture. Perhaps more importantly, we will explore the micronarrative as a vehicle for interpreting what that change might mean.

The Social Location of Religion as Backdrop

It is a legacy of its colonial identity that the Anglican Communion has defined itself largely in conversation with the social fabric of what has been named Euro-descent Western civilization. As the demographics of Anglicanism have shifted dramatically in the past fifty years, with the numerical preponderance of Anglicans growing in the global South, one must anticipate that this definition is shifting as well. Perhaps it will be the case that the micronarrative of conversation between religion and society will dominate. Perhaps it will be the case that the social context of the global South will frame a macronarrative against which the Anglican conversation will unfold. The future has yet to write that story. However, the conversation about the place of women heretofore has unfolded in the Anglican Communion predominantly formulated as a counterfoil to the conversation about gender according to evolving Western norms. As such, positing something about that conversation for our consideration is key here.

Victorian Sensibilities and the Redistribution of Religion

When the Church of England traveled around the globe as an aspect of the British Empire, it took with it a very clear notion of who a woman was and what her location was in the social discourse. The worldview of the Victorian era served as the cradle for the colonial conversation. The Victorian era embraced a concept of womanhood grounded in the notion of gender-distinct spheres of activity and expertise. It understood these distinct spheres as normative—as biologically and socially predetermined. This rigid demarcation of spheres was, in part, a response to the social, political, and economic upheaval of societies in transition from agrarian to industrial culture. Knowing what defined a "man" and a "woman" as a social construct provided a sense of stability, when it seemed that everything else was changing.

As income replaced property as a sign of successful manhood, having a woman who did not work outside the home became a badge of middle-class status. The world of men was coextensive with the world of business, politics, labor, and government. Aggression and the ruthless pursuit of individual gain characterized the public arena. Echoing themes of the warrior/hunter role of males in prehistoric times, the Victorian era saw men as providers who labored in the world outside the home, a world perceived as violent and inhumane. To fulfill this cultural construct of masculinity, it understood man to be capable of innate ruthlessness, devoid of emotion, and immoral if necessary.

In contrast, the era assigned women the domestic sphere as the arena appropriate to their gender. Assigning women to the domestic realm helped ease the moral conflicts inherent in aggressive capitalism. Modern culture redesignated the "home" as a refuge from the sullied works of the public arena. The generation of Victorian-era culture reformulated the virtuous woman to preside over the "home." This cultural construct applied only to middle- and upper-class women who did not need to work to support the survival of their families. As such, it applied to a minority of women. However, the class distinction is significant, as the Victoria era saw Protestant Christianity emerging as a phenomenon uniquely attached to the emerging middle class.[1]

How does any of this apply to the matter of women in leadership in the religious arena? As the touchstone for religious virtue, middle-class women became the keepers of morality sympathetic to Christian moral and ethical teaching, which in its heyday coalesced with colonial economic interests. All of this contributed to a shift in social location. In the Victorian era, we see the gradual migration of religion, with its idealized commitment to virtue, from the public to the private sphere. Within Western Christianity, religion became largely the preserve of women, despite, in the initial phases of this period, their exclusion from enfranchised membership and paid leadership roles, including ordination.

At first, the business of the church remained in the hands of men. However, as the third Evangelical Great Awakening inspired religious experience grounded in the heart, or the affective dimension of human life, women increasingly moved to center stage.[2] Women in turn felt justified in moving into the public realm, calling for repentance and admonishing their sisters to faithfulness. Their response to newly inspired religious experience was to galvanize legions of women into various forms of group activities aimed at promoting the mission of the church and the moral reformation of society. The explosion of involvement of women in the voluntary arena over decades led to new questions about the role and participation of women in church life overall. Women gained experience running voluntary organizations. They raised funds to pay the salaries for young single women to work in newly sown mission fields. They honed their leadership skills. As society then shifted and the twentieth century saw increasing demand to expand and eventually discard the lines that defined social roles by gender, women were ready to stand newly in the public arena with leadership skills honed in the Victorian hybridity of the then private/public world of religion.

In Western culture, the twentieth century witnessed, periods of revival notwithstanding, the increasing decline and marginalization of Christianity as a significant force in social discourse. In many locations, Christianity has migrated from serving enthusiastically as hegemonizing handmaiden of imperial discourse to a normatively disregarded and sometimes castigated bystander in the narratives of popular culture and policy making. It is against the backdrop of that social migration of the church that the redefinition of the place of women in society has in turn created a foil for the re-examination of the place of women in ecclesial leadership for Anglicans.

Structures of Decision Making at the Global Level: The Macronarrative

Given the extent to which diversity characterizes the Anglican Communion, the question of what is authoritative with reference to unity is critical to denominational ethos. Pertaining to the issue of women's work and place in Anglican structures as held within the broader communion of provincial churches, which levels of decision making and consultation have been key in defining norms and directions forward? So far as it has been attained, the Lambeth Conference and its designated commissions and working groups have been the primary vehicle for the discernment and articulation of a common mind on key matters.

The Lambeth Conference has brought together bishops from across the Communion approximately every ten years since the Conference's inception in 1867. Originally, the purpose of these conferences was to provide some basis for communication among the provinces, which might then serve as a vehicle for the formulation of agreed upon guidelines for Anglican life, work, and order. Increasingly, as diversity has grown, the Conference has served as a focus for dialogue. The Lambeth Conference does not have any authority to make or enforce legislation in the provinces represented at its gathering. However, following the proceedings and actions of the Conferences and their related bodies is our best barometer for measuring the denominational climate on many matters, including the role of women in church life. We will here consider the actions and ethos of those Lambeth Conferences at which the question of women's place in the leadership of the church was a matter of substantial discussion.

Lambeth 1920

By 1920, the question of the ordination of women to the priesthood had arisen in church circles among ecumenical groups such as the Society for the Equal Ministry of Women and Men in the Church (SWMC) and its Anglican counterpart, the Anglican Group for the Ordination of Women (AGOW). However, at the level of ecclesiastical decision making, the matter of women as deaconesses and the meaning of that order would surface as a first matter for action.

Lambeth 1920 was concerned with the issue of women's ministry as deaconesses. While deaconesses had served in the Church of England since 1861 and in some of the provincial churches from around that time, ecclesiastical structures had not made any statement about the nature of the deaconesses' work and office. By 1920, it was generally agreed that guidelines for this order should be instituted. As such, the 1920 Conference devoted a considerable amount of attention to the topic of the "Restoration of the Order of Deaconesses." A committee presented a report that made six recommendations defining the office, outlining its functions, and suggesting a form for "making deaconesses." Reflecting the notion of separate spheres, the report stressed that the office of deaconess was the one and only order of ministry for women to be recommended for recognition by the Anglican branch of the Catholic Church.[3]

The 1920 Conference passed as resolutions the recommendations of the committee with regard to deaconesses. Considerable confusion, however, still existed with regard to the status of deaconesses. Resolutions 47 and 48 appeared to create the suggestion in the minds of some that the order of deaconess and deacon were co-extensive. Such a suggestion engendered considerable conflict in the years following Lambeth 1920. Given that it was the concerted opinion of many priests and bishops that women had no place in the three-fold order of the church, feelings ran high.[4] Such was the concern over the matter, that they mandated clarification at the following Lambeth.

Lambeth 1930

In 1930, Resolution 67 resolved the definition of the meaning of the orders of the deaconess (until the resolution was undone several decades later). Resolution 67 declared that the order of deaconess was the only order open to women and that it was an order that was sui generis, or distinct to the female gender. In case there was any further equivocation as to what this meant for women, Resolution 69 went on to say expressly that the order of deaconess was not equivalent to the order of deacon.[5] A certain logical contradiction was present in these resolutions, as they effectually established a fourth order of ministry, while defending the three-fold order of apostolic tradition.

The 1930 Lambeth Conference also discussed the question of the ordination of women to the priesthood. The Lambeth Committee on the Ministry of the Church reported that it had received deputations from two separate sources supporting the idea of women in the priesthood. The first was the newly formed AGOW (mentioned earlier). The second group that wrote the committee represented a small group of women who felt a vocation to the priesthood. Although the committee agreed that the matter warranted serious consideration, it did not feel qualified to issue a statement on the subject. It confirmed that the twentieth century had introduced a shifting discourse about the place of women, as questions of equality in matters such as electoral suffrage surfaced. However, in its report to Lambeth, the committee stated that changing gender roles in society did not constitute sufficient grounds for changing the tradition of an all male priesthood.[6]

It was agreed at Lambeth to convene a commission of the Archbishop of Canterbury dealing with the ministry of women. That commission produced its report in 1935. This report covered all forms of women's ministry. It considered the question of the possibility of ordination from theological, sociological, and ecclesial perspectives.[7] According to the report, only a "fringe group" within the Church of England supported changing the existing practice of the church.

Nothing of substance happened with the 1935 report. Before the next Lambeth Conference was held, war erupted in Europe. As such, Lambeth did not meet again until 1948, some years after the conclusion of World War II. By that time, the 1935 report was ancient history, because the world had changed in several respects.

Lambeth 1948

Lambeth 1948 confronted the matter of women as priests head on. Bishop R. O. Hall of the Diocese of Hong Kong brought a proposed canon to Lambeth, sent by the General Synod of the Church in China, which, in turn, had received it from the Diocese of South China (which included Hong Kong). The canon proposed the undertaking of a twenty-year experiment in the ordination of women to the priesthood.

What is most interesting about this event is the history immediately prior to it. During the war, Bishop Hall had ordained a woman to the priesthood. He named the Reverend Florence Li Tim Oi as priest to minister to people within Japanese-occupied territory. At the conclusion of the war, the Archbishop of Canterbury was horrified to learn of the action and immediately demanded that Bishop Hall revoke Rev. Li's orders, stressing that the ordination was uncanonical.[8] Hall refused. Canterbury implicitly threatened that if Hall did not revoke Rev. Li's orders, then Canterbury would move to revoke Hall's orders. Archbishop Fisher went over Hall's head to Bishop Arnold Scott of South China (Chair of the House of Bishops of the Chung Hua Sheng Kung Hui Province) and demanded that he revoke Rev. Li's orders.[9] Still Bishop Hall refused to comply; neither did Bishop Scott take action. Rev. Li volunteered to cease functioning as a priest and slipped away quietly. Bishop Hall accepted her resignation.[10] Rather than have a political incident over her ordination, Li disappeared from history for several decades. The Cultural Revolution was unfolding in China and little is known of Reverend Li from that point, until many decades later when the possibility of ordaining women to the priesthood was again in front of the Communion.

The bishops gathered at Lambeth in 1948 did not support the proposal coming from the Synod of the Church in China. They did acknowledge there were some people who wanted the question of women's ordination considered. Resolution 115 of Lambeth 1948 referred to the fact that the *Archbishop's Commission Report* in 1935 had concluded that the time was not right for such an undertaking, and affirmed that discernment as also appropriate for 1948.[11] Lambeth responded to the Chinese proposal by stating that such an experiment would be "gravely against that tradition and order (Anglican) and would gravely affect the internal and external relations of the Anglican Communion."[12] The Conference then reaffirmed its statement of 1930 that the office of deaconess was the one and only order of ministry open to women in the Anglican Church.

Lambeth 1968

Twenty years elapsed before the question of the ordination of women to the priesthood made it back onto the Lambeth agenda. Despite some pressure from lay groups within the Church of England, the Lambeth agenda committee for 1958 did not think the matter appropriate for inclusion.[13] However, 1968 would be the last Lambeth Conference to be held before women were constitutionally ordained in the Anglican Communion. Lambeth 1968 also would serve as a turning point for the definition of women in diaconal orders, a shift from the actions of 1930.

Prior to this important meeting, the Church of England, through its Committee on Ministry, had in 1966 published a report entitled, *Women and Holy Orders*. This report, along with another by the Church of England's Women in Ministry Committee and a preparatory essay by English scholar Alan Richardson, served as background for the debates.[14] At the end of the day, the Conference undertook several actions.

Resolution 32 reversed the position taken in 1930 on women in the diaconate. By a vote of 221 for and 183 against, Lambeth 1968 declared that women who had been made deaconesses through an Episcopal laying on of hands should be declared to be within the diaconate.[15] With this action, while making no commitment to the other two orders, the Conference opened the door to women for inclusion in the historic three-fold order of ministry in the Anglican Church.

In 1968, Lambeth neither sanctioned nor forbade the ordination of women to the priesthood. At the conclusion of the debates, the Conference agreed that there were no conclusive theological arguments one way or the other on the matter of women as priests. It passed Resolutions 35, 36, and 37, asking all provinces to study the issue and to report their conclusions to the newly created Anglican Consultative Council (ACC), which would meet for the first time in Limuru, Kenya, in 1971. This council was formed in 1968 to be a body for consultation; it included laity, clergy, and bishops from all provinces of the Communion. The Conference asked the ACC to consult with other denominations on the matter of women's ordination and to distribute its findings through the Communion. The bishops gathered at Lambeth then asked that any national or regional church or province that was considering such ordinations seek the advice of the ACC before acting.[16]

Most illuminating with reference to the mindset of the bishops on the issue at that juncture is a passage included in the Lambeth report entitled, "Renewal in Ministry":

> The tradition flowing from the early Fathers and the medieval Church that a woman is incapable of receiving Holy Orders appears to reflect biological assumptions about the nature of men and women which have been generally discarded today. If the ancient and medieval assumptions about the social role and inferior status of women are no longer accepted, the appeal to tradition is virtually reduced to the observation that there happens to be no precedent for ordaining women priests.[17]

Anglican Consultative Council 1971

In 1971, there were twenty-seven provinces in the Anglican Communion. When the ACC met in Limuru, it had received reports that eight provinces had followed up on Lambeth 1968's request and had begun to study the question of the ordination of women. The remaining nineteen provinces did not provide a response. The ACC had before it, as well, a communication from the Bishop of Hong Kong, Gilbert Baker, through the Council of South East Asia, informing them that Baker's diocesan synod had approved the ordination of women in principle and that he was hoping to proceed to ordain two women to the priesthood.

Members of the Council understood that they were dealing with a matter of considerable urgency. After lengthy discussion, the ACC passed two resolutions. The first encouraged all provinces in the Communion to study the issue and report back to the 1973 meeting of the ACC. The second directly addressed Bishop Baker's request for direction with regard to his desire to proceed to ordain women in his diocese. The Council stated that his action in proceeding with such ordinations and the actions of any other bishops proceeding with the support of their synods would be acceptable to the ACC. The ACC also would encourage all members to remain in communion with any diocese that ordained women to the priesthood.[18]

Lambeth 1978

By the time Lambeth met in 1978, the ordination of women to the priesthood was *fait accompli*. That is not to say that there was universal agreement on the matter. Rather, women had been ordained in four provinces: Hong Kong, Canada, New Zealand, and the United States. Among the then twenty-three other provinces, there was no common opinion. Despite the recommendations of the Anglican Consultative Council, the threat of division within the Communion was a real one. As such, the concern of Lambeth 1978 was to find a way forward that would allow the traditional Anglican model of diversity in unity of faith to continue.

After considerable discussion and debate, the Conference passed two resolutions. Resolution 21 dealt expressly with women in the priesthood. First, it acknowledged the division and difference of opinion and practice that existed in the Communion at the time. Further, it affirmed that primary responsibility for the work of healing harm and division related to the issue was in the hands of the bishops. It also acknowledged the complexity of the issue for ecumenical relationships with several historic Anglican ecumenical partners, and it urged continued attention to dialogue in those relationships. It urged further discussion on the issue in the context of larger theological conversations about ministry and priesthood within the Communion itself.[19] Resolution 22 raised the matter of the consecration of women to the episcopate. It recommended that bishops undertake such consecrations only with the full support of the dioceses involved, "lest the bishop's office should become a cause of disunity instead of a focus of unity."[20] Further study about the issue was not mandated until the following meeting of the Lambeth Conference.

Lambeth 1988

At the Lambeth Conference of 1988, the issue of the ordination of women remained a hot topic. However, in light of developments in the Communion, the focus of the conversation redefined itself almost exclusively around the question of the consecration of women to the episcopate. By 1988, several provinces had ordained women to the diaconate and priesthood, but none had yet ordained a woman as bishop. Given the fact that women had been serving in holy orders for more than a decade in some of the provinces, the possibility of consecration was imminent.

Given the centrality of this issue to the discussion in 1988, Resolution 1 of the Conference proceedings dealt with the matter. It resolved that each province respect the decisions that individual provinces might make on the matter, and stipulated that such respect would not necessarily indicate acceptance of the principles involved. As with earlier Lambeth actions, it affirmed commitment to retaining the highest possible degree of communion across differing provinces, including bishops with differing opinions maintaining open communication and dialogue with each other.[21]

Section 3 of Resolution 1 asked the Archbishop of Canterbury, in consultation with the Primates of the Communion, to appoint a commission that would conduct an examination of the relationships between provinces within the Communion as movement into the consecration of women began and would ensure that the process of reception of women bishops included an ongoing dialogue with other churches. Monitoring the impact of women bishops on Anglican ecumenical relations was a concern.[22]

The final sections of this resolution dealt with the pastoral implications of proceeding with the inclusion of women as bishops. They noted the potential for conflict between bishops and their clergy and congregations on this issue. The bishops acknowledged the potential for harm in both directions, to those who either supported or rejected the ministry of women bishops, and they commitmed to tend to the work of dialogue where such difference of opinion resulting in harm might occur.[23] The voting members adopted Resolution 1 as follows: For, 423; Against, 28; Abstentions, 19.[24]

Lambeth 1998

By the time Lambeth 1998 was held, the emerging issue of the place of homosexual persons in the leadership of the Church had largely supplanted debates over the place of women in church leadership. Female ordination had largely ceased to function as a political issue in the Communion. This does not mean that all provinces were in agreement. As we shall see, even today there is dissent on this issue. However, it did mean that matters still to be resolved in terms of moving forward lay only in the arena of the episcopacy.

By 1998, a slim majority of the provinces had decided to ordain women.

Eleven female bishops attended the 1998 Lambeth Conference: eight were from the United States, two from Canada, and one from New Zealand. All but one were ordained as priests between 1978 and 1984. As was the case at Lambeth 1988, there was little if any discussion at Lambeth 1998 concerning female deacons and priests. Rather, the focus of the Conference was the reception of the Eames Commission report dealing with the episcopacy question. The Eames Commission (mandated by Lambeth 1988 and chaired by the Most Reverend Robin Eames) completed its work in 1994. The Commission distributed a questionnaire to the then thirty-two provinces: twenty-eight submitted a response. Members of the Commission interpreted the high rate of response as an indication of the importance of the issue in the Communion or, at the very least, of the importance of tending careful movement through diverse actions on the issue. The questions asked served to gather information on the status of this matter in the provinces and identified concerns requiring attention beyond the lifetime of the Commission.[25]

A monitoring group was put in place after the Commission completed its work; that group also produced a report for Lambeth 1998. The group estimated that, as of 1997, the number of women priests in the Anglican Communion was well over four thousand, including ten women bishops, six of whom were diocesan bishops.[26] It found that almost all provinces in the Communion were deeply attentive to the question of unity within the context of respect for particularity and that most were appreciative of the Commission's attempt to assist this process through the development of guidelines for reception in the Communion.[27]

At Lambeth 1998, the Conference thanked the Commission and monitoring group for their work and recommended the implementation of all of their guidelines in all provinces of the Communion. It also affirmed the importance of continuing to monitor the reception of women bishops both across the Communion and with ecumenical partners, to be tracked through the meeting of the Primates.[28] That action effectively closed the process tended by Lambeth over the years with regard to women and holy orders.[29]

Where Are We Now in the Macro-Story?

The Lambeth Conference of 2008 was structured differently from its predecessors. Given the level of conflict by that point about the issue of homosexuality abroad in the Communion, the Conference was designed to serve as a forum for dialogue and relationship building through an indaba process of small group conversation and Bible study. It intentionally set aside the former model of parliamentary debate and resolutions. This means that no further motions are available for consideration as we explore the current state of affairs with regard to women and the episcopacy.

We can observe, however, that by the time Lambeth met in 2008, a majority of Anglican provinces admitted women to the orders of deacon and priest. Joining those countries that had already consecrated women as bishops when Lambeth met in 1998, the Church of Australia, although divided by dioceses on the matter, ordained its first woman bishop in 2008. On November 14, 2011, the Diocese of Canberra and Goulburn also moved to ordain its first woman bishop, the third in Australia.[30] As well, in July 2012, the continent of Africa saw change in this area. The Reverend Ellinah Ntombi Wamukoya, 61, became the bishop-elect of Swaziland and the first woman bishop in any of the twelve Anglican Provinces in Africa.[31]

At its national meeting in Lampeter in 2008, the Church in Wales narrowly rejected proposals to allow women priests to become bishops. The 140-member body defeated the controversial bill by three votes, despite the bill being backed by the Archbishop of Wales.[32] The defeat of that motion left the Church of Wales and the Church of England as the only two provinces in the United Kingdom not yet canonically open to the consecration of women. The Church of Scotland had previously moved to make such action canonically possible in 2003.[33] The Church of Ireland changed its canons in 1990 to make ordination of women to all three orders possible.[34] A summary of actions taken across the Communion is contained in the endnotes.[35]

As discussed earlier in this chapter, the Church of England has been debating the broad matter of the inclusion of women in the three-fold order of the church for more than a century. However, the issue of the inclusion of women as bishops is still in process. At its 2010 General Synod, members acknowledged draft legislation aiming toward the inclusion of women in the episcopacy—in a format largely unamended from the draft presented by the General Synod legislative drafting committee. In September 2010, the draft legislation was referred to the diocese for debate and vote. If a majority of Diocesan Synods approve the draft legislation, it will return to the General Synod for final drafting. As of November 2011, of the forty-four dioceses of the Church of England, only two (London and Chichester) had voted against the draft legislation.[36] Despite enthusiastic predictions that legislation that would open the way for women bishops in the Church of England would be successfully adopted by the General Synod in July 2012, this did not happen. The legislation was indeed sent on to the General Synod, which met in July. However, prior to the Synod, in May of 2012, the House of Bishops made two amendments to the proposed legislation. Supporters of the consecration of women argued that one of these amendments, clause 5(1)c, threatened to enshrine discrimination against women into law. Clause 5(1)c stipulated that a new code of practice being drawn up should include official guidance on how to ensure that "the exercise of ministry by those [alternative] bishops and priests will be consistent with the theological convictions" of the parish that has objected to a woman. It was argued that this amendment took the former position that parishes could request alternative Episcopal oversight if they did not support women in the episcopacy and embedded it in legislation in a way that mitigated against future change.[37] Under the current timetable, it is likely that the first women bishops will be consecrated by 2014.[38]

Exploring the Canadian Experience: A Micronarrative, or How Did We Change? How Did We Remain?

Each province of the Communion has handled the matter of the ordination of women in a manner unique to its ethos and polity. Some argue that the cultural context with regard to the place of women has been determinative as to whether a church has moved to accept women in diverse leadership roles, including ordination. However, the events recounted here demonstrate that there is considerable diversity even within groups one might assume shared a relatively common cultural ethos. As noted, Western nations such as Canada and the United States were among the first to ordain women as priests. However, the African nations of Uganda and Kenya soon joined them. When we look at the current situation, we see that the Church of Wales, a Western nation, will not accept women in the episcopacy, while some nations of the global South do. What then can we say is determinative in the unfolding of particular micronarratives? What is requisite in the historical discourse for change to happen?

A consideration of the Canadian story leads to the observation that, in the end, a dialectic is necessary for institutional change of this order of magnitude to occur: both endogenous and exogenous forces must develop sufficient momentum for a shift to take place; both leadership and grassroots opinion must have a will to change if a sustainable reformulation of institutional structures is to occur. The hermeneutical lens of twentieth-century Italian philosopher Antonio Gramsci lends us tools for discussion. Gramsci argued that for there to be a sustainable shift from one historic bloc to another, the precondition of external and internal pressure is essential. Past that, there has to be both a leadership (which he called the leadership of the *organic intellectual*) with a vision for change that is sufficiently rooted in the passion and experience of the people that they will follow it and a grassroots constituency that will support change once implemented. No system that has to be maintained over time by force or coercion is sustainable and no real and lasting structural change is possible without the dialectic of complementary visions for social stasis held by intellectuals leading change and those to be affected by the change.[39] Gramsci's consideration of the organic intellectual is set in contradistinction to the traditional intellectual who spends his or her energy maintaining the status quo, even if there are indicators that the status quo is no longer working.

The process by which the Anglican Church of Canada moved to adopt the inclusion of women into the three-fold order of ministry was relatively rapid. Although women's work was a significant part of the life of the Canadian church throughout the twentieth century, the question of whether women should serve the church as ordained persons simply did not surface on the agendas of committees or synod. However, after the Lambeth Conference of 1968, Canadian bishops brought back the request that women deacons be considered as within the three-fold order of the church and a request that the matter of women in the priesthood be discussed at the Canadian General Synod of 1969. In anticipation of the synod, the church's national committee on the ministry of women was asked to prepare some initial reflections on the topic. When the committee reported to the General Synod of 1969, they stated that they saw no impediment to the ordination of women to the priesthood. Interestingly, however, they also expressed concerns about the ongoing inequality of working conditions for paid women workers in the church and argued that this should be ameliorated along with any action on women's ordination.[40]

When the Synod met in 1969, it undertook two important actions with reference to the actions of Lambeth 1968. First, it passed a motion ratifying the Lambeth action that deaconess and deacon orders be understood as one.[41] (Further confirmation by the House of Bishops authorizing the use of the service for the making of a deacon in the 1962 BCP for the ordination of both male and female deacons followed in 1970.[42] However, the first ordination of a woman to the diaconate took place in 1969 prior to that action of the House of Bishops.[43]) Second, the Synod asked the Primate to establish a task force on the ordination of women to the priesthood. It asked the task force, comprised of lay and clerical members, to study the matter and report to the next General Synod.

The report of the task force was not ready until 1972, one year after the subsequent General Synod. Its reports were tabled at General Synod 1973. The task force, in the end, produced two reports. All members of the group but one supported a *Majority Report* that argued in favor of the ordination of women. A *Minority Report*, which argued against the ordination of women, represented the views of the dissenting individual. After small group discussion and respectful debate, the Synod moved to ordain women as priests. Although the Prolocutor of the General Synod had ruled that no constitutional change was required in order to proceed with the ordination of women, the House of Bishops directed that the handling of this issue proceed as though it were a constitutional matter.[44] Accordingly, voting took place by houses with the requirement of a two-thirds majority to pass. The motion passed easily in all three houses, with the least support among the clergy.[45]

Treating this matter with caution, as though it required constitutional change, meant that the General Synod referred its motion to the House of Bishops. After much further conversation, the bishops in turn required a second vote at General Synod, by houses with a two-thirds majority in each house, before they would proceed to develop an implementation plan. A motion was brought back to the General Synod of 1975 and again passed in each house with significantly more than the requisite two-thirds. The Synod sent that motion on to the House of Bishops for implementation.[46] After the motion passed in 1975, a group of dissenting clergy prepared a text, which they signed and presented to the House of Bishops. This text, known as the *Manifesto Against the Ordination of Women to the Priesthood,* was too little too late.[47] The first women in the Anglican Church of Canada to become priests were ordained November 30, 1976.[48] The consecration of women to the episcopate would follow in 1992, with the election of Victoria Matthews as the Suffragan Bishop of the Diocese of Toronto.[49]

Not all dioceses were of a common mind in 1976 when the ordinations proceeded. It would be almost two decades before all dioceses moved to support the principle of the ordination of women. In 1975, the General Synod affirmed a conscience clause, subsequently reaffirmed by the House of Bishops, whereby no bishop or clergyperson would be compelled to accept the ordination of women.[50] This conscience clause allowed dioceses to move forward with the issue in their own time, tending to the particularities of their own demographics. The conscience clause was revoked in 1986, when the Canadian church confirmed its support for the inclusion of women in the episcopacy.[51]

What made the movement toward the ordination of women possible in the Canadian case? The relatively conflict-free and rapid process was possible because the components for a successful shift between historic blocs, as postulated by Gramsci, were in place. External pressure from the broader conversation of the Communion through the Lambeth Conference, as well as pressure from the societal context for equal access to all corridors of power in Canadian society (as a product of second-wave feminism), created exogenous pressure. The desire by women for opportunities to serve fully as ordained ministers, as well as a vision for change held by several key bishops in the Canadian church, created endogenous pressure. Pressure from within and without created fragility in the old structures, whereby it became possible for a movement toward change to grow from a desire for more inclusive forms of church life.[52] In particular, the Primate of the Anglican Church of Canada from 1971 to 1986, Archbishop Ted Scott, along with several other key leaders in the House of Bishops, including Archbishop John Bothwell of Niagara and Archbishop David Somerville of New Westminster, were enthusiastic and proactive advocates for this direction. The Canadian context had long known the ministry of women through Bishop's Messengers, deaconesses, and paid women's workers. In fact, in many isolated regions of the country, women served where male clerics had refused to.[53] As well, very active women's organizations had served the church in mission and ministry for a prior century. In the 1960s, the conversation in the church committees relating to women was working with themes of broader integration of women at all levels into the structures of the church. Lambeth added the category of ordination to a conversation already enthusiastically committed to the notion of a church framed beyond use of gender as a limiting discourse. That conversation, as reflected in the movement to integrate women's organizations into church structures per se (accomplished in 1971), contributed to a lay population at the General Synod level that was predominantly enthused about reframing the leadership models of the church to fully include women. Had either the body of the church or its key leadership been less enthused about the possibilities inherent in this reframing of social location by gender, the story would have developed otherwise.

What Did Change Mean?

How did the story unfold for Canadian Anglicans from that enthusiastic commitment to an idea of church framed as inclusive, integrated, and whole? Was a new church born from the revolution in leadership models cracked open as invitation to inclusion for all? The data is complex. An extensive survey of the experience of Canadian Anglican clergywomen and the church they inhabit, published in 2002, documents the story of mixed experience.[54] Where the vision was for mutuality and inclusion, often there has been estrangement and alienation. In places where it was hoped that the presence of women as clergy would make old things new, much has remained the same. The Anglican Church of Canada, along with its other Protestant counterparts, has continued to decline rapidly through the period of integration. Constitutional life, polity, and ways of conducting the business of the church have remained largely the same. My mother was fond of the adage, "The more things change, the more they remain the same." However, despite the empirical data that impresses upon us that perhaps not much has changed, I remain convinced that a revolution has taken place here, that in fact everything is different.

Nearly three decades ago, I studied among the first women to prepare for priesthood in the Anglican denomination. My liturgics professor was adamantly opposed to the ordination of women; he regularly shared his conviction on this matter—usually not kindly. His audience was not sympathetic, and as our unwillingness to be convinced of his views grew, so did his exasperation. One day, he shook his fists in the air and said, "Don't you see? When you change form, you change completely; you are not the same thing anymore." I see. We changed form. We changed completely. We are not the same thing anymore.

By asserting with our actions that women ontologically were capable of admission to the three-fold order of the church, we as a church changed ontologically. By our actions, we have been conformed newly to an original theology that remakes us. When it presented its *Majority Report* to the General Synod in 1973, the Primate's task force on the ordination of women considered the arguments against taking such action: the arguments from theology and from tradition and from sociology and ecclesiological orientation. In the end, they concluded that the argument that the theological case for admitting women to the ordained ministry of the church was put and agreed to when the first woman was baptized into the church and thereby into the body of Christ. Baptism, by which we move into discipleship, de facto overcomes all particularities that divide.[55]

The revolution, then, by which old forms were cracked open and new ones made possible through the inclusion of women in the three-fold order of ministry has not changed so much what we do or how we do it. To argue otherwise would incline us in the direction of unhelpful gender essentialism, the very thing our movement toward integration theoretically mitigates against. Rather, it changes who we are. Our new form returns us to ourselves, the body of Christ enfleshed in the whole people of God without any limitation or disqualification framed by the particularities and biases of our social and historical contexts. Behold, the old has passed away and the new has come.

Notes

1 See the development of the "lift theory" of denominationalism as articulated in H. Richard Niebuhr, "The Churches of the Middle Class," in *The Social Sources of Denominationalism 1929* (La Vergne, TN: Lightning Source, 2004), 80-84.

2 For a fuller discussion of this phenomenon, see Wendy Fletcher, "Through Heart and Hearth: Redefining Womanhood as a Missiological Work," in *Deeper Joy: Lay Women and Vocation in the 20th Century Episcopal Church,* ed. Fredrica Harris Thompsett and Sheryl Kujawa-Holbrook (New York: Church Publishing, 2005), 151-64.

3 *Lambeth Conference Reports and Resolutions 1897 to 1938* (Lambeth, 1949), 177-79.

4 See sentiments expressed in the local press of the time: for example, *The Guardian,* May 5, 1921.

5 Ibid., 60-61.

6 *Lambeth Conference Papers,* LC 114 (1920), 208.

7 *Report on the Ministry of Women* (Lambeth, 1935).

8 For the ordination to have been canonical, the canons of the church would have needed to have been changed to allow for the possibility of the inclusion of women in the presbyterate.

9 Correspondence between Archbishop Geoffrey Fisher and Bishop Hall can be found in the Lambeth Palace Archives. *Fisher Papers,* vol. 11, 104-5.

10 *Fisher Papers,* vol. 11, 70.

11 Roger Coleman, ed., *Resolutions of the Lambeth Conference 1867-1988* (Toronto: Anglican Book Centre, 1992), 120.

12 Ibid., 119.

13 AGOW Papers housed at the Sarah Fawcett Library, *AGOW Minutes* (1958), 7.

14 "Report of the Church of England's Women in Ministry Committee, 1968"; "Women in Holy Orders," Committee on Ministry Report, 1966; and Alan Richardson,"Women in Holy Orders," in "Preparatory Essays for Lambeth 1968," 295. All three documents are housed in the Lambeth Palace Archives, Lambeth Conference Papers, LC118 (1968).

15 Coleman, *Resolutions,* 163.

16 Ibid., 163-64.

17 "Renewal in Ministry," in *Lambeth Report* (Lambeth, 1968), 106-7.

18 Archbishop Ted Scott of the Anglican Church of Canada was a member of the ACC. His papers contain a full record of the proceedings of the 1971 meeting of the ACC. *Scott Papers,* Anglican Church of Canada Archives, M101, Record of Proceedings, 2-3.

19 Coleman, *Resolutions*, 186-87.

20 Coleman, *Resolutions*, 188.

21 Lambeth Conference 1988, Resolution 1.1 calls for respect. Resolution 1.2 affirms open dialogue between bishops. http://www.lambethconference.org/resolutions/1988/1988-1.cfm.

22 Ibid., Resolution 1.3a.b.

23 Ibid., Resolutions 1.4 and 1.5.

24 Ibid., Resolution 1 with results noted.

25 *Eames Monitoring Group Report* (1997), 1-27, http://www.anglicancommunion.org/lambeth/reports/report10.html.

26 At that point in time, the monitoring group found that there was no ordination of women at all in: Central Africa; Jerusalem and the Middle East; Korea; Melanesia; Nigeria; Papua, New Guinea; Southeast Asia; and Tanzania. Women were ordained only to the diaconate in: the Indian Ocean, Japan, and the Southern Cone. Women were ordained to the diaconate and presbyterate, but not to the episcopate in: Australia, Burundi, England, Kenya, the Philippines, Scotland, Uganda, Wales, West Africa, and the West Indies. Women could be ordained to all of the three orders in: Brazil, Ireland, Mexico, and Southern Africa. Women bishops, as well as priests and deacons, were de facto in: Aotearoa, New Zealand; Polynesia; Canada; and the United States.

27 *Eames Monitoring Group*, 4-5.

28 The conclusions of the Conference are documented in Resolution III.IV of the 1998 proceedings under the heading, *Eames Report*. This Resolution was conflated with Resolution IV.10. www.lambethconference.org/resolutions/1998/1998-3-4.cfm

29 In 1994, the three official reports of the Commission were published in one volume, *The Eames Commission, The Official Reports* (1997).

30 "Anglican Church Appoints Female Bishop," www.abc.net.au/news/2011-12-05/canberra-region-female-anglican-bishop/3712602.

31 "First Female Anglican Bishop for Africa elected in a Spirit-filled Atmosphere," Anglican Communion News Service, July 19, 2012, www.anglicancommunion.org.

32 "Church Rejects Women Bishop Bill," BBC News, April 2, 2008, http://news.bbc.co.uk/2/hi/uk_news/wales/7325877.stm.

33 "Scotland," BBC World News, January 16, 2002, www.scotland.anglican.org.

34 The Church of Ireland changed its canons to make provision for the inclusion of women in all three orders as the Anglican Church of Canada rather than separating the question of women bishops from the matter of women in the priesthood. See "Chapter IX, Canons, Part III, Section 22," *Church of Ireland Constitution*. http://www.ireland.anglican.org/information/32.

35 This table was taken from the Wikepedia site on the ordination of women in the Anglican Communion with data cross checked by information provided by provincial churches to the Anglican Communion office. www.en.wikipedia.org/wiki/Ordination_of_women_in_the_Anglican_Communion. The table illustrates the status of action with regard to the ordination of women in the Anglican Communion as of July 2010:

    Bishops (consecrated): Aotearoa, New Zealand and Polynesia; Australia; Canada; United States (including Cuba);

    Bishops (none yet consecrated): Bangladesh, Brazil, Central America, Hong Kong, Ireland, Japan, Mexico, North India, Philippines, Scotland, Southern Africa, Sudan, Uganda

    Priests: Burundi, England, Indian Ocean, Jerusalem and the Middle East, Kenya, Korea, Rwanda, South India, Wales, West Indies, West Africa

    Deacons: Southern Cone, Congo, Pakistan

    No ordination of women: Central Africa, Melanesia, Nigeria, Papua New Guinea, South East Asia, Tanzania

36 "Synod Must Decide on Women Bishops," *The Independent*, November 14, 2011, 1.

37 "Fears Church of England Vote on Women Bishops Has Begun to Unravel," http://www.guardian.co.uk/world/2012/jul/05/church-england-vote-women-bishops.

38 "Church of England Postpones Vote on Female Bishops," http://www.guardian.co.uk/world/2012/jul/09/church-of-england-female-bishops.

39 Antonio Gramsci, "Problems of History and Culture-The Intellectuals," in *Selections from the Prison Notebooks* (New York: International Publishers, 1971), 5-23. Gramsci himself most likely would not acknowledge this application of his argument. He makes a clear distinction between traditional intellectuals and organic intellectuals. For Gramsci, with a classic Marxist view of Christianity, the church per se would not be understood as anything other than a bastion of hegemony within the superstructure of the culture. The category of organic intellectual in his schema is reserved for the revolutionary who intends to entirely overturn the social order. However, I would argue that within the context of an increasingly displaced Christianity, the overturning of a model of clerical leadership that excluded women over the course of almost two thousand years warrants the designation of revolutionary change such as intended in Gramsci's description of shifts from one historic bloc to the next.

40 *Minutes of the Commission on Women (1969)*, Anglican Church of Canada Archives.

41 General Synod, *Journal of Proceedings* (1969), 47.

42 *Minutes of the House of Bishops Annual Meeting*, Anglican Church of Canada Archives, Box F 150 (October 1970), 11.

43 The Reverend Mary Mills became the first woman ordained as deacon in the Anglican Church of Canada. She was ordained by Bishop George Luxton, Bishop of Huron, on December 12, 1969. The Reverend Mary Mills, interview by Wendy Fletcher, November 15, 1991.

44 H. R. S. Ryan, "The General Synod of the Anglican Church of Canada: Aspects of Constitutional History," *Journal of the Canadian Church Historical Society* 34, no. 1 (April 1992): 52-53, 62.

45 General Synod, *Journal of Proceedings* (1973), 30.

46 General Synod, *Journal of Proceedings* (1975), M-50.

47 Two hundred clergymen signed the *Manifesto*. They were drawn from clergy in twenty-two out of the then thirty-three dioceses of the national church. They represented approximately ten percent of the clergy population. This textual lobby represents the only organized resistance to the ordination of women in the ACC.

48 Four dioceses ordained women simultaneously across the country: the Dioceses of Huron, Niagara, New Westminster, and Cariboo.

49 The Anglican Church of Canada had no exclusionary clause restraining women from the episcopacy when it moved the matter of priesthood. However, the General Synod of 1986 did affirm that such consecrations were possible in the Canadian church should a woman be nominated and elected through the usual canonical processes.

50 Anglican Church of Canada Archives, *Scott Papers*, Box M101. The *Conscience Clause* was revoked by General Synod 1986. It is now understood as a matter of ecclesiastical discipline that all clergy of the Anglican Church of Canada support women in the three-fold order of ministry.

51 Ibid.

52 For a detailed discussion of this theory of institutional shift as applied in the Canadian case, see Wendy Fletcher-Marsh, *Beyond the Walled Garden: Anglican Women and the Priesthood* (Toronto: Artemis, 1995).

53 For a fuller discussion of the paid women workers and Bishop's Messengers, see Wendy Fletcher, "The Garden of Women's Separateness," in *Seeds Scattered and Sown: Studies in the History of Canadian Anglicanism*, ed. Norman Knowles (Toronto: ABC Publishing, 2008), 280-320.

54 For a fuller conversation of findings, see Wendy Fletcher-Marsh, *Like Water on Rock: Gender Integration in Canadian Anglicanism* (Toronto: Artemis, 2002).

55 "Scripture," in *Majority Report of the Primate's Task Force on the Ordination of Women to the Priesthood*, 1972, M4Y3G2, Anglican Church of Canada General Synod Archives, Toronto.

5

WOMEN'S LEADERSHIP DEVELOPMENT FOR THE ANGLICAN COMMUNION: OH LORD, HOW LONG MUST WE WAIT . . . ?

Jenny Plane Te Paa

> *People are often unreasonable, illogical and self-centered.*
> *Forgive them anyway.*
>
> *If you are kind, people may accuse you of selfish*
> *ulterior motives. Be kind anyway.*
>
> *If you are successful, you will win some false friends*
> *and true enemies. Succeed anyway.*
>
> *If you are honest and frank, people may cheat you.*
> *Be honest anyway.*
>
> *What you spend years building, someone could*
> *destroy overnight. Build anyway.*
>
> *If you find serenity and happiness, they may be jealous.*
> *Be happy anyway.*
>
> *The good you do today, people will often forget tomorrow.*
> *Do good anyway.*
>
> *Give the world the best you have, and it may never be*
> *enough. Give the world the best you've got anyway.*
>
> *You see, in the final analysis, it is between you and*
> *God. It was never between you and them anyway.*[1]

Over the past two decades a very small number of theologically competent, qualified, and articulate women have contributed as representative leaders on various of the Anglican Communion's top-level commissions and committees, but never has our rightful representation as equally necessary, equally worthy participants in discussions and decisions on all matters pertaining to our beloved Church been an organizational given. The evidence for this is readily observed by the manner in which we still greet women's leadership appointments in the twenty-first century. Women as senior leaders in the Church are unusual, rare; we celebrate our appointments to senior roles as momentous. It seems almost heretical to suggest that the real reason we celebrate is because we are still amazed at our ability to surmount the weight of institutionally embedded patriarchal oppression (which is and always has been the structural injustice preventing women's progress).

None of this is to detract from the caliber or the deservedness of those women who have succeeded in becoming women leaders in the Anglican Communion. Rather it is to suggest that the obstacles to women's progress toward leadership are still deeply hidden behind the veil of attitudinally and institutionally mired, gendered injustice. What is needed is a sustained transformative project to both normalize and relativize the presence of women as leaders across the spectrum of ministries within the worldwide Anglican Communion. In this way, appointments based primarily on recognition of high-level professional qualification and ecclesial experience, of spirit-filled personal charism, and of proven theological competency will be the primary reasons to celebrate—certainly no less momentously.

As one privileged beyond imagining to have been "chosen"[2] to work in a variety of leadership roles across the Anglican Communion with particular intensity since the mid 1990s, it was my very early firsthand exposure to the absolute dearth of "other" women in leadership that initially motivated me to act for change. Throughout 1997, I worked alongside deeply respected global professional colleagues Dr. Denise M. Ackermann (South Africa), Dr. Kwok Pui-lan (United States), the Reverend Dr. Sathianathan Clarke (India), and (now) Bishop Ian T. Douglas (United States) to organize and then to host during the following year an inaugural gathering of contextual theologians drawn from across the Anglican Communion. We were especially committed to ensuring that significant numbers of women would be invited, even as we knew how few yet fitted our ideal attendee profile.

These were the years when postcolonial studies were particularly topical in secular universities but were only just beginning to have a tentative hearing within theological educational institutions. As a result, the lingering structural injustices, particularly the actual and attitudinal *traditional* exclusions of women and indigenous and two-thirds-world people from the theological academy were still very strongly evident. The organizers' intent was that by showcasing the theological diversity, wisdom, and insight emanating from those traditionally excluded, the deeply entrenched hegemonic discourses characteristic of the North Atlantic intellectual tradition and pervasive in seminary teaching could, at long last, be disrupted. It was time to hear the contextually grounded voices of those being popularly described as "minority"[3] Anglican theologians. In addition, and more strategically, the organizers sought to bring to bear influence beyond the academy and into the debating and decision-making forums of the Anglican Communion by promoting the range and impressive capacity of minority public theologians and leaders now eminently well qualified and available for appointments to top-level representative responsibility.

All of the papers presented at the 1998 gathering were published in what has become one of the Anglican Communion's most popularly used textbooks on postcolonial Anglicanism.[4] This gathering also produced the international Anglican Contextual Theologians Network (ACT). Its objective was to provide ongoing professional support across the vagaries of distance and "difference" and to commit to organizing global forums on a regular basis, within which multiple theological voices drawn from across the Anglican Communion could be heard and acknowledged, critiqued, and celebrated. Lacking resources to maintain, let alone enable, the network to advance its ambitious agenda for ongoing productivity and for promoting minority interests in contextual theological education and in representative leadership, the ACT project languished somewhat. However, what had been begun as professional relationships among and between its leaders soon developed very naturally into strong and enduring friendships, all of which have since proven to be extremely influential in Communion affairs.

In late 2000, the Millennium Summit held at the United Nations produced a series of aspirational goals, which quickly became benchmarks against which institutions and nations could measure their progress toward eradicating poverty, inequality, disease, violence, and indeed all forms of social, political, and economic injustice. The Anglican Communion, through the Anglican Consultative Council (ACC),[5] eventually responded to these goals at the urging of the Anglican Observer to the United Nations and the Inter-Anglican Women's Network (IAWN).[6] What follows is an account of how these two key Anglican Communion bodies, the ACC and the IAWN, have both been incrementally enabled, encouraged, and indeed expected by women to take seriously their need to be more credibly, measurably inclusive of women.

The Anglican Consultative Council and Women's (under)Representation?

As the only truly representative body out of the four Instruments of Communion, the ACC is the only one where women and lay people are officially represented. Since the ACC's formal establishment in 1971, a very small number of women have been appointed to its membership, and, to their credit, most have endeavored to advocate for an increase in their numbers. An unscientific survey of participants since 1971 nonetheless reveals an unacceptably low level of representation from among those who comprise at least 50 percent of the Anglican body of Christ.[7] And so it was that while gender (in)justice, including the issue of women's underrepresentation on the ACC was being informally noticed and occasionally spoken of by women's representatives and by a few individual male Anglican Church leaders, it was not really until the early part of the twenty-first century that ultimately transformative initiatives began to emerge.

In 2002, Archdeacon Taimalelagi Matalavea, then Anglican Observer to the United Nations, established the programmatic basis for Anglican women drawn from across the Anglican Communion to gather annually in New York as an authorized and active NGO delegation to the annual United Nations Commission on the Status of Women (UNCSW). Alongside this initiative, the IAWN, coincidentally, was revived and reorganized. Many of the IAWN's new members were also members of the UNCSW delegation. Although at times the overlapping representative roles were slightly confusing, the IAWN eventually took time to recreate for itself a distinctive and authentic internationally representative organizational framework with a clear developmental agenda.

There in New York, working within one of the world's most high-powered secular decision-making and debating forums, the enduring experience of gendered injustice affecting women and girls was writ large. As Anglican women from across God's world shared stories and experiences with women of all Christian denominations, with women of other faiths, and with women for whom faith was not a conscious life choice, the role of the church as being complicit both in the establishment and maintenance of the actual and attitudinal oppression of women through its deeply embedded patriarchal preferences and practices became far more readily understood.

It was the UNCSW experience, then, that ultimately re-energized and then positively harnessed, at a global level, Anglican women's increasing outrage about underrepresentation. This was given particular impetus when the official Provincial Anglican Delegation to the United Nations Commission on the Status of Women began officially reporting to the ACC. Thus the issue of women's underrepresentation across all spheres of church leadership received more focused and formalized *in-house* attention.

Prior to attempting a qualitative analysis of the actual experience of women in leadership, I endeavored to quantify the statistical reality of women's leadership in the Church by gathering data on how many women held representative leadership roles across the key sites of theological education, synodical governance, mission agencies, and episcopal leadership within each of the provinces. Immediately I found myself being challenged by men and women, both of whom who were skeptical. Some wanted to know what I meant by leadership (particularly those with a strongly clericalist understanding of church leadership); others wanted to know if I had taken sufficient account of cultural sensitivities (given that some provinces are inherently more sexist than others); and yet others wanted to know why it even mattered. In addition, in some provinces, the existing women's organizations were understandably protective of their primary mission field, which included advocacy and support for women's ministries. Some of these groups saw no need for surveying for current statistical data concerning women's representation.

Even in the first few years of this century, in spite of almost five previous decades of global feminist influence, it was not easy then trying to gather accurate statistics on women's leadership in the Church. My inquiries were further thwarted by encountering the reality that most provinces had neither gender-data collection requirements nor official support agencies, such as a women's desk. I could only conclude that given that most provinces apparently had no conscious desire to know anything definitively about the plight or aspirations of women, the original survey proposal was unlikely to succeed.

Somewhat sardonically then, I undertook instead to mathematically magnify the problem. I calculated that if the Instruments of Communion could, broadly speaking, be described as those entities within the Anglican Communion where representative leadership is officially located, then it would follow that a gender analysis of these four Instruments would reveal the comparative percentage of women to men in leadership at the highest levels.

On that basis, the approximate numbers (updated to 2011) are as follows[8]:

Archbishop of Canterbury	1 male	0 female
Anglican Consultative Council	56 male	21 female[9]
Lambeth Conference	800+ male	24 female[10]
Primates' Meeting	37 male	1 female
Total	894 male	46 female

While the numbers are not absolutely precise, because the data is not officially collected and thus cannot be officially confirmed, nonetheless the margin of error is negligible and therefore the disproportionate totals do not really require further analysis. The figures are stark—and surely unacceptable?

It was data such as this, together with the growing combined politicization of both the UNCSW provincial delegation and the IAWN, that finally led to a very strong submission to the thirteenth meeting of the ACC (ACC 13) held in Nottingham in 2005. In June of that year, the Provincial delegation to the UNCSW presented the following wide-ranging Resolution[11] to the ACC as the body to which it was accountable. The subsections of the Resolution were intended to encourage the Anglican Communion Office (which manages and oversees appointments to high-level Anglican commissions and committees) and all provinces of the Anglican Communion to pursue the goal of ensuring an equality of numbers of men and women in decision-making roles. Resolution 31 was easily passed in its entirety.[12]

The Anglican Consultative Council:

a. receives and adopts the Report of the ACC Provincial Delegation to the 49th UN Commission on the Status of Women (UNCSW), and affirms the work of the International Anglican Women's Network (IAWN) in responding to the Beijing Platform for Action and the Millennium Developments Goals (MDG), thereby carrying forward the full flourishing of God's Creation

b. acknowledges the MDG goal for equal representation of women in decision making at all levels, and so requests:

    i. the Standing Committee to identify ways in which this goal may appropriately be adapted for incorporation into the structures of the Instruments of Unity, and other bodies to which the Anglican Consultative Council nominates or appoints

    ii. all member churches to work towards the realisation of this goal in their own structures of governance, and in other bodies to which they nominate or appoint and to report on progress to ACC-14.

c. recommends that a study of the place and role of women in the structures of the Anglican Communion be undertaken by the Standing Committee in line with the objects of the ACC "to keep in review the needs that may arise for further study, and, where necessary, to promote inquiry and research"

d. requests that each Province give consideration to the establishment of a women's desk for that Province

e. thanks those Provinces which sent participants to the 49th Session of UNCSW, and encourages those who did not to review their decision in time for the 50th Session in 2006 in solidarity with all women of the Anglican Communion.

Notwithstanding the fact that a small number of top-level appointments of women to positions of significant leadership within the Church have been made across the Communion since 2005, it is difficult to draw a direct connection between Resolution 31 and any of those appointments. Indeed it seems that in spite of its truly noble sentiments, Resolution 31 has at best enabled some provinces to be slightly more gender-conscientious in their appointments procedures, but in general it would seem that the Resolution has largely since failed to ignite the universal spark of radical activism needed in order for the full flourishing of women as part of God's creation to even stand a chance of succeeding.

Sadly, since 2005 and although recommended by section (c) of the Resolution, there has been no official effort to establish a viable research project to assist the Church in moving forward on this most fundamental representational flaw, indeed injustice, in its own structures. The Church still needs to establish a systematic review process in order to measure progress being made toward meeting the laudable and long overdue objectives of the entire Resolution.

Theological Education and Women's (under)Representation

As a pioneering lay indigenous woman academic leader in Anglican theological education in Aotearoa, New Zealand, I was always curious to know where my peer professional equivalents were in other parts of the Anglican Communion. My first clue about just how few women there were in Anglican theological educational leadership came as a result of an international ecumenical gathering called in 2003 by Dr. Nyambura Njoroge, then working as Programme Executive, Ecumenical Theological Education, for the World Council of Churches (WCC) in Geneva. Dr. Njoroge invited to the gathering women known to hold significant leadership roles in denominational seminaries and other officially recognized centers of teaching and learning for candidates preparing for ordination. Fifty-two women attended the gathering, only two of whom were Anglican.

Inevitably, as the women gathered and shared experiences, it soon became clear that regardless of respective denominational homes, each participant found herself to be either the first, or the only, woman holding such a professional role. Virtually all were not only bereft of women peer professionals but also found themselves working in professional ecclesial environments characterized by hostility and indifference, lacking in support, and just plain difficult.

Individually and collectively, we resolved to do two things. The first was to establish a strong mutually supportive professional network among ourselves, and the second was to establish a mentoring for leadership program, whereby, notwithstanding our own challenging professional experiences, we committed to mentoring younger women for leadership roles in theological education while at the same time opening up pathways to all other forms of church leadership.

As Chair of the Ecumenical Theological Education Working Group (ETE) for the WCC for a six-year period from 2000 to 2006, I committed to offering space at my own institution in Auckland, New Zealand, for PhD candidates who could be part of the WCC foundational mentoring for leadership program. In the ten-year period beginning in 2002, five international ecumenical students were supported either partially or fully by WCC scholarships to complete either PhD or other higher-level degrees while living at St. John's College in Auckland.[13] While, for cultural reasons, not all churches were yet able to send women, the men who were selected were chosen specifically for their known feminist activism. Of the five students, two were women and both are Anglican priests.

Coincidental with my work for the WCC, there arose within certain parts of the Anglican Communion scandalous objection to the entirely legitimate election of a gay bishop within the Episcopal Church. Such was the ecclesiastical fervor provoked by the election that a special Commission[14] was established by the Archbishop of Canterbury to consider ways in which church unity might be preserved in the face of overwhelming threats to the contrary. Six women were appointed to the seventeen-person Lambeth Commission. One woman resigned after the first meeting and one was unable to attend a second meeting, which meant there was a constant presence of just four women alongside thirteen men.

The experience of working with such a high-level Commission was both profoundly humbling as well as deeply intellectually and spiritually challenging. Two standout realizations occurred during the life of the Lambeth Commission. The first was the critical importance of ensuring minority presence and voice in the key debates on how best to promote, establish, and maintain right relationships in spite of socially constructed notions of "difference." I include in this claim the traditionally marginalized or excluded voices of women (a representational rather than a numerical minority), the voices of indigenous peoples, and especially in the case of the Lambeth Commission, the voices of gay people (none of whom were included). As those continuously "designated" by dominant majorities as "other," as "exceptions," or as "different," inevitably the vantage point from which the marginalized speak is quite radically different. This was soon very obvious within the life and work of the Lambeth Commission. It was generally those members either with lived experience of social and political marginalization or those who had stood unequivocally alongside those being unjustly "set aside" in their communities or societies, who instinctively argued the God-given rightness of any duly discerned and properly elected Godly person to assume episcopal leadership. It was this same group of just five members who also came very close to proposing a minority report.

The second realization was the critical need for those of us involved in theological educational leadership to insist upon the urgency of strengthening the teaching and learning of Anglican ecclesiology and missiology. This insight was readily reinforced as submission after submission to the Lambeth Commission revealed a disturbingly consistent low level of Anglican ecclesiological knowledge, often accompanied by a decided lack of experience of being Anglican.

As a concurrent member of the Archbishop of Canterbury's inaugural Commission on Theological Education for the Anglican Communion (TEAC), I was already well aware of the alarming level of *unevenness* in terms of theological educational expectation and provision of the same to those elected or appointed as bishops across the Anglican Communion.[15] That there never has been a global standard (appropriately adjusted for theologically defensible contextual variation) developed for Anglican episcopal leadership is unconscionable. That even in 2012 there is still either resistance or outright indifference to even debating the principle of a global standard for episcopal leadership is outrageous.

It was my contention that ecclesiological ignorance or inexperience ought never to have been considered an acceptable excuse for some of the less than accurate or loving utterances and subsequently some of the less than courteous behaviors of a number of global church leaders in their responses to the Lambeth Commission. An educational intervention was clearly indicated. Unfortunately, soon after, as the focus of the Anglican Communion was turned more intently toward placating the voices of moral and theological outrage emanating from within the African continent, so too did those responsible for TEAC turn more toward the already established male-dominated network of African theologians[16] for advice and example.

In the five-year period between 2003 and 2008, as one of only two lay women of color contributing regularly at the top level of various Anglican Communion commissions and committees, Kenyan sister, treasured ACT colleague and friend, Dr. Esther M. Mombo and I began to strategize ways of using what we viewed as our positions of unique privilege to create pathways of enablement for younger women to participate and to contribute similarly. We were especially concerned to advocate for, to promote, and where possible, to academically mentor younger women, especially those from provinces where access for women to higher-level theological education was either unlikely or impossible.

Our intention was to nurture intellectually and politically a small cadre of indigenous and or two-thirds-world young women with obvious leadership potential. Our goal was to be able to advocate strongly and confidently in the future for any one of those whom we had mentored. In this way we felt we might contribute very positively to the long overdue project of broadening diversity of representation at the highest levels of debate and decision making in the Anglican Communion.

Our first step was to mobilize supportive colleagues around the Communion. We were especially keen to co-opt those with strongly established leadership experience in contextual theological education and who could readily identify young women deserving of being recruited into the mentoring program. The second step was to identify and acquire resources needed to facilitate and support the overall mentoring program. The first step was easy, and the seeds for the Global Anglican Theological Academy (GATA) were thus sown. The second step was not.

During the Lambeth Conference of 2008, however, Clare Amos, then Director of TEAC, proposed an international gathering of women theological educators drawn from across the Communion. She invited Dr. Mombo and myself to collaborate with her in the selection of women and in the planning of the gathering. The inaugural meeting of women theological educators was held at the International Studies Centre at Canterbury in the United Kingdom in February 2009.[17]

Thirty-five women drawn from across the Communion were able to attend. A very small number were women already teaching in seminaries, most attendees were completing PhD studies with a view to future teaching careers, and just five already held significant leadership roles. It was this core group of five who were the initial collaborators in the previously identified GATA mentoring project.

Of those present, virtually each one had a story of struggle to access, let alone to succeed in, theological education either as students or as administrators. Few of the students present had dared imagine themselves as potential leaders in theological education—such was and sadly still is the patriarchally embedded capture of Anglican seminaries and places of teaching and learning across many parts of the Communion.

Doubly blessed by the presence and formal contributions from both Archbishop Rowan and Dr. Jane Williams, the women gathered at Canterbury were greatly inspired by the loving encouragement and inspired wisdom both exemplary church leaders offered. Archbishop Rowan's simple edict, "It is an injustice to deprive women of the possibility of theological education," resonated powerfully with all present.

It was at the 2009 gathering that GATA was formally established as a subgroup of TEAC.[18] Following that meeting, the GATA executives met in Hong Kong to advance two of the key strategies originally established. The first of these was to host a developmental mentoring gathering of those identified as the pioneering group of deserving young women scholars drawn from indigenous and two-thirds-world communities of faith. The second of these was for the executive members of GATA to ourselves model something of the intellectual productivity that we felt was essential to the educational credibility of the entire project proposal.

An extract from the application sent to various funding agencies is instructive in terms of its articulation of the evolving vision of GATA.

> In 2008 a small group of highly qualified and highly motivated lay Anglican women theological educators drawn from across the Communion began to discuss ways in which we could use our professional status, experience and our own visions for quality theological education to enable other predominantly younger women to achieve as we have.
>
> We have long recognized to our ongoing dismay that we are among just a mere handful of women in senior leadership roles in theological education, particularly in Anglican seminaries and colleges, throughout the Communion.
>
> We further recognize, ethnic subjectivities aside, that of the Communion's current women leaders[19] in theological education, only two are women of colour and both are lay.
>
> We believe there is an urgent need for the faces of Anglican theological educational leadership to more accurately reflect the ethnic and gender diversity of the Anglican Communion.
>
> As a result of a recent global Consultation of women in theological educational leadership held at Canterbury in the UK in 2009, an executive group known now as GATA (Global Anglican Theological Academy) was officially established. Our mission objectives are three-fold.
>
> Firstly we are endeavouring to establish a global database of young, bright Anglican women of colour; women of two thirds world; women of indigenous nations and communities, who either are or ought to be in PhD programs. These young women traditionally described, as "minorities" are our primary target group.
>
> We want to identify and mentor those with real potential for theological educational leadership. We are well aware of the structural, attitudinal and resourcing constraints which militate against minority women from a good number of the Provinces of the Communion and are committed to strategizing ways of subverting these wherever possible, even if it means making provision for some to undertake their studies outside of their home context.

We have a particular preference to mentor those whose studies engage issues of Anglican ecclesiology and of missiology, broadly understood.

Secondly we are committed to exploring ways in which we may be able to establish a globally recognized PhD program with an intentional focus upon nurturing and equipping those young women in our target group for theological educational leadership within and for the Anglican Communion.

In this second objective we are seeking to contribute back to the church something of the significant leadership experience and expertise by which we ourselves have been both privileged and challenged.

We are also seeking to exemplify something of the radically creative possibilities which ought now be developed as modern technology enables us all to be more intimately and readily acquainted with one another across the previously often impenetrable divides of geography and cultural difference.

A PhD supervised by a small globally representative group of the Anglican Communion's finest women theologians would surely be second only to a PhD supervised by a small group of the Anglican Communion's finest women and men theologians! We pray for the latter to evolve as soon as this option is popularly demanded.

Thirdly by way of exemplifying/modelling scholarly excellence we have in mind to complete a publishing project drawing upon the particular expertise and academic passion each member of the executive group brings to the work of Anglican theological education.[20]

In February 2012, with generous support from the St. Augustine's Foundation, a small gathering of eight students and four mentors met at the International Studies Centre in Canterbury for a weeklong program of mentoring and intellectual exchange.[21] The seminar comprised a comprehensive program of introduction to and encounter with various key individual leaders whose work is of critical importance to gaining understanding of what it means, from both a historical and contemporary perspective, to belong to the Anglican Communion. This included an extended audience with the Archbishop of Canterbury, meetings with key senior staff of the Anglican Communion Office, meetings with key women leaders from the Church of England, and keynote presentations from the GATA mentors, all of whom are globally experienced Anglicans.

During the seminar participants were invited to present something of their own research with particular emphasis on context and potential contribution to the wider Anglican Communion. A senior executive from an established publishing house was invited to address the young scholars by way of ensuring they would understand the process and the critical importance of being published.

Following the Canterbury meetings the executive group—as the GATA mentors—has maintained contact with the young scholars group, providing constant encouragement, nurturing, and mentoring for each one of the scholars. We continue to monitor their progress and when and where possible, we work to encourage and advocate for them for advanced positions, whether as postdoctoral scholars, in positions advancing toward theological educational leadership, or other forms of representative leadership in the many official committees and commissions of the global Anglican Communion. The young scholars group has established their own social media resource and so they continue to maintain strong and powerfully supportive contact with each other across the tyranny of distance between them.

GATA is then one of the most exciting and transformative contemporary projects for Anglican women's leadership. It is slowly attracting the attention of a number of key Communion-wide leaders. Some are archbishops and bishops; some are key educational leaders, heads of mission agencies, or those who hold positions of critical influence. What is heartening is that all share passionately in our concern about the shameful statistical evidence that shows women to be virtually invisible in theological educational leadership[22] and still seriously underrepresented in all other forms of church leadership, in spite of our faithful presence and our undoubted abilities to undertake any and all forms of leadership.

Women's leadership across the Anglican Communion is still very much a fraught arena. Sadly, many consider the glacial pace of the numerical increase solution to be a satisfactory response. What this nearly always avoids is the concurrent qualitative assurance that women being selected for representative work are well-equipped and thus already enabled to be more than merely tokens. Commensurate also with this necessary assurance is the need for appropriate structural and attitudinal safeguards to protect against the unjust silencing, ignoring, distorting, or diminution of the voices and views of strong and capable women.

GATA recognizes that low numbers of women in Anglican theological educational leadership is hardly symptomatic of an inherent pathology on the part of women but rather is sadly reflective of the deep-seated structural pathology that is the patriarchal church. It is therefore the attitudinal and systemic causes of these complex injustices that GATA seeks to identify, to transform, and thus to redeem. We are convinced this can be accomplished when there is a critical mass of ecclesiologically savvy and experienced Anglican theological scholars who are prepared to take on the daunting task of transforming the unjust structures still too markedly inherent in Anglican theological education locally and globally.

We each imagine a future global Anglican Communion where all may have access to and be enabled to flourish within quality theological education—an educational experience that equips all for advancing God's mission toward a just and peace-filled world. GATA, then, was formed with faith-filled hope that women as leaders have a very significant contribution to make to the long overdue project of achieving equitable gender justice for the women of the Anglican Communion. We will continue to do so with all the generosity of spirit, the feistiness of heart, and the grace-filled yearning for God's justice that so characterized the determination of our respective foremothers, those in whose courageous pioneering footsteps we are now so richly blessed to tread.

Notes

1 This wonderful theologically aspirational poem is popularly attributed to Mother Teresa. The words resonate so closely with those often offered to me as a pioneering lay woman leader by those friends and colleagues to whom I often turned when being a servant worker for the church became especially challenging.

2 I want here to acknowledge with deep appreciation the gentle, yet determinedly feminist, advocacy of Canon John Peterson, former Secretary General of the Anglican Communion Office. John's record of personally ensuring the appointments of highly qualified women of diverse backgrounds to top-level representative leadership roles remains unparalleled.

3 Here I use "minority" in a pejorative sense to mean those unjustly underrepresented, not those numerically positioned as minority representatives.

4 Ian T. Douglas and Kwok Pui-lan, eds., *Beyond Colonial Anglicanism: The Anglican Communion in the Twenty-first Century* (New York: Church Publishing, 2001).

5 The role of the ACC is to facilitate the cooperative work of the churches of the Anglican Communion, exchange information between the provinces and churches, and help to coordinate common action. It advises on the organization and structures of the Communion, and seeks to develop common policies with respect to the world mission of the Church, including ecumenical matters. The ACC is one of the four Instruments of Communion. It is also the one high-level global Anglican Communion body that has the power to both legislate and to persuade, to advocate for change, and to give effect to decisions.

6   The IAWN was formed in November 1996 to be the organization through which the voices of Anglican women would be reported to the ACC.

7   The participant lists on the Anglican Communion website reveal that approximately forty-three women have been members of the ACC since 1971. See http://www.anglicancommunion.org/communion/ acc/about.cfm. This compares to an unknown number of men, given that many members serve for consecutive years. However, on the basis of total membership of approximately fifty-five at any one time, then (again albeit unscientifically) it is feasible to conclude that perhaps some five hundred plus men have served during this time period. The data is further rendered somewhat fraught as only laywomen are indicated by their first names—it is just faintly possible that some women are listed according to their clerical titles. The author accepts full responsibility for any inaccuracies with respect to this calculation.

8   The numbers are approximately accurate as per attendance at Lambeth 2008 and the current membership of the ACC. See http://www.anglicancommunion.org/communion/index.cfm.

9   From the Anglican Communion website 2012, http://www.anglicancommunion.org/communion/acc/ about.cfm.

10 Because no gender-based statistics are produced by the Anglican Communion office, this is a guesstimate based on the fact that since Lambeth 2008, Swaziland and Canada have elected women bishops.

11 The Resolution itself was not very well drafted. It was too generalized and non-specific in terms of solid recommendations but notwithstanding that administrative lapse, the sentiments and aspirations which lay behind the Resolution and the unbridled passion of the women who presented and spoke to it at ACC 13 left no one in any doubt about its importance to the women of the Communion.

12 "Anglican Consultative Council—ACC 13," http://www.anglicancommunion.org/communion/acc/ meetings/acc13/resolutions.cfm#s36.

13 The students selected were one each from Mizoram, Tahiti/Maohi, and Sri Lanka and two from Kenya. Four have completed PhD degrees and one has completed a bachelor's degree and gone on to PhD studies. Four of the five have gone on to become either leaders in theological seminaries back in their homelands or hold significant positions in church leadership. The fifth, who was transferred in 2008 to a full St. John's College scholarship for her PhD studies, is poised to do similarly.

14 The Lambeth Commission was established in 2003 by the Archbishop of Canterbury to consider (in short order), "the legal and theological implications flowing from the decisions of the Episcopal Church (USA) to appoint a priest in a committed same sex relationship as one of its bishops, and of the Diocese of New Westminster to authorise services for use in connection with same sex unions, and specifically on the canonical understandings of communion, impaired and broken communion, and the ways in which provinces of the Anglican Communion may relate to one another in situations where the ecclesiastical authorities of one province feel unable to maintain the fullness of communion with another part of the Anglican Communion." See "The Lambeth Commission on Communion," http:// www.anglicancommunion.org/commission/process/lc_commission/index.cfm.

15 In 2003 Archbishop Williams initiated the establishment of a Commission on Theological Education for the Anglican Communion (TEAC). A series of specialized working groups was formed to consider what might be the fundamental and ongoing theological educational requirements for those being prepared for various orders of the Church. I was a member of the Working Group on bishops' theological education.

16 ANITEPAM (African Network of Institutions of Theological Education Preparing Anglicans for Ministry) initially worked collaboratively with the Anglican Contextual Theologians group, as many were members of both. As ANITEPAM gained ascendancy as a consultative group to TEAC, it was not long before the voices of women were muted. A new group known as Anglican Communion Contextual Scholars was formed.

17 "Anglican Women Theological Educators Meet in Canterbury, England," http://www. anglicancommunion.org/acns/news.cfm/2009/3/3/ACNS4584.

18 Convened by Dr. Jenny Plane Te Paa, the inaugural GATA executive group consisted of Dr. Esther M.

Mombo from St. Paul's in Limuru; Dr Kwok Pui-lan from the Episcopal Divinity School in Cambridge, Massachusetts; Dr. Judith Berling from the Graduate Theological Union in Berkeley, California; and Rev. Dr. Beverley Haddad from the University of Peitermaritzburg in South Africa.

19 By "leaders" we mean those holding positions such as dean or principal or senior academic dean type leadership roles.

20 This book is the result of that determination to model scholarly excellence to those we are committed to mentoring.

21 "Young Anglican Women Scholars Meet in Canterbury," http://www.anglicancommunion.org/acns/news.cfm/2012/4/2/ACNS5080?pageview=print.

22 The inaugural gathering held at Canterbury in March 2011 of principals, deans, and presidents of Anglican seminaries and theological colleges drawn from across the Anglican Communion confirmed that only two women held principal type roles and maybe two or three others held academic deanship type roles. Again the statistics are fraught, as it is not known exactly how many Anglican seminaries or theological colleges there are in the Communion. However, on the speculative basis that each of the recognized provinces and affiliates of the Anglican Communion has at least one seminary, then even the minimal ratio of two to forty-four is outrageous.

PART 2

ANGLICAN WOMEN
AND GOD'S MISSION

6

GENDER, FEMINISM, AND EMPIRE: THE CASE OF THE CHURCH MISSIONARY SOCIETY

Gulnar E. Francis-Dehqani

The gradual progress of Britain as a world power, coupled with the impact of various religious revivals, resulted in Christian missionary activity burgeoning in England toward the end of the eighteenth century.[1] The geographical conquests of colonialism opened the way for those spiritually inclined to take the gospel to the farthest corners of the earth. In many cases churches were unwilling to give official recognition to such projects and left those efforts to individual initiative, reliant upon voluntary financial support. As a result, many societies were founded by groups of like-minded and committed people, eager to encourage the missionary task.

One such organization was the Church Missionary Society (CMS), set up in 1799 by several Anglican evangelical clergy.[2] During the early years, progress was slow and missionary numbers remained few. Gradually, however, public interest developed and the stature of the society heightened. Concurrently, initial emphasis upon the ordained pattern of ministry gave way and CMS—like many other missionary organizations—became a prominent vehicle for the religious expression of lay people. As the nineteenth century progressed, CMS came to rely more, not only on the membership of male lay workers, but that of women also. Discovering the advantages of influencing indigenous women through female missionaries, the society began encouraging women's participation and was soon dependent upon their involvement. By the end of the century, women provided a large amount of support for CMS, both as missionaries in the field and as fundraisers or patrons at home.[3] This chapter will focus on the work of CMS in Iran during the late nineteenth and early twentieth centuries.

During the course of the nineteenth century, CMS firmly established itself within British society and began working in many diverse parts of the world. Not until 1869, however, did work begin in Iran, or Persia.[4] Though missionary wives were present from that date, it was from 1882 and more particularly from the 1890s that single women's involvement became a major part of the missionary endeavor, which led to the founding of the Anglican Church in Iran.

There are countless books written on Iranian issues, and literature analyzing the work of Western missionaries, including that of CMS women, has also expanded considerably in recent years. In this chapter, Persian studies and the field of missionary scholarship are brought together, converging also with other issues concerning the study of history and feminism. I consider the role of CMS women missionaries in Iran, with particular interest in the changing position of Victorian women in Britain at that time. The missionary encounter reflects the broader encounter between English Christianity and Iranian Islam during that period.

By means of a theoretical approach, this chapter will assess general concerns arising from the interdisciplinary nature of the topic. The subject touches on matters pertinent to the study of history, feminism, and religion with input from post-imperialist discourses. Representing a meeting of East and West at the height of British imperial expansion, the historiographical and missiological inquiry is nuanced not only with religious and gender-based sensibilities but also with awareness of racial questions. This chapter will delineate some of the methodological issues involved, so that the topic does not fall between the various fields, but tightly weaves them together.

The chapter discusses the tensions inherent in historical research generally and offers an analysis of the Victorian women's movement specifically. I will explore the impact of imperialism upon the Iranian nation and assess the effect of the empire upon the development of feminism. Finally, I will consider the status of British women missionaries in Iran, with particular reference to the position of Persian women at that time.

Women's History, Faith, and Feminism

Women's History or Feminist History?

In recent years there has been growing concern to distinguish between what is meant by women's history as distinct from feminist history.[5] Women's history tends to be defined more by its subject matter, demonstrating a concern for the retrieval and exploration of the lives of past women. This task of restoring visibility dates back to the nineteenth century, which saw the publication of many hagiographies celebrating the lives of exceptional women. While modern biographies show greater interest in ordinary women and are generally more analytical, the emphasis remains on description and retrieval.[6] By contrast, feminist history has been defined as "a pursuit committed to the present,"[7] which, while imbued by concern about the past, is fueled primarily by a desire to contribute to contemporary social change by challenging the continued oppression of women.

Scholars have criticized both approaches as unsatisfactory and unhelpful. Compensatory history is accused of merely "filling in the gap" and falling short of the full potential of feminist analysis. Critics argue that the method risks focusing on exceptional women involved in activities traditionally regarded as important. This not only undermines the majority of women but judges the minority on the basis of how successful they were in a "man's world." Moreover, a methodology limited to simplistic replication of historical documents by and about women fails to appreciate the constraining effect that pressure to conform has upon such evidence.

Feminist historiography arose from "a need for a past with which the feminist movement and women individually could identify."[8] It has caused concern regarding its tendency to judge women of different eras according to present-day ideological and practical priorities. Gizela Bock warns of the danger inherent in such "professional vice," which sees the past merely as "a function of, and as an instrument for, the present."[9] Ignoring historical diversity, this methodology often refuses to allow women to emerge as individuals in their own right with concerns that may conflict with ours but are no less significant. Women in all ages speak with a variety of voices, and while some undermined the confines of nineteenth-century patriarchy, others found collusion to be their only method of survival. They may seem unenlightened and insignificant now; however, today's priorities are only possible because of those early context-specific attempts to improve the condition of women. The intrusion of late twentieth-century assumptions as an absolute by which previous generations are to be judged neither gives credit to the past nor truthfully helps make sense of the present. Unless we try to understand Victorian women within the context of their own concerns and realities, we present a one-sided and over-simplified reading of history. Forced to falsify their part in our present, we deny ourselves true dialogue with them and fail to appreciate the historical complexities of the choices facing them.

We need elements from both women's history and feminist history if a balanced approach is to emerge. Furthermore, the boundaries between them need not be as sharp as some commentators suggest. There is no such thing as one feminist- or woman-orientated methodology. Indeed, feminism itself confronts the notion that one person or group has the right to impose definitions of reality on others. The same, then, is true of feminist scholars (and scholarship) who should "avoid doing the same thing in research situations."[10] Instead of searching for a single method-ology, it is better to work under the standard of a feminist epistemology, which presents an alternative way of seeing reality, without imposing specific investigative conditions. This style sees research not in terms of particular techniques, but offers "a feminist perspective on the research process,"[11] permitting greater flexibility in the application of various methodologies. Retrieval of women's past remains vital in the restoration of a more accurate historical narrative, and it would be foolhardy to give up too soon what we have barely had at all. Meanwhile, maintaining a critical edge on historical events through the concerns and priorities of feminism today need not result in methodological or political deter-minism that only succeeds in smothering the diversity of past voices.

The Impact of Faith and Feminism on Victorian Women

A more holistic approach to a feminist epistemology is particularly appropriate when considering the role of religion in the lives of Victorian women. While traditional accounts of Victorian church history have included little by way of gender analysis, contemporary feminist histo-riography has largely ignored or treated with suspicion the religious ele-ment in women's history. Despite the efforts of a few commentators to bring the disciplines closer, they still remain markedly disparate, with secular scholars wary of including religion as an analytical category in gender studies.[12] Those willing to admit the significance of Christianity and the Church mostly regard the impact as negative. Religious women, evangelicals, and those involved in purity campaigns and the defense of Christian morality, in particular, are often seen as betrayers of the women's movement, acting as a kind of brake on its forward motion. Meanwhile, scholars happy to accord religion a more positive status in the progress of women do so primarily on the basis of a broader understanding and more comprehensive definition of nineteenth-century feminism.[13]

The 1960s witnessed the advent of what is often described as the "second wave" of the women's movement. During this period feminism was frequently defined, somewhat narrowly, in terms of a doctrine of equal rights for women, based on a theory of sexual equality. Nineteenth-century religious women, concerned less with political, legal, or economic equal rights with men, and more with basic welfare rights for women, were easily excluded from this definition and placed outside the historical women's movement. Historians, however, soon found such straightforward classifications crude and unsatisfactory. There was growing realization that a comparative historical approach necessitated a broadening perspective if the wide-ranging activities of earlier women were not to be condemned.

A twofold understanding developed that leads to a deepening appreciation of the past. First, scholars increasingly acknowledged that "feminist theory is not monochrome,"[14] but holds within itself a plurality of reflective analyses and practical strategies. Second, feminism came to be regarded as context related. Women's opportunities and priorities differ according to time and place, resulting in changing manifestations of feminism, which is always deeply embedded in its surrounding culture:

> There have been significant shifts in the range of ideas, attitudes, and concerns of feminists . . . but these were changes within feminism rather than involving a change from something which was pre-feminist or non-feminist to feminism.[15]

Such a broadening notion helped historians redefine feminism along very different lines. Olive Banks, eager to reappraise the relationship between nineteenth-century evangelicalism and gender, uses the term "feminism" in referring to those "that have tried to change the position of women, or ideas about women," while Karen Offen regards it as "the impetus to critique and improve the disadvantaged status of women relative to men within a particular cultural situation."[16]

In a strictly historical sense, the use of the term "feminism," however it is defined, is problematic in relation to British Victorian women. Coined in France during the nineteenth century, the word did not find common usage in England until after 1910.[17] Moreover, the CMS women in Iran never used it to describe themselves or their work. While recognizing an inherent anachronism in this situation, it remains possible to continue using the expression. Quite simply, in the absence of a suitable alternative, "feminism" is a useful shorthand too convenient to lose. More positively, no other term adequately conveys the extent or intensity of concern regarding the position of women or the sense of injustice at the oppression many experienced. Above all, "feminism"—utilized in its inclusive form—encourages appropriate analysis of the complex and multilayered nineteenth-century "woman question" as more than just the radical suffragette movement, which developed as a branch of contemporary liberalism during the early twentieth century. Accordingly, the entire nineteenth-century women's movement, in all its diversity, can be acknowledged as predecessor to today's feminist concerns. The religious element can thereby claim its place as one strand in the historical evolution of feminism. For while placing more emphasis on women's Christian duty and less on their equal rights, religious feminism strengthened the women's movement by bringing into it many who would not have been motivated by a desire for equality.

Of course, Victorian religious feminism, far from representing a hegemonic entity, was itself "a cause with many sides."[18] It included radicals who joined the fight for suffrage and raised controversial issues such as women's ordination, and moderates eager to persuade church authorities through committed philanthropic service that the female force was strong and valid. Many in the latter category, including most missionaries, would never have explicitly aligned themselves with a radical feminist cause. Nevertheless, they were part of the broader movement, in terms described by Philippa Levine, as distinct due to its "conscious woman-centeredness."[19] In contrast to active engagement in organized politics or ecclesiastical controversies, this form of feminism represented a change in outlook. It involved the adoption of alternative values, which, common to much nineteenth-century feminism, was interested in improving the rights of women without showing undue concern for achieving equality with men.[20]

This brand of feminism, rooted in the dominant ethical value of its day, was based on the philosophy of separate spheres and steeped in the evangelical culture of Victorian Christianity. Negotiating and manipulating acceptable parameters, churchwomen were walking an ideological tightrope. Had they proved too radical they might have fallen off without achieving anything. Therefore, many played according to conventional social rules, all the time carving out for themselves ever-growing niches in which their potential blossomed. We should be wary of determining the success of Victorian feminism only in terms of public achievements by assuming these women were passive objects compared with their more radical sisters. To be sure, domestic ideology and evangelicalism provided the language for their cause, which, based on sexual difference, stressed the Christian duty of women and the "centrality of potential or actual maternity."[21] This notion that the women's movement apparently included distinctly anti-feminist values, serving only to restrict women, could be regarded as an unacceptable contradiction. Alternately, it could represent the extraordinary achievement of countless women who successfully used their subordinate position as an ideological vehicle for expanding their possibilities.

I have tried to argue for diversity as the essential feature of Victorian feminism. Indeed, the sheer breadth of the movement was a factor in its refusal to submit to one formal organizational principle. There is no single women's movement or phenomenon describing the position of all feminists. Moreover, Barbara Caine rightly warns against a simplistic division of moderate feminists (those stressing women's "difference" from men) and radicals (emphasizing "equality").[22] For when paired dichotomously, these constitute an impossible choice, belying the reality whereby most women worked with the advantages of both.

The modern missionary movement and women's participation within it remain unpopular and much maligned by secular critics, in particular, regarding it as an exploitative arm of British imperialism. Women's role is often seen only in terms of a futile power struggle between superiority lauded over indigenous women and ultimate submission to the male authority of mission hierarchy. Such ideas fuel the notion that the Victorian church was an anti-feminist institution and that the closing years of the nineteenth century represent a blank period in the history of Britain's religious feminism.

In fact, we should regard female participation in the missionary movement as one strand in an increasingly diverse movement.[23] Struggling with very different concerns, many of them controversial today, missionary women were no less involved in conscious woman-centered work. This resolute concern for the welfare of their sex is a common theme among female missionaries, evidenced by one worker in India who expressed her calling in terms of "a passion for woman."[24] To be sure, their involvement was based upon a reinterpretation of the separate spheres philosophy and the essential difference between men and women. However, even the harshest critics of missionary activity admit that female missionaries helped stimulate the movement toward women's emancipation in the East.[25] Though they did not call themselves feminists and were far from aligning themselves with radical groups demanding sexual equality, missionary women's participation in the development of feminism should not be undermined. Nor should it be forgotten that conditions abroad were often more favorable than those at home in allowing the possibility for change:

> It was . . . in the mission field, far away from the institutional and social confines of Victorian England, that the greatest opportunities for women to exercise responsibility and initiative . . . occur[red].[26]

A comprehensive historical understanding of Victorian feminism acknowledges that the multifaceted movement, steeped in the dominant values of its day, expressed itself through prevailing linguistic tools. This approach denies feminism a false hegemony, and acknowledges a place for religious and missionary women within the developing movement. Underlying it is the paradox of the faith/feminism dialectic in which religion both empowered and shackled women. Christianity was central in the lives of all Victorians and for women it frequently provided strength and self-belief in taking up their cause. Concurrently, the Church imposed the full weight of the separate spheres ideology upon women, drastically limiting their opportunities. In response, religious women ingeniously used the domestic ideology to their advantage, thus becoming active agents in the making of their history. The very essence of what impeded them became the source of their liberation. Despite their limitations and shortcomings, these resourceful women should not be denied their rightful place in the making of modern feminism.

The Genderization of Missionary Imperialism

While it is possible to place the CMS women within the context of feminism's development in Britain, there are also significant factors differentiating their situation from that of women in England. The missionaries were venturing into new racial and religious terrains as well as grappling with gender and class issues. In this section I examine the connection between the missionary movement and imperialism, exploring in particular gender questions pertinent to the position of women. The link between missionary work and imperial expansion has long been established, although the manner in which commentators interpret the relationship varies.[27] By comparison, the more specific field of gender and empire is relatively new and one that both secular and religious scholars are only just beginning to tackle.[28]

Defining Imperialism in a Postcolonial Context

Any study of imperialism is fraught with difficulties. A complex etymology means its contemporary usage is controversial, polemical, and loaded with ideological premises. The term entered the English language during the 1840s, having originated in France with unpleasant conno-tations from its earliest days.[29] Attempts were made to improve its rep-utation during the 1860s and by the end of the century two diverse interpretations had emerged. To the majority, it was "a larger patrio-tism,"[30] growing from pride in an expanding empire. Accordingly, the imperial mission—a topic of unembarrassed attention in Britain—was based on an obligation to spread the benefits of Western civilization to less fortunate peoples. This philosophy was founded on an unconsciously held view of "natural" English superiority operating across society, pro-viding "cultural hegemony" and a "unified discourse."[31] Though the vocabulary of the time is littered with value-laden terms such as "infe-rior," "subject races," and "subordinate peoples," the underlying premise of this understanding of imperialism was an eagerness to act responsibly for the benefit of those being ruled. Conversely, a different strand associ-ated imperialism with wars, bloodshed, exploitation, and the search for profit. Later it was absorbed into Marxist ideology, and since the advent of postcolonialism in particular, it has been a convenient multi-purpose, anti-Western slogan.

Despite the efforts of a number of commentators to elucidate it, impe-rialism remains difficult to define and, carrying strong emotional over-tones, is often confusing rather than clarifying. It is, therefore, a word to be used with extreme caution. According to Edward Said, imperialism is "the practice, the theory, and the attitudes of a dominating metropol-itan centre ruling a distant territory," in contrast to colonialism, which, "almost always a consequence of imperialism, is the implanting of settle-ments on distant territory."[32] Similarly, C. C. Eldridge refers to it as an "umbrella-word" encompassing not only events that led to the establish-ment of colonies, but also the motives behind those events and the theo-ries underlying them.[33] In other words, imperialism includes aspects of a theoretical ideology as well as practical implications. Though the political idea failed in that the empire as a political reality did not last, faith in the idea remained alive in the thought and action of governing classes in Britain until the end of World War II. Iran is not commonly included among the acquisitions of the British Empire. However, taken as a prin-ciple or idea, the impact of imperialism was as strong in Iran, which was never colonized, as it was anywhere. For empire was more than physical invasion; it was

> a relationship, formal or informal, in which one state con-trols the effective political sovereignty of another political

society. It can be achieved by force, by political collaboration, by economic, social, or cultural dependence.[34]

It is in this context that Said uses the term imperialism in his book
Culture and Imperialism. Arguing that cultural links are more potent
than direct domination through physical force, he considers imperialism
to be

> an ideological vision implemented and sustained . . .
> much more effectively over a long time by *persuasive
> means* . . . [through] . . . the daily imposition of power
> in the dynamics of everyday life, the back-and-forth of
> interaction among natives, the white man, and the insti-
> tutions of authority.[35]

The cultural imperialism implied here was at the root of the
informal imperialism operating in Iran during the Victorian/Qajar era.
Throughout the empire, Western culture "constructed privileged norms
and unprivileged deviations,"[36] against which it judged indigenous societies. Missionaries are frequently accused of having been "a quintessen-
tial feature of British expansion" as primary agents in the transmission of
cultural imperialism.[37] Perhaps surprisingly, in *Culture and Imperialism*,
Said makes no explicit mention of missionary activity. However, in
his seminal work, *Orientalism*, he identifies religion as a primary area
of interest over which Britain felt it had legitimate claim and, quoting
Tibawi, accuses the missionary societies, including CMS, of "openly
join[ing] the expansion of Europe."[38]

Feminist Imperialism

Empire was, essentially, a patriarchal structure founded upon mas-
culine ideologies. Firm views on traditional gender roles helped maintain the male balance of power.[39] Nevertheless, women, often accused of
"complicity with patriarchy and imperialism,"[40] are not immune from the
charge of imposing an imperial agenda, and feminists still struggle with
how best to include women in the process of historical analysis. British
women throughout the empire had no authoritative part in formal organizational and administrative structures. However, they did influence
official policy in important ways. The majority were infused by the widespread values and beliefs of an imperial worldview and, at some level,
strongly identified with its masculinist ideologies. Others, however,
attempted to develop a feminine version of "benevolent imperial social
reform."[41] Often displaying condescending elements, this adaptation

involved a dualistic approach toward indigenous women. It regarded them as sisters whose stereotypical role in society should be challenged, but at the same time, as "passive and silent victims in need of the protection of white women."[42] Antoinette Burton interprets this as a kind of feminist imperialism, prevalent among the middle classes, which regarded white women as prime agents of Western civilization, motivated in their work by a sense of duty to help their Eastern sisters.[43]

Whatever it is called—maternalistic, benevolent, or feminist imperialism—its roots were in the dominant evangelical culture of the time. This promoted the notion that spreading the gospel was a duty resulting from God's munificence showered upon Christendom. It provided moral justification for imperialism in a doctrine of trusteeship over so-called "backward" races. The feminization of this theology in the missionary movement resulted in women colluding with its basic ideology, while at the same time challenging it through their very presence. The continuation of Christian civilization was still considered dependent upon women conforming to the traditional role of wife and mother. However, single women missionaries stepped outside the traditional bounds of the domestic sphere both in their own social context, by rejecting marriage and working outside its confines, and by questioning the position of indigenous women in relation to Persian cultural norms. Due to their self-perception as better equipped (through their Western and Christian heritage) than Iranian women to ensure the latter's liberation, and in common with much contemporary evangelical and imperialist thought, "their charity seems often to have been accompanied by a patronising attitude."[44]

The Status of Women in the Mission Hierarchies

The mixture of "complicity and resistance,"[45] common among women of the empire, indicates their ambivalent position within the hierarchical structures. According to Michel Foucault's concept of power as omnipresent and decentralized,[46] the CMS women were active participants in the politics of the mission field. However, they played different roles according to whether they were reacting to the dominant male mission culture or the perceived inferior indigenous culture of Persian women. In the former case, the CMS women were involved in "reverse discourses," subverting and resisting institutional power where they could and following the "path of convention" where it best suited.[47] By contrast, in the inverted non-egalitarian relationship between them and Persian women, the missionary women became the dominant activators to which their

Eastern sisters reacted with their own reverse discourses. In short, like many other Western women in the empire, the CMS missionaries "played ambiguous roles as members of a sex considered to be inferior within a race that considered itself superior."[48] The result was equivocal, enabling identification with the oppression of Persian women, while at the same time nurturing a sense of superiority.

The nature of the unstable power relationships with which the CMS women continually juggled is evident in their racially orientated approaches to the separate spheres philosophy. Recognizing the strictures created by the Iranian version of the domestic ideology, the missionaries aimed to help Persian women toward liberation. What they actually did was to impose their own (often subconscious) Western version of the ideology on a new context. In other words, they wanted to *improve* the private world of women rather than eradicate it in favor of equality with men. While the CMS women themselves had rejected traditional roles as wives and mothers, they endeavored to teach Persian women about the inherent virtues of this model, hoping they would adhere to it in the new Christian society imagined for Iran.

The CMS missionaries were not simply attempting the regeneration of a new Persian womanhood, but were also in the process of clarifying their own role and identity. In *Orientalism*, Said argues that all societies or groups acquire their identities by developing a notion of "self" based upon some "other" in binary opposition. Thus, the Orient, while representing one of the Occident's "deepest and most recurring images of the Other," more importantly helps the Westerner "define Europe (or the West) as its contrasting image, idea, personality, experience."[49] Thus the "Orientals" Said writes about are little more than Western innovations (equivalent to Foucault's insane, perverts, and criminals) who, deviating from imposed European norms, are falsely constructed and at the same time help construct the Westerner.[50]

This concept of "otherness" may be applied methodologically to other disciplines, geographical entities, or historical settings, and it proves particularly fruitful in areas of feminism and racism. Its application in this case underlines how, during their time in Iran, the CMS missionaries developed their own self-identity, not just through new and groundbreaking work, but in direct opposition to their construction of indigenous women as "other." Comparable to their role in the convoluted power relationships (mentioned earlier), the women were part of a structural hierarchy that also regulated their sense of "self" and "other." In relation to their male colleagues they were the "other" fabricated in opposition to the male notion of "self." Concurrently, however, they formed the dominant group, defining "self" according to their perceived version of the Persian women as "other." Jane Haggis writes about London Missionary Society (LMS) missionaries in India involved in "a process of 'othering' which construct[ed] Indian women as the converse of their English 'sisters.'"[51] The CMS women in Persia were doing likewise, but all the time they were also being categorized as the "other" invented by male colleagues.

Exposing the Myths of Imperialism

There are dangers in portraying the West-East relationship in crude terms, as a straightforward superior/inferior power domination. A number of qualifications are necessary to avoid simplistic conclusions akin to a battle between the virtuous, idyllic East versus the evil, destructive West. Notwithstanding the strength of Western technology, economics, and ideological self-confidence, the success of both imperialism and the missionary movement necessitated cooperation on both sides. Just as women colluded, to a degree, in the ongoing dominance of patriarchy, so the East chose to accept elements of imperialism, and the missionary movement endured because of its perceived benefits.[52] The entire imperialist enterprise provided a mixture of humiliation and benefits for indigenous recipients. This was equally true of the missionary movement, perhaps especially respecting women's contribution.[53]

It is, moreover, demeaning and patronizing to assume that when faced with the Christian message brought by missionaries, Persians simply surrendered to the might of Western power. First, this presupposes far greater contact and assimilation of ideas than was actually the case. The extent of social interaction between missionaries and Persians was modest at best, and the number of converts infinitesimally small. Second, it is based on the model of Persians as gullible, hopeless victims with scant capacity to think for themselves and filter the missionary message. Indeed, many enjoyed the benefits of missionary education and medical care without any inclination toward conversion. Finally, it undermines the decision of those who did convert, often in the face of hostility and opposition. Several writers have shown how the missionary message was embraced as an attractive alternative, addressing important aspects of everyday life inadequately dealt with by indigenous religions. For women in particular it offered hope in the face of social evils such as poverty and disease, helping them to face death in very different ways.[54] It is not surprising, therefore, that the missionaries in Iran found many of their early converts among poorer women.

We should note a further important point regarding the nature of Western cultural hegemony and/or the Christian civilizing message and its supposed impact upon Eastern societies. Andrew Porter is extremely suspicious of the notion that missionaries were involved in the process of cultural imperialism.[55] He believes it is based on a mistaken assumption that there was an identifiable entity, called imperial culture, which missionaries were trying to transmit. Rather, he argues, the inherent difficulties with the term "imperialism" are further compounded by the addition of a qualifying adjective such as "cultural," itself open to contrasting interpretations. It is wrong, therefore, to present Western culture as highly integrated, persistent, monolithic, and immune to change, imposing itself on some idyllic version of indigenous civilization, which, fragile and weak in comparison, crumbles in the face of its superior counterpart. Said agrees, maintaining that such a view envisions the "outlying regions of the world [as having] no life, history or culture to speak of, no independence or integrity," leaving Westerners "at liberty to visit their fantasies and philanthropies upon a mind-deadened Third World."[56]

In reality, cultures do not survive in isolation but are interconnected and interdependent. This presupposes that any social contact between two groups impacts both sides, rather than influencing one and leaving the other in its original state. Therefore, the missionaries and their Christianity must have been affected through contact with Persian society. Indeed, for their universal message to enjoy any form of efficacy it required negotiating and adapting to fit its new localized context. Compromise and malleability were essential elements in the meeting of these two worlds and missionaries unable to comprehend this soon found "the penalty for inflexibility was commonly rejection."[57]

The question remains whether the CMS women were *aware* of this need for the fusion of ideas and cultures, and whether they were open to change for themselves as well as for the Persians they tried to influence. "Was the glass two-way? Did [they] learn from the culture . . . they sought to transform? How far were their own values modified by their experiences?"[58] Brian Stanley believes most nineteenth-century missionaries did allow "their personal experience of other cultures to re-define their norms of civilization to the limited extent that their moral and theological convictions allowed."[59] This, however, raises serious methodological difficulties due to the nature of the original sources available. Limited by their language and the audience for whom they wrote, missionary letters and articles must be read with care. Literal interpretation is often inadequate, for it does not necessarily serve as an accurate indicator of the authors' real views.

If their language was restricted by prevalent Orientalist ideologies,[60] then we too must be wary of the boundaries that fence us into all too narrow conclusions of our own time. Historiography that is overly concerned to maintain "political correctness" (racial- or gender-based) is in danger of limiting its insights. Ronald Hyam, for example, writes about the "poverty of feminism," with its "self-imposed parameters" and "humourless rules," which operate only according to the militant agenda, consistently hostile to any study of women as victims who, through their resilience, could turn their exploitation into advantage.[61] Similarly, Maxime Rodinson warns against a kind of distorted Orientalism that simply classifies the "other" in a diametrical manner. Rather than rendering it diabolic, it goes to the other extreme and through an extraordinary "ideological about-face . . . practically sanctif[ies] Islam" and the East. This European version of "Muslim apologetics," through its refusal to be critical of Islam in any way, loses its analytical advantage and becomes little more than indulgent description.[62] There must be no discrimination, vilification, or scorn, but there is no obligation to applaud all Muslim ideas and deeds. If past voices are to speak on their own terms, scholars must be wary of imposing such a heavily biased twentieth-century agenda that it silences their sources. An anti-imperialist sentiment, when combined with Christian ecumenism (eager to make amends for past enmity), can result in distorted historiography based on fear that any racial or religious criticism will exacerbate old imperial attitudes.

Conclusion

The CMS women lived, worked, and were influenced by dominating contours of their era: high imperialism, missionary confidence, and feminism. Caught between the "interplay of imperial mission and gender imperatives,"[63] they sometimes challenged the predominance of restrictive ideologies and at other times did not. Negotiating the converging and conflicting fields of gender, race, class, nationality, and religion, they were forced to improvise and innovate while operating within a paradoxical feminized empire. Despite offering women benefits of a lifestyle and responsibilities they could never have achieved at home, the empire still contained them within overall Victorian gender norms. Able to identify with Persian women on some level, the missionaries recognized various social problems and sought to alleviate them. However, they were too easily persuaded that these resulted from the evils of indigenous culture and religion, failing to see them as a product of gender oppression from which they too suffered in different ways. Believing that they possessed the key to Iran's problems, they regarded Christianity as the source of Western greatness and the solution for Persian society. East was compared unfavorably with West, and Islam denounced as the cause of Iranian (especially women's) degradation.

Away from home for long periods at a time, it was easy for the missionaries to remember a glorified version of Britain, far from the real country they had left behind. Forgetting the tensions at almost every level of social, political, and religious life, each struggling with new ideas of modernism and feminism, they presented a distorted image of Victorian Christian Britain as a shining example of civilization, particularly in respect to women and the exalted position it accorded them. "Victorian class and gender stereotypes were transferred into racist ideology"[64] as their convictions molded by the tenets of empire proved stronger than their will to question the conventions of imposed sexual norms. The former placed distance between the British and Iranian women, while the latter, a cross-cultural issue, brought them closer than either side recognized.

Notes

1   Theories about the reasons and motivation for the development of the modern missionary movement are many and varied. Most commentators, however, agree that a combination of spiritual and sociopolitical factors were at play. For a variety of views, see, for example, Stephen Neill, *A History of Christian Missions*, rev. ed. (Middlesex: Penguin, 1986); Brian Stanley, *The Bible and the Flag: Protestant Missions and British Imperialism in the Nineteenth and Twentieth Centuries* (Leicester: Apollos, 1990); John Kent, "Failure of a Mission: Christianity Outside Europe" in John Kent, *The Unacceptable Face: The Modern Church in the Eyes of the Historian* (London: SCM, 1987), 177-202; Max Warren, "The Church Militant Abroad: Victorian Missionaries," in *The Victorian Crisis of Faith*, ed. Anthony Symondson (London: SPCK, 1970), 57-70; Max Warren, *I Believe in the Great Commission* (London: Hodder & Stoughton, 1976), 112-14; and B. Worrall, *The Making of the Modern Church: Christianity in England Since 1800* (London: SPCK, 1988), 184-89.

2   On April 12, 1994, the organization changed its name from Church Missionary Society to Church Mission Society. For an account of how CMS started and details of its early years, see Eugene Stock, *History of the Church Missionary Society*, vol. 3 (London: CMS, 1899), 68ff.

3   Within the last ten years, scholars have begun publishing on the phenomenon of female involvement in the nineteenth-century missionary movement and its significance for the broader women's movement. See, for example, Fiona Bowie et al., eds., *Women and Missions: Past and Present, Anthropological and Historical Perceptions* (Oxford: Berg, 1993); *Women's Studies International Forum* 13:4 (1990)—several articles in this issue of the journal are dedicated to the subject of women and missions; Sean Gill, *Women and the Church of England: From the Eighteenth Century to the Present* (London: SPCK, 1994), 173-98; Frank Prochaska, *Women and Philanthropy in 19th Century England* (Oxford: Clarendon Press, 1980), 19-72;

and several chapters in Robert Bickers and Rosemary Seton, eds., *Missionary Encounters: Sources and Issues* (Surrey: Curzon Press, 1996).

4 For more details on the early work of CMS in Iran, see Hassan Dehqani-Tafti, *Masih va Masihiyyat Nazd-e Iraniyan*, vol. 1, *Sayr-e Ejmali Dar Tarikh* (*Christ and Christianity Among the Iranians*, vol. 1, *A Short Historical Survey*) (London: Sohrab Books, 1992), 59-76; Robin Waterfield, *Christians in Persia* (London: George, Allen & Unwin, 1973), 87ff.; Gordon Hewitt, *The Problem of Success: A History of the Church Missionary Society, 1910-1942*, vol. 2 (London: CMS Press Ltd, 1977), 375ff.; and Gulnar Francis-Dehqani, "Religious Feminism in an Age of Empire: CMS Women Missionaries in Iran, 1869-1934" (PhD thesis, University of Bristol, 2000), 54-57.

5 See, for example, Susan Morgan, "A Passion for Purity: Ellice Hopkins and the Politics of Gender in the Late-Victorian Church" (PhD thesis, University of Bristol, 1997), 33-37.

6 There are now a growing number of such studies concentrating on all aspects of nineteenth-century women's lives. See, for example, Gail Malmgreen, ed., *Religion in the Lives of English Women 1760-1930* (London: Croom Helm, 1986); Pat Jalland, *Women, Marriage and Politics, 1860-1914* (Oxford: Clarendon Press, 1986); Jane Lewis, *Women in England 1870-1950: Sexual Divisions and Social Change* (London: Harvester Wheatsheaf, 1984); and Lilian Lewis Shiman, *Women and Leadership in Nineteenth-Century England* (London: Macmillan, 1992).

7 Patricia Hilden, "Women's History: The Second Wave," *The Historical Journal* 25, no. 2 (1982): 501.

8 Gill, *Women and the Church of England*, 3.

9 Gizela Bock, "Women's History and Gender History: Aspects of an International Debate," *Gender and History* 1, no. 1 (1989): 8-9.

10 Liz Stanley and Sue Wize, "Feminist Research, Feminist Consciousness, and Experiences of Sexism," in *Beyond Methodology: Feminist Scholarship as Lived Research*, ed. Mary Fonow and Judith Cook (Bloomington: Indiana University Press, 1991), 281.

11 Verta Taylor and Leila Rupp, "Researching the Women's Movement: We Make Our Own History But Not Just As We Please," in ibid., 127.

12 For a notable attempt to bring religion and gender into closer association, see Judith Plaskow, "We Are Also Your Sisters: The Development of Women's Studies in Religion," *Women's Studies Quarterly* 21, no. 1-2 (1993): 9-21.

13 For negative approaches to the role of religion in the lives of British women, see, for example, Shiman, *Women and Leadership*, 43; and Patricia Crawford, *Women and Religion in England 1500-1720* (London: Routledge, 1993), 4. For more positive interpretations, see, for example, Gill, *Women and the Church of England*, especially 98-103; Morgan, *A Passion for Purity*, especially 67; Barbara Caine, *Victorian Feminists* (Oxford: University Press, 1992), 12; and Prochaska, *Women and Philanthropy*, 222-30.

14 Elaine Graham, *Making the Difference: Gender, Personhood and Theology* (London: Mowbray, 1995), 26.

15 Caine, *Victorian Feminists*, 6.

16 Olive Banks, ed., *Faces of Feminism: A Study of Feminism as a Social Movement* (Oxford: Blackwell, 1993), 3; and Karen Offen, "Defining Feminism: A Comparative Historical Approach," *Signs* 14, no. 1 (1988): 132.

17 For a historical account of the word feminism, see Offen, "Defining Feminism," 126-27.

18 Brian Heeney, "The Beginnings of Church Feminism: Women and the Councils of the Church of England 1897-1919," *The Journal of Ecclesiastical History* 33, no. 1 (1982): 91.

19 Philippa Levine, *Victorian Feminism 1850-1900* (Tallahassee: Florida State University Press, 1987), 18.

20 Offen, "Defining Feminism," 128, has pointed out that, like many other nineteenth-century "ism" words (such as liberalism, conservatism, and socialism), feminism was used by different groups to mean different things. Frequently, however, it referred to the "rights of women" rather than "rights equal to those of men."

21 Caine, *Victorian Feminists*, 52.

22 Ibid., 16-17.

23 From the 1880s in particular, feminism expanded rapidly to include new and varied ideas. For example, having been a predominantly middle-class phenomenon, it increasingly involved working-class women whose participation diversified feminist theory and practice. For details of changes within feminism during this period see, for example, Caine, *Victorian Feminists*, 241-50, and Levine, *Victorian Feminism 1850-1900*, 15-16.

24 Lavinia Byrne, ed., *The Hidden Journey: Missionary Heroines in Many Lands* (London: SPCK, 1993), 10.

25 See, for example, Kent, "Failure of a Mission," 192.

26 Gill, *Women and the Church of England*, 168.

27 Traditionally, in the days of uncritical histories of missionary societies earlier in the twentieth century, the link between British colonialism and imperialism was acknowledged as a natural product of its time. See, for example, Neill, *A History of Christian Missions*, 273-334. More recently, writers influenced by post-imperialist theories have been much more critical of missionary expansion as an exploitative arm of Western imperialism. See, for example, Kent, "Failure of a Mission"; and Greg Cuthbertson, "The English-speaking Churches and Colonialism," in *Theology and Violence: The South African Debate*, ed. Charles Villa-Vicencio (Johannesburg: Skotaville Publishers, 1987), 16-17. Others more committed to the missionary movement find themselves struggling with the subject. Stanley, *The Bible and the Flag*, 184, for example, concludes that the missionary relationship to imperialism was complex and convoluted and while the missionaries were not indifferent to oppression and the desire for justice, their perceptions were too easily molded by prevailing Western ideologies.

28 A number of secular studies have recently been published concerning the role of women in the colonial services. For example, Helen Callaway, *Gender, Culture and Empire* (Urbana: University of Illinois Press, 1987); Hilary Callan and Shirley Ardener, eds., *The Incorporated Wife* (London: Croom Helm, 1984); Clare Midgley, "Ethnicity, 'Race' and Empire," in *Women's History: Britain 1850-1945, An Introduction*, ed. June Purvis (London: UCL, 1995), 247-76. For the relationship between missionary women and empire, see Judith Rowbotham, *"This is no Romantic Story": Reporting the Work of British Female Missionaries, c. 1850-1910*. NAMP Position Paper Number 4 (Cambridge: University of Cambridge, North Atlantic Missiology Project, 1996); Margaret Strobel, "Gender and Race in the Nineteenth- and Twentieth-Century British Empire," in *Becoming Visible*, ed. R. Bridenthal et al. (Boston: Houghton Mifflin, 1987), 374-96; and Nupur Chaudhuri and Margaret Strobel, "Western Women and Imperialism," *Women's Studies International Forum* 13, no. 4 (1990): 289-94.

29 For details of its early history, see C. C. Eldridge, *Victorian Imperialism* (London: Hodder & Stoughton, 1978), 1.

30 Rosebury quoted in A. Thornton, *The Imperial Idea and its Enemies* (London: Macmillan, 1959), x.

31 Edward W. Said, *Orientalism: Western Conceptions of the Orient* (London: Penguin, 1995), 7; and Edward W. Said, *Culture and Imperialism* (New York: Knopf, 1993), 132.

32 Said, *Culture and Imperialism*, 8.

33 Eldridge, *Victorian Imperialism*, 3.

34 Michael Doyle, *Empires* (Ithaca: Cornell University Press, 1986), 45.

35 Said, *Culture and Imperialism*, 131-32.

36 Judith Bennett, "Women's History: A Study in Continuity and Change," *Women's History Review* 2, no. 2 (1993): 174.

37 Ronald Hyam, *Empire and Sexuality: The British Experience* (Manchester: University Press, 1992), 179.

38 Said, *Orientalism*, 100. It is commonly maintained that missionary societies followed in the path forged by British imperialist expansion. A number of commentators argue from a somewhat different angle, emphasizing instead the notion that a great deal of imperial ethos arose as a direct result of evangelicalism and its cultural influence upon British society. See, for example, Hyam, *Empire and Sexuality*, 56-57; and Kathryn Tidrick, *Empire and the English Character* (London: Tauris, 1990), 3.

39 For more detail, see Callaway, *Gender, Culture and Empire*, 30.

40 Rowbotham, *"This is no Romantic Story,"* 30.

41 Midgley, "Ethnicity, 'Race' and Empire," 263.

42 Ibid.

43 Antionette Burton, "The White Woman's Burden: British Feminists and the Indian Woman, 1865-1915," *Women's Studies International Forum* 13, no. 4 (1990): 295-308.

44 Worrall, *The Making of the Modern Church*, 8.

45 Nancy Paxton, "Feminism Under the Raj: Complicity and Resistance in the Writings of Flora Annie Steel and Annie Besant," *Women's Studies International Forum* 13, no. 4 (1990): 333.

46 Michel Foucault, *The History of Sexuality*, vol. 1, *An Introduction* (New York: Pantheon, 1978), 26.

47 Foucault, *The History of Sexuality*, 101; and Jane Haggis, "Professional Ladies and Working Wives: Female Missionaries in the London Missionary Society and its South Travancore District, South India in the 19th Century" (PhD thesis, University of Manchester, 1991), 33.

48 Strobel, "Gender and Race in the Nineteenth- and Twentieth-Century British Empire," 375.

49 Said, *Orientalism*, 1-2.

50 For more on the connection between Foucault and Said's theories of "otherness," see Mehrzad Boroujerdi, *Iranian Intellectuals and the West: The Tormented Triumph of Nativism* (Syracuse: Syracuse University Press, 1996), 1-7.

51 Haggis, *Professional Ladies and Working Wives*, 336.

52 Boroujerdi has written about this Eastern desire to emulate the West, referring to it as "orientalism in reverse," a phrase coined earlier in the twentieth century by the Syrian philosopher Sadik Jajal al-Azm. Orientalism in reverse is the process by which "oriental" intellectuals aim to appropriate their true identity on the basis of many of the biases imposed by orientalism. It cannot satisfactorily be called occidentalism, for its point of departure is essentially introverted. Primarily concerned with understanding its "own" Orient, it is only secondarily interested in the "other's" Occident. While it shares the assumption about a fundamental ontological difference between East and West, orientalism in reverse begins from the point of infatuation with the dominating West. See Boroujerdi, *Iranian Intellectuals and the West*, 10-14.

53 According to Neill, *A History of Christian Missions*, 220, regardless of missionary strategy, converts were frequently imitative, requiring everything to be done in its traditional Western way. For a discussion of the mixed benefits of empire, see, for example, Said, *Culture and Imperialism*, 18-19. For the views of several writers concerning the positive influence of women missionaries, see, for example, Hyam, *Empire and Sexuality*, 49; and Andrew Porter, *"Cultural Imperialism" and Missionary Enterprize*. NAMP Position Paper Number 7 (Cambridge: University of Cambridge, North Atlantic Missiology Project, 1996), 19-22. Kent, a vehement critic of the missionary endeavor, has already been quoted acknowledging female missionaries as among the positive influences of the age of empire (cf. note 25 above).

54 Isichei has underlined this in her study of African missionary work, concluding that female converts, far from resenting the imposition of Christianity, generally experienced it as beneficial and empowering. See Elizabeth Isichei, "Does Christianity Empower Women? The Case of Anaguta of Central Nigeria," in *Women and Missions: Past and Present, Anthropological and Historical Perceptions*, ed. Fiona Bowie et al. (Oxford: Berg, 1993), 209.

55 Porter, *"Cultural Imperialism" and Missionary Enterprise*, especially 6.

56 Said, *Culture and Imperialism*, xxi.

57 Porter, *"Cultural Imperialism" and Missionary Enterprize*, 25.

58 Gill, *Women and the Church of England*, 191.

59 Stanley, *The Bible and the Flag*, 160.

60 Said, *Orientalism*, 205, argues that during the nineteenth century there was a distillation of essential ideas about the Orient: its sensuality, for example, and its tendency toward despotism, its aberrant mentality, habits of inaccuracy, and backwardness, etc. This meant that when the term "oriental" or "Orient" was used, it provided sufficient reference to be identified as a specific body of information, which was, moreover, considered morally neutral and objectively valid.

61 Hyam, *Empire and Sexuality*, 16-18.

62 Maxime Rodinson, *Europe and the Mystique of Islam* (Seattle: University of Washington Press, 1991), 78, 106, 127.

63 Strobel, "Gender and Race in the Nineteenth- and Twentieth-Century British Empire," 383.

64 Hyam, *Empire and Sexuality*, 202.

7

MOTHERS' UNION: FROM VICTORIAN VILLAGE TO GLOBAL VILLAGE

Cordelia Moyse

The Mothers' Union (MU) must be counted as one of the great success stories of the Anglican Communion. The longevity and popularity of the Mothers' Union contrasts sharply with that of other Anglican voluntary membership organizations.[1] Begun in 1876 as a mothers' meeting in a rural English parish, today it has four million members in eighty-three countries around the world. As a consequence, it has sometimes been referred to as an essential instrument of unity for the heterogeneous Anglican Communion. Throughout its history it has had to negotiate the dramatic changes and challenges of worldwide Anglicanism, among them: imperialism, decolonization, the indigenization of Christian leadership and practice, the phenomenal growth of the Church in the global South, and the articulation of different biblical, ecclesial, and moral perspectives on family life and sexuality. This negotiation has involved it in periodically, and often painfully, re-evaluating the relationship between the identity of its membership and its mission.

The historic interplay between its organizational identity and global mission as it wrestled with the issue of divorce is the key to understanding the MU today.[2] This interplay and its impact on lay leadership and formation, as well as on women's spirituality, provide some surprising grounds for hope for the Anglican Communion struggling to survive when its member churches voice deeply held but opposing views on contentious issues such as the place of homosexual people in the Church.

At the conclusion of the MU's Provincial Presidents 2005 meeting in Wydale, England, they issued a remarkable statement to the Anglican Communion, offering a real but costly way forward:

> In our journeying together, we have recognised that there are many differences in our cultures, the ways in which we express our faith, our approaches to membership of the organization: we have recognised these differences can cause us pain. We have, however, celebrated our unity, our shared vision and mission. This has empowered us and brought us great joy. Today we affirm our belief that the things that hold us together are greater than the things that divide us.[3]

This statement was not born out of cheap grace or facile hope. Rather it was the fruit of an organization that had nearly fatally lost its way, fixating on one desirable feature of stable Christian family life—namely lifelong marriage—at the expense of practically and spiritually supporting both adults and children in diverse and often less than ideal contexts.

Earlier in its history the MU had come to see "witnessing" to its definition of "the sanctity of marriage" as requiring its members to forgo divorce irrespective of their situation. By so doing, it had created an image of itself as anti-divorce, rather than as a pro-family-life organization with a wider aim of supporting women in their spiritually challenging vocation as mothers. This resulted in a crisis in the 1960s that scarred the MU, even though it managed to deal courageously with the problem and has since continued to grow in membership and effectiveness in mission. This chapter offers both the cautionary tale of the MU's search for organizational purity prior to the 1960s and an institutional conversion narrative that explains why the MU today promotes a vision of its members living out their faith in action, wherever they are, through the common value of Christian service in a organization that has internalized the values of global partnership and inclusivity.

The Mothers' Union's Early Years

Mary Sumner née Heywood (1828–1921) started the Mothers' Union because she believed that motherhood was a moral and spiritual vocation for which women were largely unprepared. Her own experience as a mother and then as a leader of the Girls' Friendly Society convinced her that mothers needed to come together in Christian fellowship if they were to find the necessary support to fulfill their common vocation. The initial purposes of the MU were therefore: "to awaken in mothers a sense of their responsibility in the training of their boys and girls (the future fathers and mothers of England)" and "to organise in every place a band of mothers who will unite in prayer, and seek by their own example to lead their families in purity and holiness of life."[4] Sumner's idea found a ready audience because it spoke not only to Victorian ideals of motherhood but also to a missional desire to promote an inclusive and relevant Anglican identity in a time of heightened class antagonism and increasing secular thinking. Furthermore, it built on the mission and structure of the Girls' Friendly Society, with branches in parishes usually led by the vicar's wife, dioceses headed by a president (usually the bishop's wife or sister), and a national (later international) organization with a central president.

Quickly the MU took root beyond its home diocese of Winchester, spreading throughout the United Kingdom and overseas.[5] It established its earliest known branches overseas in Canada and New Zealand in the late 1880s. More followed in Australia, China, India, and Japan. What these branches had in common was that membership was primarily expatriate British women. Branches in army regiments were initially responsible for the wide geographical spread of the new organization, accounting for many branches in India. MU membership offered a spiritual home in a new place, as well as a vital link for members with their home country thousands of miles away.

The MU made ecclesial, missional, and theological sense in an imperial age. At the heart of the MU's understanding of its mission in relation to the empire was the concept of "divine patriotism."[6] The phrase embodied not only the expression of Christian duty and mission but the inherent rightness of British identity as an imperial power. Like many Christians, MU leaders ascribed imperial rule to the providence of God, not to base motives of wealth or adventure. To Mary Sumner, true imperialism rested "upon moral righteousness, upon the individual character of the citizen for its justification and its hope."[7] Women were key to the foundations of empire, because the Christian home was the foundation of British moral superiority and imperial power. The MU moved from rhetoric to practical action in support of its imperial mission following the Anglo-Boer War (1899-1902) by sending out speakers from England to set up branches. While seeking both Boers and British as members, the MU seemed oblivious to the reality of a leadership made up of the British ecclesiastical and colonial elite in the context of an imperial victory.

By the turn of the twentieth century, the organizational growth in an imperial context was not limited to expatriate or white women. The MU believed women to be central to "divine patriotism" because Christian motherhood and its responsibilities were universal values that needed to be brought out in all women. In Hong Kong, the Indian Subcontinent, Madagascar, and South Africa, missionaries saw the MU's potential as a vehicle for nurturing newly converted Christian disciples. It created branches based on racial or language identity usually led by white missionaries or clergy wives, thereby duplicating the imperial hierarchy.

The 1908 Pan-Anglican Congress was the single most formative experience in forging corporate imperial identity. The Congress, designed to awaken all Anglicans to their missionary responsibility, brought together in London for the first time hundreds of bishops, clergy, and laity from around the Anglican Communion. The historian Steven Maughan argues that Bishop Montgomery, secretary to the Society for the Propagation of the Gospel (SPG) and organizer of the Congress, wished to further his goal of welding Christianity and empire into "a single popular programme" and to add the bond of Anglican spiritual loyalty to the many other ties between mother country and her colonies.[8] As if this were not appealing enough to the MU, the Congress emphasized the growing importance of women's work for the empire. The immediate effect of the Congress was to draw the MU formally into the overseas mission field. Starting with India in 1909, it began to fund some SPG, Church Missionary Society (CMS), and the Church of England Zenana Missionary Society missionaries to establish branches of newly converted "native women" in the Indian Subcontinent and Africa.

A New Direction

Prior to the creation of a new constitution in 1912, the MU was largely a movement rather than an institution. Its first constitution in 1896 had set some parameters for participation and membership, but their limited nature and the fact that the dioceses rather than the new Central leadership were the driving force behind expansion meant that there was a wide range of interpretations of mission and membership. The 1912 constitution was designed to bring greater coherence and focus to the MU, and in fact it set the MU on a trajectory that was only to end when the organization had to fight for its survival in the late 1960s.

The first of the 1912 constitution's three significant changes concerned what the MU came to call "overseas membership."[9] Prior to 1912, the MU had made no distinction regarding the location of members. However, it increasingly thought that "overseas members," as opposed to "home members," had different needs and problems, not the least of which was communication with headquarters. The solution was the creation of the Overseas Committee, largely made up of representative correspondents for the overseas dioceses. To ensure that the correspondents spoke with authority, they were appointed by the local bishop in conjunction with the local diocesan council and were required to have resided in that country. Along with distributing grants for overseas work and helping formulate policy, an important duty of the Committee was to elect fifteen representatives according to regional numerical strength to serve on the MU's Central Council, its governing body. At first Australia had four representatives and India three; South Africa, Canada, and the so-called "scattered dioceses" had two; and New Zealand and the West Indies had one representative each.

The 1912 constitution created formal relationships, but the MU still was primarily a fellowship of women seeking to fulfill their vocation as Christian mothers as caring and praying women. The MU outside the UK needed funding for literature and workers who could not be found locally and a common sense of purpose for members geographically, and often culturally, thousands of miles away from the UK. It tackled the first need through the creation of the Overseas Fund in 1919. It addressed the second need through the creation of the Wave of Prayer, "linked branches," and worldwide conferences that from 1930 took place alongside the decennial Lambeth Conferences for Anglican bishops. Beginning in 1925, each member was expected to pray daily for MU members in every diocese in a yearly cycle of prayer. By 1929 there were links between British and 1,391 out of a total of 2,187 overseas branches. These, combined with the worldwide conferences, provided cross-cultural learning opportunities within the context of a common lay vocation and spirituality.

The draw of mission led to the second important difference between the 1896 and 1912 constitutions—the legal establishment of the MU as an Anglican society.[10] The Dowager Countess of Chichester, who succeeded Mary Sumner as Central President in 1909, believed that the MU needed to choose between being "a handmaid of the Church" or "an imperial Union of Motherhood, without cohesion, without a standard of teaching."[11] One did not need to be an Anglican to join the MU in 1896, but those in leadership positions had to be members of the Church of England—although there was an exemption for Scotland and the colonies. The 1912 constitution removed the blanket exemption. Instead, the local bishop could relax the rule "under special circumstances," which, with increasing denominational competition, bishops were less inclined to do.[12] (Anglicanization was completed when a constitutional revision in 1926 in pursuit of operating under a royal charter removed the by then never-used bishop's exemption. The commitment to a denominational society caused the MU to cut the funding of its workers in 1951 following the creation of the ecumenical United Church of South India and to no longer officially support the Mothers' Union of the Church of South India, which was part of the newly formed Women's Fellowship.)[13]

The third important change in the 1912 constitution was to its membership rules, which defined the Mothers' Union identity and mission for the next sixty years. In 1892, a new first object had been added to the original two: "to uphold the sanctity of marriage."[14] For the MU this made sense, as it saw faithful marriage as the bedrock of the home and family. What this object meant in practical terms was not articulated at the time. However, it was to draw the organization into the public sphere to campaign against liberalizing marriage and divorce reform in the first decade of the twentieth century. The MU began its advocacy interpreting "the sanctity of marriage" as meaning that both Jesus and the Church held that marriage was indissoluble and could only be ended by death and that any other view was theologically wrong and socially dangerous to the Christian family.[15] In 1910, three MU leaders gave evidence to the Royal Commission on Divorce and Matrimonial Causes. On the face of it, the MU's opposition to divorce was theological, not sociological, but the bulk of its evidence was designed to refute the argument that the respectable working class felt aggrieved by the existing limited law and was demanding reform.

This was a transformative experience and led in 1912 to marriage rather than motherhood becoming the definitive feature of full MU membership. The fateful decision defined members as married women, with or without children, and associates as unmarried women. By so doing, the MU emphasized it was a pro-marriage rather than pro-family organization. Furthermore, the Constitution now read that "divorce must be regarded as a disqualification for membership." It was no longer enough to be married. The organization had to be made up of "pure" members— women who, while knowledgeable of the stresses of marriage, had (often at great personal cost) forgone a solution that was held to be theologically and socially unsound. It was believed that one could only "witness" to the indissoluble nature of marriage if one had not been divorced oneself.[16]

The consequence was that as an Anglican laywomen's organization, the MU's internal and external identity became inextricably linked with its views on marriage and divorce. Members remained committed to the other two objects and at monthly meetings in parish halls continued to learn about faith and family life and pray for themselves and fellow members. But the organization's position as a stakeholder in limited provision for divorce transformed its membership, mission, and identity. It became better known for being "the anti-divorce society" rather than one supporting mothers and family life. The attempt to maintain itself as a "pure" organization with members intellectually, theologically, and personally against all divorce required a great deal of effort, as this identity was always under pressure both internally and externally. Many Anglicans believed in the authenticity of the so-called "Matthean exception" where Jesus was recorded as forbidding divorce *except for unchastity*. Some MU members believed that it was unjust to exclude an innocent party to a divorce, the faithful wife of an adulterous husband, from the organization. In 1920 however, a majority of the Central Council adopted the 1920 Lambeth Conference definition of marriage as the meaning of its first object, namely that marriage was a "lifelong and indissoluble union, of one man with one woman to the exclusion of all others on either side."[17] Those MU members who could not accept this definition were made to feel unwelcome and were asked to consider resignation.[18]

In the first few decades of the twentieth century, the MU was seen as more hard-line than even some episcopal leaders. In 1923, Randall Davidson, archbishop of Canterbury, justified extending divorce by giving women the right to divorce for a husband's adultery on the ground that it helped establish an equal moral standard. His successor, Cosmo Lang, adopted a neutral position in 1937, when faced with a bill that sought to address injustices and abuses of the current law by, among other things, allowing new grounds for divorce. Believing that it was no longer possible to impose a Christian standard on what he considered a largely non-Christian population, he stated in the House of Lords that as a citizen he could not vote against the bill and as a churchman he could not vote for it.[19] Both archbishops were happy for the MU to take a different position. The same was true for overseas bishops when the MU adopted membership criteria for so-called "native" branches that set narrower criteria for MU membership than for church participation. In 1913, the Executive Committee ruled that in future *all* native branches should be run on a communicant basis and that no member should be allowed to continue her membership after she had been through a divorce court even if the disciplinary laws of the Church would admit her to Communion after so many years. Bishop King of Madagascar, who had requested affiliation to the MU, was perhaps surprisingly content to defend this decision, writing, "communion is necessary to salvation, and belonging to the MU is not."[20]

Despite its pursuit of purity and Anglican sectarianism, membership continued to increase, reaching a total of 615,000 before World War II. The MU experienced an eight-fold increase in the number of overseas members between 1910 and 1940. Overseas membership stood at just under eighty thousand in 1940 and represented about twelve percent of total membership. The combined drive of missionary-minded women and the imperial vision of the Central MU worked together to create and nurture an indigenous membership. The shift is most clearly illustrated by the fact that in 1910, the MU's overseas heartlands were the white dominions and India, but by 1940, Africa was the continent with the largest overseas membership.

Crisis

Following World War II, the MU, like much of the world and church, wanted to get back to "normal"—the normal of the pre-war world. Yet this was not to occur. Internationally, the Central MU in London had to grapple with the implications for its membership of decolonization and the creation of autonomous churches around the world. Slowly, depending on the country, indigenous women and councils representative of the rank and file replaced the white leadership and paid workers.[21]

Of greater concern was the hostility to the MU of some UK clergy who saw it as impeding the mission of the Church. The origins of much of the clerical criticism, and of the resulting identity crisis within the MU, lay in developments in the Church's own pastoral practice around divorce. Despite the provisions of the 1937 Matrimonial Causes Act, the Church ignored clergy's freedom of conscience and officially was committed to refusing marriage to those who had divorced. Yet while Church policy recognized no *right* of admittance to Holy Communion for those who had divorced and remarried, bishops could sanction their readmission under certain circumstances. By so doing, the Church demonstrated its pastoral responsibility for the divorced and remarried. The MU's exclusive membership policy, by contrast, did not recognize concepts such as reconciliation, repentance, or individual circumstances or make any distinction between those who were divorced and those who had divorced and remarried. This policy laid the MU open to the charge that it, a mere church society, had a higher and harsher moral standard than that of the Church it claimed to serve. It was one thing for the MU and Church leaders to adopt different approaches to public policy but another when the difference touched on internal church discipline. As a consequence, the MU faced an increasing barrage of criticism from both within its ranks and from the wider church, which found public expression in church newspapers. The MU's response was to downplay its own importance. It claimed it had never intended to be *the* Anglican women's society but rather a society committed to lifelong marriage and family life. Yet it had often promoted itself as the guardian of the Church's doctrine of marriage. In the eyes of Joanne Hallifax, Central President (1962-70), the MU had a nobler standard and was a sign not only to a permissive society but to a permissive Church.[22]

Events outside the control of Mary Sumner House in Westminster, the MU's headquarters since 1925, were to propel the MU to re-evaluate its identity and mission.[23] One event was the publication in 1966 of the report, *Putting Asunder, A Divorce Law for Contemporary Society*, by the Archbishop of Canterbury's group on divorce law. This marked a decisive break with past Anglican thinking and changed forever the entire context in which Church members considered divorce. It recommended "that the doctrine of breakdown of marriage should be comprehensively substituted for the doctrine of matrimonial offence," as "breakdown" reflected the reality that responsibility for the failure of a marriage as a meaningful and healthy relationship often lay with both parties.[24] A court's role was not to assign blame but to establish that the marriage was irretrievably broken as a recognizable relationship. Perhaps surprisingly under Hallifax's leadership, the MU's position on divorce shifted. Crucially, according to her, the report did not propose changing the Church's doctrine of marriage nor did it envisage marital breakdown as a "means of easier divorce." Therefore the MU, while affirming that "the Christian principle that marriage is a life-long, indissoluble relationship," was able to recognize for the first time that "this doctrine is not always accepted by, and cannot be imposed upon society."[25] *Putting Asunder* allowed the MU to abandon its policy of total opposition to divorce reform and instead to engage in shaping the content of any proposed legistlation for the better. This it has done with varying results beginning with the bill that became the 1969 Divorce Reform Act.[26]

While the MU's understanding of its mission was reshaped by new thinking, the MU was more resistant to rethinking the relationship between its mission and its identity as an organization of women who upheld the sanctity of marriage by personally eschewing divorce. However, pressure to change even that relationship came when first the

Canadian Dominion Council in the mid-1960s and then New Zealand presented the Central Mothers' Union with the problem of members having to choose between their loyalty to the purpose of a worldwide organization and their full participation in the life and work of their local church.[27] The autonomous Anglican churches in both places had recently allowed the remarriage of divorced people in church under certain circumstances. As the churchwomen's organizations of the Anglican Church of Canada and New Zealand, the MU in those countries believed that in order to minister to the practical and spiritual needs of local women and families, it had to open up membership to all women whose marriages the Church had sanctioned. While the Canada MU made it clear that it would admit divorced women and was therefore disaffiliated, the New Zealand MU wanted the Central Council to change the rules so that both those receiving holy communion who were divorced but not remarried and those readmitted to communion by the bishops after a second marriage could join. It also wished the Council to acknowledge the principle of provincial autonomy regarding membership rules.

Following New Zealand's failure to win sufficient support for its views at the World Wide Council in 1968, a commission was set up to look into the MU's purpose and how it could develop its witness to Christian family life, considering the lifelong nature of marriage and changes in civil and ecclesiastical law. The Willesden Commission, chaired by Bishop Graham Leonard, issued a report in 1972, after having heard the views of clergy and MU members from around the world. The Willesden Report, *New Dimensions*, did not present the MU with one route forward but with a choice. The explanation Willesden gave for the difference between "the alternatives" was that it gave different weight to the concepts of witness and ministry.[28] While both alternatives supported five new objects offering a more holistic understanding of the MU's commitment to Christian family life, *Alternative One*, signed by the bishop, proposed no membership rule change except that women who had been divorced and had not remarried could join. By contrast, *Alternative Two* recommended that membership be open to baptized women "who in good conscience support the Objects of the Society." While supportive of provincial autonomy, the reports contained two definitions based on different understandings of the relationship between the MU and provincial churches of the Anglican Communion. *Alternative One* envisaged corporate unity based on uniform membership rules. It recommended that the MU should only exist where autonomous churches had not passed canons that permitted remarriage of divorced persons in church. If the churches had done so, then the MU should become an independent society and sever its formal links with the local church. *Alternative Two* offered autonomy irrespective of the marriage policy of the local church. Autonomy meant that overseas provinces and dioceses could decide qualifications for their own membership and officeholders. Unity would in this case be located in a commitment to common aspirations, not to uniform behavior.[29]

Renewal

The world into which *New Dimensions* was born was very different from that in which it had been conceived. While the Willesden Commission sat between 1969 and 1972, the MU lost 46,000 members in England. The 1969 Divorce Reform Act, replacing a fault-based system in England and Wales with one based on "irretrievable marital breakdown," led to those formerly called "innocent parties" being divorced against their will. The MU's Executive decided that, with the approval of the bishop and diocesan president, a member divorced under the Act could remain in the MU. Externally, the church landscape had changed, too. The revision of canon law on marriage was now proceeding in many provinces of the Anglican Communion. The Church of England was also grappling with new theological and pastoral insights about the nature of marriage following the publication in 1971 of the *Marriage, Divorce and the Church* report of the Commission on the Christian Doctrine of Marriage (the Root report), which looked at breakdown primarily in terms of a personal relationship rather than a social or sacramental institution.[30] Furthermore, the MU that received *New Dimensions* was no longer led by Hallifax but by Susan Varah, who was sympathetic to meeting the contemporary needs of families. On receiving the report, she declared that it was on the objects

> that we shall build our foundations and it will be for these
> that members everywhere will work and it will be within
> their Church whatever part of the world they live in. It will
> not, I believe be on membership rules but on our aims that
> our future can be built.[31]

At the Central Council meeting in July 1973 at Royal Holloway College, the MU made historic decisions. Two-thirds of the Council endorsed a simplified version of the Commission's five new objects. The first object now read: "to uphold Christ's teaching on the nature of marriage and to promote its wider understanding." The rewriting of the second, fourth, and fifth objects reflected the desire to make the MU sufficiently flexible and inclusive in order to support Christian marriage and family life. The second object now read: "to encourage parents to bring up their children in the faith and life of the church." This recognized that it was not only mothers who had responsibility for children's faith. The fourth and fifth objects showed how far the MU had come in its thinking about engaging with the reality of marriage and family life rather than simply holding up, and witnessing to, an ideal. It was now committed to promoting "conditions in society favourable to stable family life and the protection of children" and to helping "those whose family life has met with adversity."[32]

The decisions about membership and autonomy evidenced a full commitment to a paradigm shift in identity and mission. The Council adopted the most inclusive membership option before it. By an overwhelming majority, it decided that there was one class of membership open to all women who were baptized, and it declared support for its objects. It also granted autonomy to overseas provincial and diocesan councils where there was "full acceptance of the aims and objects of the society,"[33] thereby decoupling autonomy from any definition of membership. Varah believed that the significance of this vote was that "with joy . . . we could at long last recognise those who have called themselves our daughters as full partners."[34] New attitudes toward membership, combined with the new third object "to maintain a worldwide fellowship of Christians united in prayer, worship and service," had the potential to make the MU more of a movement engaged in a common vision rather than an institution with rigid boundaries: one that might not only engage women in very different family and social contexts but also across denominational divides. In time the ecumenical Women's Fellowships of the Churches of North and South India were to affiliate with the MU.

Revisioning

While the 1974 constitution, with its new objects and membership rules, set new horizons for the organization, it did not describe how they were to be achieved. This was a blessing, because the MU has had to navigate immense global social and economic changes as well as developments within the Anglican Communion. Three overlapping themes characterize the development of the MU's identity and mission today: global partnership, inclusivity, and service.

The granting of autonomy to various local councils around the world marked the first real attempt to move away from a centralized colonial model of organization and power with the Central MU at Mary Sumner

House in London controlling the agenda of a worldwide organization. The earliest places to obtain autonomy were Australia, Barbados, Canada, New Zealand, Papua New Guinea, and South Africa. It was hoped that the freedom to customize the MU locally would make it more attractive to potential members and more effective in its mission. Unsurprisingly, autonomy was not a guarantee of local success. Despite its innovative work in support of families and its open and flexible attitude to membership, the Australian membership continued its long-term decline.[35] In parts of Africa where widows, unmarried women, single mothers, the divorced, and the customarily married are either officially or unofficially excluded, growth continues.

The involvement of the worldwide membership in the decision-making processes of the Central MU has evolved slowly, due to UK charity law and the financial difficulty of creating a genuinely democratic worldwide organization when the organization is growing in the global South and contracting in the global North. In 1997, UK membership contributed approximately 140,000 to a total membership of 750,000. The 1990s saw the MU seeking to internationalize its decision-making processes. One development was the periodic meeting of provincial presidents. Of her experience of the 1999 meeting in England, Worldwide President Christine Eames wrote, "we were partners in leadership, there was mutual trust and a longing to understand the conditions that shaped one another."[36]

Another development seemed initially to go against this process. In 1995, due to changes in UK charity law, the Central Council, made up of hundreds of representatives from across the world, was replaced by a board of twenty-two trustees. In response to Charity Commission rules that required a majority of trustees to be resident in England and Wales, the MU ring-fenced three positions for members from around the world and fully funded the positions. It divided the world into three zones, each containing broadly the same number of dioceses. Africa made up zones one and two, and the rest of the world made up zone three. The result of the first election in 2001 was the appointment of representatives from Australia, Rwanda, and South Africa.[37]

The need to create an organization more reflective of its mass membership, combined with long-term membership decline in the UK and Ireland and consequent fall in financial support, continues to push the MU to greater organizational and financial devolution. The most public manifestation of this was the decision in 2008 to break the link between the Worldwide Conference and the Lambeth Conference and instead set up a series of smaller regional conferences around the world where representatives from across the organization could meet to increase understanding of the issues affecting different societies and to share solutions.

The history of the MU is more than that of its constitutional changes. The mission of the MU has evolved in significant ways since the early 1970s, giving it resilience in the face of the centrifugal forces of the wider Anglican Communion. One way is a movement from a sole focus on promoting and supporting marriage to a commitment to affirming and improving the quality of all familial relationships. The new first object must have seemed initially to have been an inspired solution to an organization trying to distance itself from the liability of upholding "the sanctity of marriage." Yet it became increasingly evident that in an era characterized in Western countries by falling church attendance and the weakening of orthodox belief—with persistently high rates of divorce, greater tolerance of homosexuality, and new patterns of family formation—even this modest object stood on shaky ground. Furthermore, members were confronted by the reality of contemporary family life, not only in their own homes but also by their organization's commitment to engagement in the messiness of family life through standing alongside those who faced difficulties. Members were no longer just running parent and toddler clubs in church halls, but befriending and supporting parents and children visiting family in prison or maintaining in contact centers relationships following divorce.

These experiences, along with a propensity of the Church of England in the 1990s to connect to the nation through grassroots service and pastoral care for all, led the MU to engage with many of the social and economic forces shaping family life.[38] It has done so by embracing the inclusive concept of "relationship," while at the same time minimizing the use and theological content of the word "marriage." Today the MU's first objective is "to promote and support married life." Its vision "is to bring about a world where God's love is shown through loving, respectful, and flourishing relationships"[39] and each member is charged with demonstrating "Christian faith in action by the transformation of communities through the nurture of the family in its many forms."[40] In recent years the MU has successfully relaunched itself as a stakeholder in parenting, producing useful resources for families and visibly participating in public debates on family issues. No longer is the MU "witnessing" to a totemic and uniform understanding of marriage and family on which its purity and unity stands or falls. Instead, it values global membership, interconnectedness, and relationship. The MU now believes that the admitted diversity of members on "family values" is not something to be feared or contained, but rather "the ability to maintain and sustain such a diversity of opinions, cultures and lifestyles is one of the MU's strengths."[41]

As the 2005 Wydale Provincial Presidents' statement declared, MU unity was built on "our shared vision and mission" and "the things that hold us together are greater than the things that divide us."[42] At the core of this shared mission is turning faith into action and focusing on women's economic and social development and empowerment in the global South. The reality of the MU being a mass women's movement within the Anglican Communion with its strength of numbers in sub-Saharan Africa made this a logical development.

The MU's thinking was shaped by the Anglican Consultative Council's five marks of mission articulated in the Mid-point Review of the Decade of Evangelism in 1995, which called Christians "to live like Christ in concern for the poor, the weak, the oppressed and to uphold the integrity of Creation" and urged the churches "to pray and work to overcome structures and systems that perpetuate poverty, oppression and environmental degradation."[43] That year also saw the Provincial President of Uganda attend the UN Fourth World Conference on Women and the former Central President take part in the NGO Forum in Beijing. Out of that conference emerged the *Platform for Action for Equality, Development and Peace*, detailing the objectives and required actions for women to take an equal place in the world with men.[44] Now the MU viewed its mission, particularly in sub-Saharan Africa, in the context of equality, justice, peace, poverty eradication, and economic and social justice. In its 1995-96 *Annual Review*, the *Platform for Action* was said to be not only "challenging the MU...to monitor and evaluate its work against these stated aims of universal concern" but also urging it to identify "fresh challenges [and] areas of Christian work which clearly contribute to the international agenda of justice for women and families."[45]

The drive to integrate Christian faith and social transformation in the MU has led to a flourishing of HIV and AIDS education; the creation of the Literacy and Development Program, which has improved the literacy and numeracy of more than 50,000 people in Burundi, Rwanda, and the Sudan; and the establishment of the Literacy and Financial Education Program in Burundi to enable formation of savings groups and teaching of business skills. These programs not only involve local members in the developing world. Much of the funding or seed money comes from outside the global South—predominantly from the UK and Ireland, although increasingly through development partners.[46] The commitment of members outside of developing countries to a shared vision is more than a financial one. The needs and concerns of members outside the UK are no longer dealt with by a separate department. The Action and Outreach Unit is the umbrella unit for social justice issues, members' campaigns, and projects wherever the MU is active. One of the early successes of this approach was involvement in the campaign to secure debt relief for the poorest countries in the late 1990s. The campaign fell within the fourth object, but, perhaps more importantly, members lived in twenty-one of the fifty-two severely-indebted countries. The MU not only formally joined various campaign networks but encouraged members to learn about issues, sign petitions and attend demonstrations at G8 summits.[47] In its work, the MU drew together the experience of its poorer members with the lobbying power of their more affluent sisters. This is a model that it continues to apply when lobbying the UN through the Commission on the Status of Women.

As of today the MU works in thirty-four provinces of the Anglican Communion. Like the Anglican Communion, the MU is a work in progress, seeking to find a model of unity in a diverse world and church still shaped by a legacy of colonialism and the competing forces of globalization and indigenization. It is still an organization with its headquarters in London, largely funded by members and institutions of the North. Yet it is trying to create an organization that shares knowledge and learning about parenting, family life, and women's roles and undertakes organizational planning regionally.[48] At this time the MU, perhaps wisely, stakes its unity on deeds, not words. The valuing of orthopraxis regarding economic justice and empowerment of women over an agreed orthodoxy on marriage and family life runs the risk of postponing disagreement and crisis. It also exposes the MU to the heresy of Pelagianism, namely reducing Christianity to making things right on a range of moral, economic, and political issues. Yet notwithstanding those dangers facing both it and a liberalizing Christianity, the MU continues to offer a valuable witness to the wider Anglican Communion as its seeks to build communion on the basis that the things that hold Anglicans together are greater than the things that divide them.

Notes

1 Cordelia Moyse, *A History of the Mothers' Union: Women, Anglicanism and Globalization, 1876-2008* (Woodbridge: Boydell Press, 2009), 245.

2 The MU also has wrestled with the issues of birth control and the ordination of women. While, until 1959, it supported "self-control" as the ideal for Christian men and women, it never made views on birth control a test of membership. Regarding women's ordination, it claimed the subject was outside its mission. Ibid., 126-31, 182, 194-97.

3 Ibid., 233.

4 Members were supposed to achieve these purposes by such actions as preventing gossip and angry words in their homes, not giving alcohol to children, and keeping their children from bad books and doubtful companions. They were supposed to teach their children to pray and worship. See Moyse, *A History of the MU*, Appendix 1.

5 Ibid., chap. 4, for this account of overseas expansion.

6 Ibid., 81.

7 *Mothers in Council,* July 1908, 131; Mrs. Sumner, *A Mother's Greatest Duty,* 9th ed. (Winchester, n.d.), 22.

8 Moyse, *A History of the MU,* 84.

9 Ibid., 141-43.

10 Ibid., 98-102.

11 Mothers' Union Executive Committee minutes, December 14, 1910, MU/EX/001/05, 96-97, Mothers' Union archive held at Lambeth Palace Library, London (hereafter cited as MU archive).

12 Mothers' Union Central Council minutes, June 6, 1912, MU/CC/001/04, 52-53, 59, MU archive.

13 Moyse, *A History of the MU,* 204-7.

14 Ibid., 63-64.

15 Ibid., 117-19.

16 Mothers' Union Central Council minutes, October 18, 1912, MU/CC/001/04, 79-80, 82, MU archive.

17 Lambeth Conference 1920, Resolution 67, http://www.lambethconference.org/resolutions/1920/1920-67.cfm.

18 Mothers' Union Central Council minutes, December 1-2, 1920, MU/CC/001/05, 266-68, MU archive.

19 Moyse, *A History of the MU,* 122, 124.

20 George King to Mrs. Maude, Central Secretary, July 13, 1917, MU/OS/005/13/08, MU archive.

21 Moyse, *A History of the MU,* 203. Ibid., 207-11, for example of Ghana. Ibid., 211-16, for example of South Africa.

22 Ibid., 170-74.

23 Ibid., 190-93.

24 Jeffrey Weeks, *Sex, Politics, and Society: The Regulation of Sexuality Since 1800,* 2d ed. (London: Longman, 1989), 251-52; Jane Lewis, *Women in Britain Since 1945: Women, Family, Work and the State in the Post-War Years* (Oxford: Blackwell, 1992), 56.

25 *Mothers' Union News,* November 1966, 2.

26 Ibid., March 1968, 10.

27 Moyse, *A History of the MU,* 173-74.

28 *New Dimensions,* the Bishop of Willesden's Commission on the Objects and Policies of the Mother's Union (London: S.P.C.K., 1972) (hereafter cited as ND). See Willesden's presentation to the press conference, June 20, 1972, MU/CO/003/17, MU archive.

29 ND, paragraphs 308, 357.

30 Root Commission, *Marriage, Divorce, and the Church: the Report of the Commission on the Christian Doctrine of Marriage* (London: S.P.C.K., 1971).

31 Central Council minutes, June 23, 1973, MU/CC/001/19, 68-69, MU archive.

32 See new objects in the 1974 constitution of the Mother's Union in Moyse, *A History of the MU*, Appendix 4.

33 Recommendations, ND, paragraphs 306, 354.

34 Central Council minutes, July 2-6, 1973, MU/CC/001/19, 151, MU archive.

35 Moyse, *A History of the MU*, 225.

36 Mother's Union Annual Review, 1999-2000, 2.

37 Moyse, *A History of the MU*, 228.

38 For example, see the Church of England's Board for Social Responsibility, *Something to Celebrate: Valuing Families in Church and Society* (London: Church House Publishing, 1995).

39 "Theme for 2010 Relationship not Rules 2010," Mothers' Union, http://www.themothersunion.org/theme_for_2010.aspx.

40 "Our Vision: Purpose, Aim and Objectives," Mothers' Union, http://www.themothersunion.org/vision.aspx.

41 Moyse, *A History of the MU*, 243.

42 Message from the Provincial Presidents of the Worldwide Mothers' Union, Wydale, July 2005.

43 See Cyril Okorocha, "Evangelism in the Anglican Communion: an Overview," in *Anglicanism: a Global Communion*, ed. Andrew Wingate et al. (London: Church Publishing, 1998), 328.

44 *Beijing Platform for Action for Equality, Development, and Peace*, http://www.un.org/womenwatch/daw/beijing/beijingdeclaration.html.

45 *Mothers' Union Annual Review*, 1995/96, 3, 12-15.

46 Report of the Trustees and Consolidated Annual Accounts for the year ended 31 December 2010, 8,13, Mothers' Union, http://www.themothersunion.org/MOTHERS_UNION_-_2010.pdf.

47 Moyse, *A History of the MU*, 238.

48 "Blueprint for Mission, Mothers' Union Annual Review, 2010-11," 24, Mothers' Union, http://www.themothersunion.org/documents/annual_review/Annual_Review_2011.pdf.

8

THE CHURCH AND POVERTY ALLEVIATION IN AFRICA

Esther M. Mombo

It is generally accepted these days that Africa is caught up in a trap created by the global culture of power vested in the private institutions of the market. As the Arusha Charter states, "We are united in our conviction that the crisis currently engulfing Africa is not only an economic crisis but also a human, legal and social crisis. It is a crisis of unprecedented and unacceptable proportions manifested not only in abysmal declines in economic indicators and trends, but more tragically and glaringly in the suffering, hardship and impoverishment of the vast majority of African people."[1] Those who advocate for poverty reduction programs would argue that the way out of this is through reparation, debt relief, and/or fair trade. Although this is a familiar argument, it is too simplistic when applied to the African situation. Indications are that Africa's marginalization and poverty have continued to worsen. This is true among Africans in the diaspora too. The situation is viewed as an entanglement of complex systems that results in a poverty trap. You cannot disentangle yourself from one system without dealing with the other. In that complex, you have material poverty, physical weakness, isolation, vulnerability, powerlessness, and spiritual poverty all working to reinforce the chains of poverty that are so hard to escape.

In the cities of Accra, Nairobi, Johannesburg, and Kingston, where I visited as part of a Pan-African religion and poverty project, it was clear that the majority of people in those cities were poor, particularly those living in areas that were slums. A visit to Mathare, Kenya, and to one of the churches there was a case in point. It is in this connection that Carol

Mandi observes that "there is a grinding poverty humorously referred to as Kenya's only growth industry at the moment—that is now becoming a cliché as the government continues with the Poverty Reduction Strategy Paper talks in various provinces."[2]

The contemporary basic concern of people worldwide seems to be with economic matters. This is evident from a simple content analysis of any randomly selected issue of a newspaper anywhere in the world. One can always find a newspaper filled with consumer advertisements and references to banks, globalization, debt relief for poor nations, and poverty alleviation programs. In the same newspaper one also finds ads from religious circles dealing with the issues of poverty alleviation in various ways, including prayers of deliverance from poverty. The interaction between spirituality and materiality has manifested itself, particularly, in the emergence of a new phenomenon of religious commercialization. There is a visible mushrooming of seemingly "Christian" religious groups, which interpret salvation in terms of material relief and the quick-fix solution of material poverty of individuals. The theological content of their preaching is popularly known as "prosperity gospel."[3]

From a secular perspective, methods for poverty alleviation include (as noted above) reparation, debt relief, and/or fair trade. And indeed, movements such as Jubilee 2000 emerged from discussions among the World Bank, the Anglican Provinces in Africa, and the Anglican Lambeth Conference of 1998.[4] Jubilee's goal was later adopted by Protestants, Catholics, and others round the world. This chapter seeks to investigate the historical developments of such poverty alleviation specifically by the Church and the involvement of the Church in debt relief.

I argue that if the Church is going to be involved with poverty alleviation, it needs to seek a more permanent strategy than merely putting food into people's mouths or coins in their wallets. Such a strategy would transcend the bounds of mere religion and theology and would seek to integrate the best of other disciplines such as economics, science, and ethics, to name but a few.

The Beginnings of the Church and Poverty Alleviation in Africa

Material poverty is a relative concept. People in precolonial Africa may have been poor by contemporary Western standards, but they did not necessarily regard themselves as poor.[5] In fact by their own criteria, some of them might have been extremely rich. But the interaction between Africa and the West through the European voyages of world discovery, the transatlantic slave trade, and colonial and missionary expansion was motivated by the impulses of religion, commerce, and politics.[6] The effects of the three motives cannot be rubbed out or swept aside easily. The way Europe viewed Africa helped formulate their policies and mission programs.

The Christian mission in particular had a conviction to convert the people to Christianity, through which they would improve the living standards of the African peoples whom they saw as poor in comparison to themselves. The Africans were depicted as people who were both poor and living in deplorable situations.

David Livingstone, who came to Africa with the London Missionary Society, said in a lecture at the University of Cambridge on December 4, 1857, "I beg to direct your attention to Africa. I know that in a few years I shall be cut off in that country, which is now open. Do not let it be shut again! I go back to Africa to try and make an open path for Commerce and Christianity; do you carry out the work which I have begun. I LEAVE IT WITH YOU!"[7]

It is in this context that most mission societies developed ways to alleviate poverty. The first way was to introduce Christianity through evangelism; this was meant to deal with the spiritual life of the person. The second way was through health and or medical work to deal with health issues. The third way was through formal education, so that people would be employed to earn a living. Formal education was gendered, so men got more education, which equipped them with knowledge and skills to participate fully in society and have more central and secure positions in society. Women, on the other hand, received education to help them become evangelists and Christian mothers. In terms of poverty this led them to be among the poorest and most vulnerable people in society. The fourth way was through industrial training in order for people to learn skills to improve their living. It was the responsibility of God to change the inside of the human beings while the missionary improved the outside with what were seen as adequate skills.

Across Africa these were ways that the mission societies used to help people alleviate poverty, as it was seen then.[8] During this period of mission establishment, there was a strong link between spirituality and materiality. Those who managed to join the mission schools or stations at the time were the ones who benefited from material prosperity. They changed their lifestyles and modeled them on the missionary styles, even in simple things like housing.

The missionary experience as a modernizing experience was supported by the colonial enterprise. This type of modernization did not fit into the indigenous legacy. Instead, the colonial and missionary projects took their stand from the assumption that useful history in Africa was that which started with them taking over. Anything that had existed before was considered valueless to the needs of the African society at the time. Africans, unlike other human beings, were prevented from modernizing from a basis of their own culture. Instead, modernization was within the framework of existing economic, political, and military domination and racist attitudes and behavior. These behaviors and attitudes undoubtedly infected mission societies and their personnel.[9]

During the colonial administration some mission societies in some African countries received financial assistance through what were called grants-in-aid to run health care and education services under their management. Most contemporary mainline churches inherited the mission structures without the necessary resources to run them, and they were thus not able to deal with the situations of poverty.

The people who were able to pass through the colonial economic and social systems managed to gain material things, which moved them from one class to the other. But even within this class there were those who did not make it and remained an underclass. The mission societies, together with colonial systems, helped create cities, and it is in the cities that one now finds people living in abject poverty; examples are Mathare and Kibera Valley in Nairobi, Kenya.[10] These places, where the majority of poor people live, are also places where there is too much religion. There are more churches than toilets, and one wonders how the people cope with the call of nature. One may ask what the connection is between religion and toilets. There is a connection, in that the role of religion is seeing the development of the whole person. And if cleanliness is next to godliness, then a religion that ignores the living conditions of its members is deficient.

Although the mission societies acted to alleviate poverty from the African people during the colonial period, Africans who fought for their independence viewed them as linked up with the colonial forces. Consequently, most of those who sought independence founded their own churches rather than stay in the churches that preached equality but did not practice it. These churches were known as African independent churches and later as African instituted churches. In Kenya, for example, some of the adherents of the original independent churches are those whose families physically fought in the war of independence. After the war of independence, most of these people were pushed to the periphery of society because they did not have resources that could help them in the independent states. Most of their churches are on the periphery of the cities, especially in the slums.

Poverty Alleviation during the Independence Era

When most African countries gained independence from colonial rule in the 1960s, the feeling of well-being that swept across the continent was infectious. Leaders such as Dr. Kwame Nkrumah of Ghana counseled Africans to seek first the political kingdom and the rest would be added later; his advice captures not only the naiveté at the heart of this choice but also brings out the ironic commitment of Africans to the inheritance of the colonial state structures, which have remained almost unchanged in most African countries. This is despite the fact that the leaders could see the problems of poverty, disease, and ignorance and called on people to work hard.[11]

For a while there was a marked economic growth in the world, which was extended in a marginal way to Africa as well. But this prosperity was short-lived because of the leadership wrangles among the leaders, leading to coups-d'état in a good number of governments. What followed was a rapid increase in poverty levels as the economies that had been thriving began to collapse. Infrastructure became dilapidated; school buildings and the quality of education deteriorated. Real income per capita dropped by 14.6 percent from its levels at independence. Several reasons account for this decline. Some of them are external, while others are internal. Africa became a testing ground for developmental policies by foreign agencies.

In the meantime, African leaders became obsessively preoccupied with the issue of their own survival, so much so that they had no time to improve the lives of the poor in their respective countries. As a result, the ideals that were embodied in the people's wars of independence were abandoned and the nationalistic cause ultimately betrayed. The result of this was that political independence did not lead to economic autonomy as had been predicted with the coming of independence.

As this was happening, the churches that had become independent from mission societies began to look at the issue of poverty alleviation to help their members. In Kenya, for example, the National Council of Churches established village polytechnics from 1966 to provide youth with marketable skills.[12] The village polytechnic scheme was a challenge to the elite education given in schools, which led to many school dropouts, who joined the vicious circle of poverty. After the polytechnics, the Church developed colleges of technology to help give people skills that they could use to earn a good living and thus move away from being poor. In order to alleviate poverty the Church had to invest in people skills so that they could be self-employed. The sector of self-employment later to be known as *jua kali* has continued to be a major aspect in resisting or alleviating poverty.[13]

As well as the development of village polytechnics, the National Council of Churches and its member churches embarked on large development projects that had to do with basic health, agriculture, gender issues, animal husbandry, and small-scale businesses. The Church's aim was to alleviate poverty by empowering people rather than giving them handouts.[14] Development in terms of small-scale business was one way the Church was responding to poverty and taking note of economic issues.

One church leader who took seriously the notion of poverty alleviation was the late Rt. Rev. John Henry Okullu. He served in a rural region, which was riddled with poverty, unemployment, degraded social services (schools, hospitals), and other shortcomings. Bishop Okullu noted that if people had access to credit facilities they could improve their lifestyles. He, together with others, started a micro-lending program. Since the banks in this area did not offer poor people credit, the poor were not able to participate in economic development because they lacked access to loans.[15]

The situation of people in the poor nations got worse in the 1980s with the introduction of structural adjustment programs (SAPs). This was a policy encouraged by the International Monetary Fund as a way to economic recovery for poorer nations that were struggling. The loans given to a country were granted or rescheduled on conditional principles of austerity, reduction in government spending, and devaluation of the currency.[16] As a result, funding for education, health, and agriculture was cut. These were, however, the most important sectors for the poor nations because they dealt with issues of life. Thus the poor were denied a chance to live even modestly well.

The eighties and the nineties saw such deterioration of the poor nations that they were worse off than they had been during the colonial and independent periods. By the end of the century, one in five of the world's people lived on less than one dollar a day.[17]

The alleviation of poverty was high on the agenda of most churches and nongovernmental organizations (NGOs). Some of the NGOs were faith-based; others were not. Several reasons account for the proliferation of NGOs in poorer countries, the most salient of which was "a broad public concern in the West with poverty, coupled with the emergence of a popular form of third worldism among young people. NGOs were able to connect with this public sentiment, either in its more conservative apolitical humanitarian form, as was important with the big US NGOs or in its more radical politicized form in which it challenged the West."[18] The NGOs worked with communities on projects to help alleviate poverty. The churches in Kenya for example began the Christian Community Services (CCS) to develop their people and help them move out of the trap of poverty. The CCS were to do this through income-generating projects for groups. The NGOs and the CCS were taking over the roles the mission agencies had played in the preindependence era in Africa, when they provided services in all sectors of the community life.[19] The two groups were to nurture "holistic development," which would contribute to poverty alleviation. However, development that is based on income-generating projects seems not to have had much effect on the alleviation of poverty, as observed by S. I. Oladeji. "Targeting the poor by means of social programs is the most direct approach, followed by the adoption of specific programs to enhance the earning capacity of the poor. Both of these select the particular groups to be reached and therefore, presumably, reduce poverty immediately within these groups. The problem with these strategies in practice is the possibility of leakages of benefits to unintended groups. Administratively, they can be expensive to implement, inefficient in operation and outcome and lack sustainability."[20]

The reason why poverty alleviation by the NGOs, the religious institutions, and the government appears not to be taking root lies in the development models of modernization. These models go back to World War II, when the concept of development was synonymous with economic reconstruction and growth. In its classical sense, development theory referred to the level or mode of production of a given society's economy.

According to this model, African countries are somewhere between second and third stage, and depending on the policies they adopt, they can either stagnate or fast-track their development processes. While this version of development is no longer mainstream, it continues to linger in the models of some theorists.[21] The funding of the development programs run by the Church was through donor agencies of the West, which saw themselves bringing progress to a "backward" world. The philosophy that informed such thinking was a linear historic process that links all nations' histories and experiences on a single plane, putting some ahead while others lag behind. Development thus became an alienating and humiliating process for the people who helplessly remain undeveloped.

This model of development was criticized by liberation theologians because it implied that the solution to poverty alleviation in the poor countries lie in mimicking the rich countries. At the same time the advantages that the rich countries enjoyed were a consequence, directly or indirectly, of their historic relationship with the poor countries.[22] This historic relationship includes slave trade and colonialism, which exploited Africa's wealth and sowed the seeds of poverty. The crucial issue here is that alleviation of poverty must of necessity be related to a particular context and that it must be comprehensively construed in relation to the diversity of factors that impact on the totality of human existence.

Alleviation of poverty through SAPS, NGOs, and CCS seems to have failed. This is because none of them worked toward making policies that the governments would adopt and implement for the sake of the poor. Policy implementation on poverty alleviation remains a matter of discussion.[23] The next move for the churches was the Jubilee 2000 proposal, which called for a cancellation of debt that the poor countries were paying to the World Bank and the International Monetary Fund.

The models of the so-called Bretton Woods institutions (i.e., the World Bank and the International Monetary Fund) applied to Africa were wrong prescriptions, mainly because the principal governing themes were devised after World War II and need revision in order to be relevant to third world countries in our time. The models and policies have produced few socioeconomic benefits but eroded a great many of the traditional strengths of the African society. Africa has been trying to develop herself out of wrong and inappropriate experience of Europe, rather than drawing on her own history and culture to benefit her people.

Break the Chains: The Jubilee 2000 Campaign for Debt Relief

"Must we starve our children to pay our debt?" Julius Nyerere once asked.[24] His remarks on that occasion were made in a wider move to relieve the third world of the yoke of debt through a campaign called Jubilee 2000. The history of Jubilee 2000 goes back to 1990, when Martin Dent, a fellow of Keele University, together with staff and students at Keele, founded the campaign. It was based on two incompatible requirements that had to be reconciled: on one hand, the need to uphold the general principle on which all banking and commerce depend, that is, that debts must be honored, and on the other, the need to remove the monstrous imbalance whereby poorer parts of the human family owe unpayable debt to the richer part.

The only way Dent and others considered to reconcile these two requirements was to have a special time (a jubilee) leading to a moment at the end of which there could be a new beginning. The idea was to seek for a period of time to forgive all debt, as in the old jubilee in ancient Israel. Such remission would break the continuous chain of special measures to reduce debt, an immensely tedious and time-consuming rescheduling process that was hobbling the poorer countries.

The religious basis of the jubilee concept is found in the Bible, and especially the books of Leviticus, Deuteronomy, Nehemiah, Isaiah 58 and 61, and Luke 4:18-19 (where Jesus speaks of a time of deliverance and liberty, the "acceptable year of the Lord"). The proximity of the year 2000 offered great potential to associate debt remission with the ideas of jubilee. According to Jonathan Sacks, "The Bible is candid in its appeal to lenders. Not only is debt relief a moral duty, it is in the long run a key to collective prosperity."[25]

The Christian Aid organization in Britain took up the Jubilee 2000 campaign as a move to help alleviate the poverty of the poor nations. The campaign for debt cancellation of the poorer nations was necessary because debt had brought untold miseries to many innocent people. First, paying off debt meant that the governments had less money to spend on education and other essentials like safe water and sanitation. It meant that the poor continued to suffer when money was diverted to rich countries and to the International Monetary Fund and World Bank. In many of the poor countries debt servicing had been the largest expenditure.

Second, when a country builds up debts that are too large for it to have a reasonable chance ever to pay off, it is said to have debt overhang. The problem with debt overhang is that it puts off investors, making it even more difficult for a country to get the resources it needs to develop.

Third, foreign debt has to be repaid in hard currency. So debtor countries had to find hard currency. This is why they had problems servicing their debts, as their sources were aid money and export earnings. But most poor countries did not earn enough through exports to manage their debts easily, and of course they also needed to import items like oil simply to keep going at all. So there is also an immediate cash flow problem. Poor countries are currently being pushed hard to export as much as possible, without much regard to the environmental or social consequences. The problem underlying the debt issue is that of trade and development.[26]

It is in this connection that Sacks notes, "Nothing is more effective in alleviating poverty than giving individuals the chance to create small business. But to allow debt to accumulate is also wrong. The economic system must encourage freedom, not financial slavery. That is why periodic debt release is necessary. It enables people to begin again freed of burdens of the past."[27]

In view of this the Jubilee 2000 campaign was twofold. First, it was aimed at asking the governments of the North to cancel bad, unpayable, and odious debts; and second, it was to make proper plans to avoid the further buildup of unpayable debt after the millennium. As much as there were good reasons why the third world debt should be cancelled, there were also reasons from the rich countries why the matter was not that simple.

The reasons against cancellation of debt put forward were, first, the moral hazard of debt cancellation. That is to say, if debt is cancelled it will encourage reckless future borrowing. The immorality of this argument came from allowing "children to starve to pay debt," in the words of Nyerere. The idea of moral hazard also wrongly placed all blame for debts on the borrower, but not the lender, who may have acted irresponsibly.

The second reason against debt cancellation was that of future creditworthiness. Would debt cancellation undermine the credit worthiness of poorer countries? While countries remained heavily indebted, they found it hard to attract credit; yet opponents of relief said cancellation would further undermine credit worthiness. Even the World Bank recognized that the vast majority of the highly indebted poor countries would never be able to pay off their crushing debt.

The third reason against cancellation of debt was corruption, through which aid was being lost. While this may have been a valid claim, corruption was not only an issue in the poor nations; it is a human issue. Both the poor and the rich were involved in corruption; both the lender and the receiver survived through networks that supported corruption in one way or another. In many ways it was in the interest of the rich nations to bolster the position of corrupt administrators because they were, and still remain, good markets for the export of arms and military equipment.

The fourth reason against debt cancellation was military spending. Why should the North cancel the debt of countries that spend money on arms? Arms spending is not the issue of one continent but of most countries. In fact the North spends more on arms than the South or the poor countries. The arms industries based in the North encourage the manufacture and sale of arms, while the South consumes them.

The Anglican conference of bishops held every ten years at Lambeth, England, met in 1998 and addressed the issue of debt cancellation. James Wolfensohn, then president of the World Bank, addressed the gathering. In his address on the debt cancellation, he acknowledged the fact that "in many countries the payment of debt is a principal reason that social services could not be provided," but he argued that debt cancellation was not an easy thing to do. In reality, he said, "debt is part of life and there is a level where you can live with debt. That is both on an individual level and also as a country . . . . If the World Bank has to forgive debt then how will it survive?"[28]

In the Lambeth Conference, the Church called for an economy that enhanced full humanity, arguing that the Church can make the poor present and their voices heard. The Church condemned the double standards of the debtor nations and the fact that money had more powerful rights than human rights.

Both the Lambeth Conference and the Jubilee 2000 campaign succeeded more in sensitizing the masses to the plight of poor countries than in making the rich governments cancel the debts of the poorer nations in order to alleviate poverty. This was yet another attempt to alleviate poverty—yet all these economic, political, social, and religious arguments about debt failed.

Conference of Anglican Provinces in Africa and the World Bank

From what I have recounted, there seems not to have been much collaboration between Church and governments for poverty alleviation. With the Jubilee 2000 campaign the churches were in solidarity with one another in challenging the governments on debt cancellation. The Lambeth Conference also issued its challenge to the World Bank, without engaging the bank in the deliberations. From the Lambeth Conference of 1998, it was agreed that since Africa is adversely affected by poverty, a conference on poverty alleviation should be held. The aim of the conference would be to provide a forum for dialogue between the Church and the World Bank on the issues of poverty alleviation on the continent.

In January 2000 the World Bank held a consultation in Johannesburg, where the major focus of debate was the issues of poverty. It was revealed that, among economists, cultural anthropologists, and sociologists alike, there was agreement that any measurement and definition that did not include the religious dimension would be inadequate.[29]

In March 2000, there was a conference on alleviating poverty specifi-cally in Africa, sponsored by the Council of Anglican Provinces of Africa (CAPA) and the World Bank. It was held in Mbagathi, Nairobi, partly as a follow-up to the Lambeth 1998 Conference, where poverty and debt can-cellation had been featured. The conference brought together bishops of the Anglican Church and other church people drawn from the National Council of Churches with World Bank officials from both Africa and abroad.

Through the presentation of papers, the conference considered various areas of poverty, especially among women and children; the HIV/AIDS pandemic in the midst of abject poverty; the crisis in education; and debt repayments as a burden on the economies of many poor countries, The conference resolved that in order to alleviate poverty there was a need to put people at the heart of development, to prioritize women, children and youth, and to address education and health issues, especially HIV/AIDS. At the same time it was important to deal with conflict prevention and to pursue postcolonial conflict reconstruction.

For the first time, the religious sphere and the World Bank had come together to talk about poverty alleviation; not only that, but the two groups had resolved to work together on poverty alleviation by targeting the most vulnerable groups in society. Women in the rural communities are the most vulnerable group affected by gender inequality, by a lack of access to education, and by poor health services. The agreement between the World Bank and the Anglican Church stated that "the World Bank can work with the church to assess the impact of programs of both institutions that are targeted to this group and to enable men and women to work together in mutually supportive partnership in the home and the community."[30]

This paradigm shift was significant for the religious groups because it justifies the role of religious groups in poverty alleviation in discussing economics with the authorities. The Church was to bring into the discus-sions the human face to development, in which development is a mission of God, as noted by Carl E. Braaten: "As long as Christian faith is oriented by the history of promise and eschatological significance of Christ, there will be a Christian mission in world history—the universal scope of the history of promise posits the whole world as the horizon of mission—the world is not something that can be added on. The world stands within the horizon from the beginning or simply comes too late to prevent evan-gelistic backlash or ecclesiastical retrenchment . . . The doctrine of the Church needs to be reconceived within the horizon of the eschatological mission of the God in world history."[31]

The involvement of the Church in poverty alleviation is not optional; it is the extension of God's mission on earth. The mission societies began doing this when they set up the fourfold strategy of mission work, but they seem only to have created a new form of poverty. The many policies and models that have been tried in the continent have produced few social and economic benefits.

The move by the Christian churches to be involved in poverty alleviation is wonderful, but it is superficial and does not go to the root causes of why Africa is in the current state. One cannot ignore the fact that burgeoning technological advancements and profound geopolitical realignments are presently shaping and directing our world, and the two together are inexorably leading to an alarming marginalization of Africa. At the same time Africa at the present moment has neither the technological power nor the kind of political muscle that would make her respected in the global forums. It appears then that Africa has no choice other than to use all available opportunities to transform herself while resisting the pressure and influence of the very powerful neighbors with whom she shares the planet.

So how does Africa meld the worthwhile societal systems and elements of the present and those elements of the "global civilization" that are impinging on the entire continent? This constitutes the enduring challenge with which Africa is faced. Although the major forces of poverty alleviation programs continue to come from outside the continent, it is true that it is ultimately only those who live in the continent that will transform Africa. But the chances that they can carry it out alone without the help of the outside are slim. It is no service to the African cause to ignore the problems involved or make them look lighter that they actually are. There is the indomitable will of African peoples, coupled with their faith in the future of Africa, that provides us with a basis of thinking and believing that African leaders will, in time, put aside their parochial visions for a more inclusive one that would weaken the hold of the myth of national sovereignty and personal power.

Conclusion

In this chapter I have sought to look at the Church's involvement in poverty alleviation in historical context. I have tried to show that the route taken to develop Africa created a poverty trap. So how does Africa break out of the vicious circle of poverty in which she is trapped? This is a worrying situation, which cannot be dealt with in simplistic ways but needs to be looked at in a wider context. The fundamental problem in the poverty reduction debate is the link between the widening unequal distribution of income or wealth in general and poverty. As a structural phenomenon, poverty cannot be erased by providing the poor with welfare and opportunities; we need also to transform larger underlying structures like the nation-state apparatus and income and asset distribution mechanisms that are today in operation in many countries in Africa. Such a strategy would transcend the bounds of mere religion and theology by integrating the best of other disciplines—economics, politics, science, ethics, and sociology, to name but a few.

Notes

1 African Charter for Popular Participation in Development and Transformation (Arusha, 1990), 17. During the week when Nelson Mandela was released from prison, the International Conference on Popular Participation in the Recovery and Development Process in Africa was held in Arusha, United Republic of Tanzania, February 12-16, 1990. The conference comprised a large assembly of peoples' organizations, government and nongovernmental representatives, and United States agencies, all searching for the role of the populace in Africa's transformation. It was the third such conference organized by the United Nations Program of Action for African Economic Recovery and Development (UN-PAAERD) and crafted what would be known as the Arusha Charter.

2 Carol Mandi, "The Poor Die Everyday, Everywhere, Anyway," *Daily Nation*, May 10, 2001.

3 Kenneth Copeland, *The Laws of Prosperity* (Fort Worth, TX: Kenneth Copeland Ministries, 1978); Kenneth Hagin, *How God Taught Me about Prosperity* (Tulsa, OK: Kenneth Hagin Ministries, 1978); Otabil Mensa, *Enjoying the Blessings of Abraham* (Accra: Altar International, 1992); Otabil Mensa, *Four Laws of Productivity: God's Foundation for Living* (Accra: Altar International, 1992).

4 Jubilee 2000 was an international campaign in over forty countries that sought the cancelation of third world debt by the year 2000. It later split into an array of organizations round the world driven by the same aim. The concept derives from the biblical idea of the year of the Jubilee in Leviticus when all the people were set free from their debts to begin anew on an equal footing rather than remaining hindered by the debts of the past.

5 Africa cannot be treated as a homogenous cultural set, nor can Africans be treated as members of a homogenous cultural system. At best, Africa is merely the name of a geographical continent and Africans are natives of that continent.

6 Roland Oliver, *The Missionary Factor in Africa* (London: Longman, 1952); Brian Stanley, *The Bible and the Flag* (Leicester, UK: Apollos, 1990).

7 Quoted in Stanley, *The Bible and the Flag*, 70.

8 W. B. Anderson, *The Church in East Africa* (Nairobi: Uzima, 1977); John Karanja, *Founding an Anglican Faith: Kikuyu Anglican Christianity* (Nairobi: Uzima, 1999); Carl-Erik Sahlberg, *From Krapf to Rugambwa: A Church History of Tanzania* (Nairobi: Evangel Publishing, 1986); Zablon John Nthamburi, *A History of the Methodist Church* (Nairobi: Uzima, 1982).

9 Margaret Crouch, *A Vision of Christian Mission: Reflections on the Great Commission in Kenya, 1943-1993* (Nairobi: NCCK, 1993), 5.

10 J. O. Oucho, *Urban Migration and Rural Development* (Nairobi: Nairobi University Press, 1996), 16.

11 Felix Kiruthu, *Voices of Freedom: Great African Independence Speeches* (Nairobi: Cana Publishers, 2001), 75.

12 Crouch, *A Vision of Christian Mission*, 39.

13 Kenneth King, *Jua Kali Kenya: Change and Development in an Informal Economy, 1970-1995* (London: James Currey, 1996).

14 Mutava Musyimi, "Building God's Kingdom through Microenterprise Development," *Transformation: An International Dialogue on Mission and Ethics* 20, no.3 (July 2003): 152-53.

15 Henry Okullu, *Quest for Justice: An Autobiography of Bishop Henry Okullu* (Nairobi: Shalom Publishers, 1997), 173.

16 Graham Bird, *IMF Lending to Developing Countries: Issues and Evidence* (London: Routledge, 1995).

17 Jessica Williams, *50 Facts That Should Change the World* (London: Icon Books, 2004), 56.

18 Julie Hearn, "'The Invisible' NGO: U.S. Evangelical Missions in Kenya," *Journal of Religion in Africa* 32, no. 1 (2002): 45.

19 Agnes Chepkwony, *The Role of Non-Governmental Organisations in Development: A Study of the National Council of Churches of Kenya (NCCK), 1963-1978* (Uppsala: University of Uppsala, 1987).

20 S. I. Oladeji and A. G. Abiola, "Poverty Alleviation with Economic Growth Strategy: Prospects and Challenges in Contemporary Nigeria," *Journal of Social Development Africa* 2 (July 2000): 45.

21 Tim Allen and Alan Thomas, *Poverty and Development in the 1990s* (Oxford: Oxford University Press, 1992).

22 Gustavo Gutiérrez, *A Theology of Liberation* (Maryknoll, NY: Orbis Books, 1973).

23 Government of Kenya, *Kenya Interim Poverty Reduction Strategy Paper, 2000-2003* (Nairobi: Government of Kenya, July 13, 2003).

24 E. Wayne Natziger, *Economic Development*, 4th ed. (Cambridge: Cambridge University Press, 2006), 561.

25 Jonathan Sacks, The *Dignity of Difference: How to Avoid the Clash of Civilization* (London: Continuum, 2003), 115.

26 Ann Pettifor, *The Coming First World Debt Crisis* (New York: Palgrave, 2006), 26.

27 Sacks, *The Dignity of Difference*, 117.

28 James Wolfensohn, "International Debt I," speech given at the Lambeth Conference 1998, in *Report of the Lambeth Conference, 1998* (London: Morehouse, 1999), 5-52.

29 Molefe Tsele, "The Role of Religion in Development," *Transformation* 17, no. 4 (2000): 136.

30 Conference paper on poverty alleviation in Africa, for a conference hosted by the Council of Anglican Provinces in Africa and the World Bank, March 6-10, 2000, Nairobi, Kenya.

31 Carl Braaten, *The Flaming Centre: A Theology of the Christian Mission* (Philadelphia: Fortress Press, 1977), 54.

9

TAMAR'S CRY: THE AFRICAN CHURCH AND THE HIV AND AIDS PANDEMIC

Denise M. Ackermann

The AIDS pandemic in South Africa is a complex mixture of issues. Gender inequality, attitudes toward human sexuality, the scarring and fragmentation of large sections of society, our history of migrant labor and uprooting of communities exacerbated today by increased poverty, unemployment, and a tragic period of denial of the cause of AIDS by leading politicians are all part of the South African AIDS story. I shall comment briefly on the HIV and AIDS pandemic in South Africa. Thereafter, I reread the story of Tamar in 2 Samuel 13:1-22, a story of rape and violence that took place in David's household. The last half of this chapter is devoted to the search for clues of resistance and hope in the midst of AIDS. This chapter aims to introduce certain theological themes for the churches in South Africa to pursue as they struggle with their role in combating the AIDS pandemic.

HIV and AIDS in South Africa

The statistics of the AIDS pandemic are a nightmare. According to UNAIDS, the Joint United Nations Programme on HIV/AIDS, at the end of 2010, an estimated 34 million people were living with HIV worldwide, up 17% from 2001. Sub-Saharan Africa remains the region most affected by HIV. About 68% of all people living with HIV live in Sub-Saharan Africa, a region with only 12% of the world's population. This region also accounted for 70% of the new HIV infections in 2010, although there is a notable decline of the regional rate of new infections. The proportion of women living with HIV has remained stable at 50% globally, but women are more affected in Sub-Saharan Africa (59% of all people living with HIV). Since 1998, AIDS has claimed at least one million lives annually in Sub-Saharan Africa.[1]

The statistics from UNAIDS also indicate that the epidemic is most serious in southern Africa, with almost half of the deaths from AIDS-related illnesses in 2010 occurring in this region. South Africa has more people living with HIV (an estimated 5.6 million) than any other country. That is one out of nine of South Africa's population.[2] According to the South African National HIV Survey of 2008, an estimated 16.9% of people between 15 and 49 years old were infected with HIV and AIDS. The annual number of deaths as a result of HIV and AIDS rose by a massive 93% between 1997 and 2006. The rise was 173% among those aged 25-49 years old. In 2008 alone, more than 590,000 people have died due to AIDS-related illnesses.[3]

Despite this grim picture, South Africa is slowly moving from pariah status to one with progressive programs for HIV prevention and is now fully compliant with the World Health Organization's guidelines for HIV treatment. This change started in 2009 when new policies for HIV prevention were introduced that are having far reaching consequences for mother to child transmission and for the general treatment of those infected with the virus.[4] However, despite recent progress, there are no South Africans who do not know someone or of someone who has died of AIDS or is living with HIV. Statistics and forecasts are numbing. Yet they cannot convey the suffering of decimated families, the despair of orphaned children, the fear induced by stigma, and the material and physical needs of those who are losing loved ones.

In southern Africa HIV and AIDS is in reality a pandemic that has everything to do with gender relations and conditions of poverty. South Africa is a society in which cultural traditions of male dominance, bolstered by a particular understanding of the place of men in the Christian tradition, have resulted in continued inequity for women.[5] Furthermore, domestic violence, rape, and the sexual abuse of women are rife. Poverty, both in the rural areas and in the informal settlements surrounding our cities, is a further grinding reality. Understanding this unholy alliance should be at the heart of all HIV and AIDS programs whether located in the churches or in state structures. Gender inequality coupled with sexual violence against women and the snail-like pace at which poverty is being tackled are the main problems blocking effective HIV and AIDS prevention. Women who are HIV-positive are at the receiving end of prejudice, social ostracism, and violence. This gendered pandemic requires a theological response that is prepared to wrestle with the implications of gender inequity in our traditions and our practices as well as the reasons for continuous grinding poverty in sub-Saharan Africa. Today we are all infected by this pandemic. The Church has AIDS.

Rereading an Ancient Text: The Story of Tamar

I am a white, South African academic theologian with no expertise in biblical scholarship. I read the Bible as does the general Christian reader, from the perspective of faith, seeking resources for life in a context with its own particular problems and challenges. My reading of the Tamar text is tempered by an acute awareness of the gendered nature of the HIV and AIDS crisis in which women and children are too often the victims. At the same time it is also a reading that seeks hope and affirmation for life.[6]

The story in 2 Samuel 13:1-22 is well known yet seldom preached.[7] King David's son Amnon falls in love with his beautiful half-sister Tamar. He is tormented and consults his friend Jonabab, a "very clever man." They hatch a plan. Amnon pretends that he is sick, and at his request David sends Tamar to him to make cakes "in his sight." He refuses to eat the cakes, sends the servants away, and asks Tamar to bring the cakes "into the chamber, so that I may eat from your hand." She does so, he grabs her and says, "Come lie with me, my sister." She resists: "No my brother, do not force me; for such a thing is not done in Israel; do not do anything so vile! As for me, where could I carry my shame? And as for you, you would be as one of the scoundrels in Israel." But Amnon will not listen, he is stronger than Tamar, and he rapes her. Once the deed is done, Amnon is "seized with a great loathing for her" and he says: "Get out!" Tamar protests at her treatment. Again Amnon is deaf to her entreaties, and he calls a servant and instructs him to "put this woman out of my presence, and bolt the door after her." After this is done, Tamar puts ashes on her head, goes away, and "remains a desolate woman, in her brother Absalom's house." Later we learn that Absalom kills Amnon as revenge for Tamar's rape.

Such are the bare bones of this rapacious tale. Its truths are multiple, conflicting, and resistant to being read as a simple story of a rape. It is a text that echoes through the ages and that resonates with women's experiences today in a number of ways. Tamar is a victim of rape, betrayal, and abandonment. She is the obedient daughter who pays a price in a patriarchal clan. She does as she is told; she obeys her father and serves her "sick" brother. When she realizes what is about to happen to her, she cries out: "No, my brother, do not force me, *for such a thing is not done in Israel.*" The immorality and injustice of the violation is more than just hers. It is a shame on the name of Israel. Her words are honest and poignant. While they acknowledge female servitude, they speak of a moral vision that is tragically in contrast with that of Amnon.

Tamar is not only a victim of rape. She is betrayed by her family, raped, and then despised. She is no longer "my sister," but "this woman." Amnon ends up hating her.[8] His love for his sister is a disordered love driven by morbid desire. Once the rape is committed, he is confronted by his own morbidity mirrored to him in the tragic figure of his victim. This he cannot bear and she is "put out" of his presence. She is also a victim of her father's abdication of his responsibility as king and as father. There is no record of him responding to this outrage with an appropriate punishment. She is also a victim of her brother Absalom's plans for revenge when she is coopted by him into concealing them: "Be quiet for now, my sister; he is your brother; do not take this to heart." The victim is made silent. Finally, she is cast out. We last hear of her as remaining in Absalom's house "a desolate woman." Condemned to a quiet life of despair and desolation, her social and spiritual needs are not acknowledged or addressed and she disappears into the mists of history. I agree with James Poling that "the latent message of this story is that sexual violence against women is not about the humanity of women but about power between men."[9] Finally, there is no restitution or justice for Tamar.

The brutal rape in this text speaks stridently into my context in South Africa. Rape, incest, and violence are endemic in South Africa.[10] Human Rights Watch/Africa's *Report on Violence against Women in South Africa* states: "What is certain . . . is that South African women, living in one of the most violent countries in the world, are disproportionately likely to be victims of that violence."[11] Unlike domestic violence, which cuts across all barriers,[12] recorded victims of rape are mostly concentrated among poor and disadvantaged women in South Africa.[13] This is not surprising, as poor women do not have private transportation, need to walk long distances and live in areas plagued by crime, gangsterism, overcrowding, and poverty and, in order to work, are often required to leave and return home in the dark. We have our Tamars, our Amnons, our Davids, and our Absaloms.[14]

Women's vulnerability to abuse is unflinchingly portrayed in Tamar's story. It speaks truth to my context. While poverty is not Tamar's lot, this text names the evil: our human proclivity for abuse of power. It appears to leave us with little hope. But does it really? Tamar's cry: "for such a thing is not done in Israel," is a cry of resistance. The very fact that this woman's voice is heard in this text in this manner is unusual enough to leave some ground for hope, slim as it may be. The quirky power of scripture to uncover new ways of seeing, to point to less obvious paths, and to evoke hope when despair seems the only legitimate reaction can allow clues for resistance and hope to slip through this reading that could assist the churches as they struggle to find a way forward in this present crisis.

The Tamar Text: Clues for Resistance and Hope

"Saying It as It Is"

Tamar's story "says it as it is." Why is this important? There is no prevarication, no avoidance of the horror, no cover up. Miroslav Volf speaks about "the geography of sin" and "the ideology of sin."[15] In the case of Tamar "the geography of sin" is the scene of the crime in which her violated body is at the center. "The ideology of sin" is the context backed by eons of patriarchal traditions and practices that result in women's status being secondary to that of the male in familial relations. "Saying it as it is" is the place to begin. What would it take for the churches to accept responsibility publicly for our role in the promotion and maintenance of gender inequality? And when will we make the link between this woeful tradition and the present deadly impact of HIV and AIDS on the lives of women and men? Positively put, the churches can begin to deal with the present erosion of sexual morality, with its devastating consequences for women and children, by esteeming women—our entire being, our bodies, our status, and our humanity—in every respect, as well as by speaking out unambiguously about the reasons for the present scourge of HIV and AIDS.

Once the Body of Christ is able to make the connection between power, gender relations, and HIV and AIDS within its own infected body, the question then is this: What will it take for the Body of Christ to be a body that can bring hope to those living with HIV and AIDS? Given the existing conflicting models for being Church, I suggest that a common starting point is found in our creeds. As Anglicans, we confess the Church as being "one, holy, catholic, and apostolic."[16] What does this mean in the midst of this HIV and AIDS crisis?

These statements are made in faith and are integral components of the confession of the Triune God. As the Church acquires its existence through the activity of Christ, the marks of the Church are, in the first instance, marks of Christ's activity. Unity of the Church lies in Christ's unifying activity. Holiness is not initially ours but is the holiness of Christ who acts on sinners. Catholicity is really about the limitless lord-ship of Christ. Apostolicity refers to Christ's mission in the Spirit. Seen in this way these confessions of faith are statements of hope—indicators of the new creation of all in Christ.[17] They are also statements of action. If we are truly *one*, we are the Church with HIV and AIDS. People living with HIV and AIDS are found in every sector of society and every church denomination. We are all related; what affects one member of the Body of Christ affects us all (1 Cor. 12:26). We are all living with HIV and AIDS. There is no "us" and "them." We dare not forget that inclusion, not exclu-sion, is the way of grace. If we are *holy*, we are not living some super-human mode of existence, as Marjorie Suchocki reminds us: "Holiness does not require a transcendence of our human condition, but a full uti-lization of our condition toward the concrete reality of love."[18] Holiness is not withdrawal from the smell of crisis but engagement, often risky, in situations where God is present. If we are *catholic*, we are in solidarity because we are connected, in communion, with those who are suffering and who experience fear of rejection, poverty, and death. If we are *apos-tolic*, we stand in continuity with the Church in its infancy, and we strive to live as Ignatius of Antioch put it, "in the manner of the apostles."[19] This means that we are true to the heart of our confession, that we are zealous for the Word, and that we continuously examine the ideals of the early church and measure ourselves against them. This is nothing new. It is no more than a call to put the words we mouth in the creeds into practice. Clearly we all fall short in this regard. The marks of the Church do, however, offer solid, practical guidelines for measuring our actions as members of this one universal body, a body infected with viruses strug-gling to live faithfully.

The Power of Narrative

Tamar's story raises the issue of the power of narrative. Human beings cannot survive without a narrative identity. Telling stories is intrinsic to claiming one's identity and in this process finding impulses for hope. For those living with HIV and AIDS there is a need to claim and to name their identities in order to move away from the victim status so often thrust upon them. Narrative has a further function. Apart from claiming identity and naming the evil, narrative has a sense-making function. The very act of telling the story is an act of making sense of an often incomprehensible situation, of a suffering and chaotic world in which people wrestle with understanding and in so doing seek to experience relief.

The stories of people living with HIV and AIDS are not only stories of suffering. They are also stories of triumph, of resistance, and of hope. Stories such as these need to be heard in communities of faith. Churches can offer a supportive and empathetic environment for storytelling in the search for meaning. The stories of people living with HIV and AIDS are individual tales within the metanarrative of the pandemic. Hearing and engaging with these stories in communities of faith has the potential to draw members into relationship. We all have stories to tell. As our stories intersect, they change. We become part of one another's stories. In this process, we are all changed. Hearing and telling stories begins a process of openness, vulnerability, and mutual engagement that challenges stigmas, ostracization, and the loneliness of suffering, and hopefully leads to acts of engagement, affirmation, and care. Most importantly, narrative has the power to break the silences surrounding this crisis and to give it a human face.

The real metanarrative is *the* story of our faith: the story of the God of Israel acting to create and redeem culminating in the ministry, the suffering, death, and resurrection of Jesus Christ. Storytelling becomes a two-way conversation—hearing stories of suffering and triumph, and retelling *the* story of suffering and triumph in our communities of faith. The intersecting of our life stories with the Jesus story is our ultimate hope.

Embodiment

The HIV virus enters, lurks, and then makes forays into the immune system until ultimately it destroys the body. This pandemic is all about bodies. Unfortunately, writes William R. LaFleur, "in spite of doctrines of incarnation, resurrection, and *imago dei*, and theories about the ingestion of the very body of Christ in the mass, both the Catholic and Protestant Churches, perhaps especially during some of the modern centuries, have conceived their principal domain as that of the soul and its salvation."[20] Thankfully, the Tamar story is a tale about embodiment. This text challenges the recurring Christian refrain that the body is secondary to the soul and that the material is less praiseworthy than the spiritual. Our social reality is an embodied reality. Our bodies are more than skin, bone, and flesh. Our bodies encompass the totality of our human experience, our thoughts, our emotions, our needs and memories, our ability to imagine and to dream, our experiences of pain, pleasure, power, and difference, as well as our beliefs and our hopes. Our bodies are, in fact, the intricate tracery of all that is ourselves. In Elaine Graham's words, "embodiment is more than an 'issue' exciting our compassion; rather, it points us to the performative, incarnational nature of all theology. Bodily *praxis* is the agent and the vehicle of divine reality and the faith practices of the Body of Christ are 'sacraments' of suffering and redemption."[21] The Tamar text opens up the issue of the body and challenges any thoughts of separating soul and body, mind and emotions.

For women and children who are infected, the body is at the center of political, social, and religious struggles. This is hardly surprising. The female body has, for instance, been the subject of ridicule, adulation, envy, discrimination, abuse, and stigma. The question of stigma is particularly relevant to persons suffering from HIV and AIDS. Ignorance, prejudice, stereotypes, and issues of power and dominance all conspire to stigmatize sufferers and in so doing to label them and to distort their true identities. You simply become "an HIV positive," a statistic whose identity is now subsumed in your status. This denies the active, meaningful, and contributing lives led by increasing numbers of HIV positive people.

Women who are known to be HIV positive are stigmatized by a large section of South African society. Tamar's cry is a poignant reminder of what happens when stigmas prevail. Fortunately, within the body of people living with HIV and AIDS there is an increasing band of people who are slowly gaining power by defining their experiences and claiming their reality, speaking out, and breaking the silence around the disease. The social activism of the Treatment Action Campaign, which had bodies marching in the streets in South Africa demanding affordable treatment for HIV and AIDS, is a case in point.

When, on the one hand, the body is seen merely as a vehicle for the soul, or, on the other, as some kind of a trap, it has been maltreated, vilified, and abused. This is an important clue for the churches to seize in the struggle against HIV and AIDS. Bodies are at the center of this crisis— sick, poor, and too often women's and children's bodies. The gospel demands embodied acts of care, comfort, support, and acceptance.

Ethical Codes

Tamar's cry, "for such a thing is not done in Israel," raises the issue of the ethical codes of a people. She does not only cry out for the protection of her own body but for the honor of her people. Her people are God's people. In reality, her cry is a cry to God. It is a cry for the integrity of life. It is a cry of resistance against the disordered and morbid nature of Amnon's love and a cry for love expressed in relations of trust and respect.

In South Africa today there is much talk, and very necessary talk, about abstinence, prevention, and medication in the face of the HIV and AIDS crisis. The Roman Catholics say abstinence is the only answer. The Anglicans say yes, but if you must, use condoms. There is very little being said, however, about the moral and ethical issues raised by the HIV and AIDS pandemic. So far the churches have not grasped this nettle. The recognition that the Body of Christ is a community of sexual human beings is slow in coming, and centuries of ignoring any matter related to human sexuality is merely feeding the silences around HIV and AIDS.[22] It simply is not good enough merely to preach fidelity and abstinence in sexual relations. This message cannot be heard, understood, or followed as long as it is communicated without a properly constructed debate on what constitutes a moral community. Moral choices and moral account-ability and a community in which women are respected as equal partners in the Church itself are essential to this debate.

What makes a moral community? Christian ethics are communal ethics. How people live with one another and our faithfulness to God are two sides of the same coin. In Amnon's world the people of Israel received the law, according to Rowan Williams, "when God had already established relations with them, when they were already beginning to be a community bound by faithfulness to God and to each other."[23] Williams continues:

> When the Old Testament prophets announce God's judg-ment on the people, they don't primarily complain about the breaking of specific rules (though they can do this in some contexts) or about failure to live up to a moral ideal; they denounce those actions that signify a breaking of the covenant with God and so the breaking of the bonds of faithfulness that preserve Israel as a people to whom God has given a vocation.[24]

In the New Testament Paul deals with ethical dilemmas (for example, Rom. 14 and 15, 1 Cor. 10) by arguing that any decisions taken should be guided by the priority of the other person's advantage, by avoidance of judgmentalism, and by acceptance of one another and thus by the ultimate imperative of building the Body of Christ more securely. For Christians, ethical actions flow from involvement in community with God and with one another. Actions that promote the good of another are actions, which are designed to be for the good of the Body of Christ. As Bruce B. Birch and Larry L. Rasmussen note, to be a member of the Body of Christ means "the formation and transformation of personal moral identity in keeping with the faith identity of the community."[25]

Brazilian bishop Dom Helder Camara meditated in the middle hours of the night about the attitudes of the rich toward the poor and wrote a poem. This poem speaks to those of us in the Church who are not HIV positive and who may be tempted to feel virtuous about our status, perhaps even indifferent to those who are infected.

> I pray incessantly
> for the conversion
> of the prodigal son's brother.
> Ever in my ear
> rings the dread warning
> "this one [the prodigal] has awoken
> from his life of sin.
> When will the other [the brother]
> awaken
> from his virtue?[26]

Life and Death

Tamar is lost in the mists of history, and we do not know how she lived out her life. Her rape undoubtedly affected her quality of life and her ability to live abundantly. Discovering that one is infected, coping with subsequent opportunistic infections and finally with full-blown AIDS challenge one's quality of life. How to live productively and hopefully with the knowledge of premature death and then how to face imminent death raise questions about the relationship between life and death that demand attention in the Body of Christ. What has the Good News to say to someone who is infected with HIV or who is dying of AIDS?

I suggest that the place to begin is to affirm that God is a lover of life, so much so, that life continues into eternity. Certainty about this comes from the promise of the resurrection of the body. Hope is the key to questions about life and death. Not "pie in the sky when you die" kind of hope, which is nothing more than the thin skin of religious optimism, but creative, imaginative, expectant, and risky hope, maintained only with struggle. Hope is demanding, because we have to live our lives in such a way that that which we hope for can come about. This kind of hope takes our confessed belief in "the life everlasting" as not only something for one day when I die but as a confession of how I will live my life this day, in this moment. It is the kind of hope that enabled Dietrich Bonhoeffer when he took leave of a fellow prisoner in Flossenbürg concentration camp and went to his execution, to say: "This is the end—for me the beginning of life."[27]

Life, death, and resurrection all belong together: they make up the whole of life. Resurrection cannot be reduced to life after death alone. When John (1 John 3:14) writes, "We know that we have passed from death into life, because we love one another," he stresses that love is passionate about life, that we must say a hearty "Yes" to life. What the resurrection of the body means is the subject of theological speculation; resurrection talk, however, remains body talk according to our creeds. Resurrection does not mean a deferred life—something we put off until after we die. In Jürgen Moltmann's words: "I shall live *wholly* here, and die *wholly*, and rise *wholly* there."[28] Eternal life is all of me, all of everyone, all of creation, all healed, reconciled, and completed. Nothing will be lost. Christian faith is shaped by the experience of the dying and the death of Christ and by his resurrection. The process of the resurrection of the dead begins in Christ and continues in the Spirit, "the giver of life" and will be completed in the raising of all the dead.[29] So, I would say to the person dying of AIDS, "Death is not your end. *Every life remains before God forever.*" For Moltmann, to be raised to eternal life means that nothing has been lost for God—"not the pains of this life, and not in moments of happiness."[30] Thus, death both separates and unites. "Eternal life is the final healing of this life into the completed wholeness for which it is destined."[31]

Unfortunately, there are Christians who believe that AIDS is God's punishment for sin. In her book *AIDS and Its Metaphors*, Susan Sontag says that "plagues are invariably regarded as judgments on society."[32] We are very quick to link any sexually transmitted disease with sin as if there are no innocent victims. Insensitive zealousness has resulted in persons dying of AIDS being told: "Your sin has caused your death." I am cautious, even suspicious of this language of fear. Despite those terrifying medieval pictures of judgment that were designed to encourage women and men to seek comfort and salvation in the arms of the Church, people have not stopped sinning. The mere mention of HIV and AIDS raises fear. It seeps into places where we did not know it before: fear of sexuality, fear of bodily fluids, fear of the Communion cup—as Sontag comments, "fear of contaminated blood, whether Christ's or your neighbor's."[33] Death can be caused directly by sin. We kill one another. We are destroying our environment. But death is not God's ultimate judgment on us. Admittedly, Christian thinkers like Paul, the old church fathers, and Augustine saw death as punishment for "the wages of sin." James writes that "then, when that desire has conceived, it gives birth to sin, and that sin, when fully grown, gives birth to death" (1:15). Undeniably death can be caused by sinful acts.

There are other traditions in Christianity that do not see death as a judgment on sin. Schleiermacher and liberal Protestant theology of the nineteenth century disputed the causal connection between sin and physical death.[34] Moltmann argues that death may be called the "wages of sin" but that this can only be said of human beings. Angels are dubbed immortal but according to 2 Peter 2:4 they sinned! Animals, birds, fish, and the trees don't sin, yet they die. Through human beings death has been brought into nonhuman creation. Death has been with us from the beginning. God's first commandment to human beings was "be fruitful and multiply" (Gen. 1:28). We were mortal right from the beginning. From a pastoral point of view, theological speculation about the relationship between sin and death is not particularly helpful for the person dying of AIDS.

The body is implicated in the process of sin. The very context in which we live is affected by sin. Innocence suffers. Everything that is "born" must die. It is part of our condition. Our responsibility is to live and to die in loving solidarity with that sighing and groaning community of creatures described by Paul, all waiting for "the redemption of our bodies" (Rom. 8:23).[35] We all need redemption. "The death of all the living is neither due to sin nor is it natural," writes Moltmann. "It is a fact that evokes grief and longing for the future world and eternal life."[36] We all await what Letty M. Russell calls "the mending of creation."[37]

At the center of our efforts to understand the link between life and death is Christ. For Paul, community with Christ, who is the subject of our hope, extends to the living and the dead: "For to this end Christ died and lived again, that he might be Lord of both the dead and of the living" (Rom. 14:9). Moltmann reads this verse as follows:

> I understand this in the following sense: In dying, Christ became the brother of the dying. In death, he became the brother of the dead. In his resurrection—as the One risen—he embraces the dead and the living, and takes them with him on his way to the consummation of God's kingdom.[38]

As we struggle to understand what it means to live hopefully, we are reminded that life remains unfinished. We have tried to live according to the plan for our lives, but we have failed. We are wounded, incomplete, not yet the persons that God intends us to be. We mourn the death of those we love. There is no quick fix for those who suffer. Life in the midst of suffering and death is a constant struggle; it risks moments of despair and loss of trust, and it seeks hope even in the darkest places.

Eucharist

So far my rereading of the Tamar text has raised issues of honest awareness, narrative, embodiment, moral community, and issues of life and death. At heart, Tamar's story portrays what can happen when human relationships become corrupted. It is a story of failure and loss of hope, as both Tamar and Amnon are violated, albeit in different ways. Yet when it is read within the wider context of the canon, it is a story of resistance to abuse and to evil power and an affirmation of the moral code of a people who knew the better way.

By grace, failure does not have the last word in the Christian life. Our hope is in Jesus Christ, the embodiment of our faith, whose life, death, and resurrection we celebrate in the Eucharist. Michael Welker reminds us that the Eucharist was instituted "in the night that Jesus Christ was betrayed and handed over to the powers of this world."[39] Its origins do not lie in success or triumph but in the human betrayal of the Son, and it is precisely here that we dare to hope. I want to conclude my search for clues on hope with a few thoughts on how the Eucharist links up with the themes that I have already raised and how it offers hope in our present context. The Anglican Church believes in sacramental theology and the Eucharist occupies a central place in its worshipping life and spirituality. Rethinking the meaning of Eucharist helps the Anglican Church to envision a more inclusive church community and develop strategies to respond to the AIDS pandemic and offer help to those suffering from HIV and AIDS.

At the outset of this essay I said that the Body of Christ has AIDS. I see a link between the violated body of Tamar, the abused bodies of women and children, the bodies of people living with HIV and AIDS, and the crucified and resurrected body of Jesus Christ, whom we remember and celebrate in the bread and the wine at the Eucharist. Deep inside the Body of Christ, the AIDS virus lurks, and as we remember Christ's sacrifice we see in his very wounds the woundedness of his sisters and brothers who are infected and dying. Our hope is in Christ, who takes the Church as his bride, makes it his body, and through this nuptial act sets before us the possibility of relationships in love that are the antithesis of the disordered and morbid expressions of love found in Tamar's story.

The Eucharist is the bodily practice of grace. Nancy Eisland writes: "Receiving the Eucharist is a body practice of the church. The Eucharist as a central and constitutive practice of the church is a ritual of membership . . . . the Eucharist is a matter of bodily mediation of justice and an incorporation of hope."[40] Because God chose to live with us in the flesh, sacramentality takes physical reality very seriously.[41] We are bodily partakers of the physical elements of bread and wine, Christ's presence in our lives and in our world. The very bodiliness of the celebration of the Eucharist affirms the centrality of the body in the practice of the faith. "The Supper," writes Welker, "centers on a complex, sensuous process in which the risen and exalted Christ becomes present. The Supper gives Christians a form in which they can perceive the risen and exalted Christ with all their senses."[42]

The celebration of the Eucharist makes the reign of God present "to us" in the form of Christ's body broken "for us" and Christ's blood shed "for us." Christ invites us to the feast, and he is "both the giver of the feast and the gift itself."[43] In other words, the gift of the reign of God is quite simply present in the person of Christ himself—Christ crucified and risen. Thus, the Communion meal mediates communion with the crucified One in the presence of the risen One. It becomes a foretaste of the messianic banquet of all humankind. It is the meal at which all are welcome. In Christ's Body, the Eucharist is *the* sacrament of equality. Only self-exclusion can keep one away. At the Communion table we are offered the consummate step in forging an ethic of right relationship, across all our differences. "We who are many are one body for we all partake of the one bread," as the Eucharistic liturgy says. This visible, unifying, bodily practice of relationship with all its potential for healing is ours. For the Eucharist to have meaning in our lives, we need to feel its powerful pull to the radical activity of loving relationships with those who are different. As Ducan Forrester writes, "The Eucharist involves a commitment (*sacramentum*) to sharing with the needy neighbor, for Jesus said, 'The Bread that I shall give is my own flesh; given for the life of the world' (John 6:51)."[44]

A covenanted Eucharistic community is a community in relationship with one another and with God. Paul describes us as the Body of Christ, a body which though it has many members, is one body: "If one member suffers, all suffer together with it; if one member is honored, all rejoice together with it" (1 Cor. 12:26). It is a body in which the weakest are to be treated with respect for "God has so arranged the body, giving the greater honor to the inferior member, that there may be no dissension within the body, but the members may have the same care for one another" (1 Cor. 12:25). The picture here is one of solidarity in suffering, of mutual support, and of a moral community in relationship with one another and with God.

Finally, much has been made of the text in 1 Cor. 11:27-29, 31-32 about eating the bread and drinking the wine in an unworthy manner, about examining ourselves, and about the threat of judgment. Welker comments that then "the Supper is no longer a feast of reconciliation but rather an anxiety-producing means of moral gatekeeping. In a sad irony, the feast of unconditional acceptance of human beings by God and among each other was misused for intrahuman moral control!"[45] There is a tension here. Welker points out that in the celebration of the Eucharist, God accepts us unconditionally, while at the same time Paul's concern is that Christians celebrate the meal in accordance with the meal's identity. Rightly so. How we partake of the meal is deeply significant for how we live as a moral community. "The Eucharist may be understood as nourishment for moral growth and formation," writes Forrester.[46] A community with a moral code and a moral identity partaking in a meal of grace, memory, and new life brings resistance to evil and hope for now and tomorrow for the Church with HIV and AIDS.

In conclusion, while conceding at the outset that the Tamar text did not give much apparent cause for hope, I have tried to find clues for resistance and hope that could be useful for church praxis in our present crisis. We live in what Edward Schillebeeckx terms a world that is an "enigmatic mixture of good and evil, of meaning and meaninglessness."[47] In the midst of this bewildering mixture of experiences, there is the human capacity for indignation and moral outrage. Tamar's cry, "for such a thing is not done in Israel," allows us to find hope where there is little cause for it, enables us to say "yes" when all else shouts "no," and allows chinks of light to help us find footholds in a context that in John Chrysostom's words is "grazed thin by death."[48] Her cry jars our reality. We know what should *not* be done in Israel. Tim Trengove Jones writes, "'We know what to do' is a formulation that takes us to the very heart of the scandal that is AIDS; it situates us on the frontier between hope and despair, between action and inertia, between those with the means to 'do something' and those who have little to 'do' but suffer."[49] HIV and AIDS are our *kairos*. It is a time when the ordinary rhythm of life is suspended. Will it be a time of doom, or will we find a new unveiling of God's presence and love for us here and now?

Notes

1 Joint United Nations Programme on HIV/AIDS, *UNAIDS World AIDS Day Report, 2011*, http://www.unaids.org/en/media/unaids/contentassets/documents/unaidspublication/2011/JC2216_WorldAIDSday_report_2011_en.pdf.

2 Ibid.

3 "South Africa HIV & AIDS Statistics," in *Alerting AID and AIDS*, http://www.avert.org/south-africa-hiv-aids-statistics.htm.

4 Yogan G. Pillay, C. White, and N. McCormick, "How Times Have Changed: HIV and AIDS in South Africa in 2011," *South African Medical Journal* 102, no. 2 (2012): 77-78.

5 This is illustrated by the fact that there are mainline denominational churches in South Africa in which Communion is served in the following order: first the men, then male adolescents, then women, and lastly female adolescents—as a confirmation of leadership of men (see 1 Cor. 11:3).

6 In passing, a comment on my personal experience of Bible reading. Long before I was aware of the technicalities of different kinds of reading, I was in fact familiar with a nascent form of interpretation used by women when studying the bible in groups. For well over thirty years I have belonged to women's bible study groups. We read the biblical stories through women's eyes, seeking meaning for our lives, understanding of our faith, and affirmation for our experiences. Often the texts were and are difficult, even off-putting to women. After studies in hermeneutics my approach to such contentious texts in Scripture took the route of a *sachkritiek* and I simply rejected them. This I no longer find satisfactory. My present approach is to try and deal with the whole of Scripture with its fundamental contradictions, to mull over them, often with irritation and anger, to ascertain how I can live with such texts fruitfully.

7 In 1999 I conducted research for a workshop on homiletics and found that of the eighty-four people interviewed (which included clergy and lay people) only one had heard a sermon on this text.

8 According to Phyllis Trible, "Tamar: The Royal Rape of Wisdom," in *Texts of Terror: Literary-Feminist Readings of Biblical Narratives* (Philadelphia: Fortress, 1984), 47, the repetition in this passage emphasizes the hatred focused on Tamar. "*Then-hated-her* Amnon *a-hatred* great indeed *(mĕ'ōd)*. Truly *(kî)* great(er) *the-hatred* which *he-hated-her* than-the-desire which he-desired-her."

9 James N. Poling, *The Abuse of Power: A Theological Problem* (Nashville, TN: Abingdon, 1991), 158.

10 See Jane Bennett, "Gender-based Violence in South Africa," *African Gender Institute Newsletter* 6 (2000): 3.

11 Human Rights Watch/Africa, *Report on Violence against Women in South Africa* (New York: Human Rights Watch, 1995), 44.

12 See Mmatshilo Motsei, "Detection of Women Battering in Health Care Settings: The Case of Alexandra Health Clinic," *Women's Health Project* paper no. 30 (January 1993): 5, which states that contrary to conventional wisdom, research has shown that "the perpetrators of violence against women include men who hold respectable jobs and positions in society. . . .These include lawyers, doctors, psychologists, psychiatrists, priests and business executives."

13 Human Rights Watch/Africa, *Report on Violence*, 52.

14 As a sample, see Anne Mager, "Sexuality, Fertility and Male Power," *Agenda* 28 (1996): 12-24, and Promise Mthembu, "A Positive View," *Agenda* 39 (1998): 26-30.

15 Miroslav Volf, "Original Crime, Primary Care," in *God and the Victim: Theological Reflections on Evil, Victimization, Justice, and Forgiveness*, ed. Lisa Barnes Lampman (Grand Rapids, MI: Eerdmans, 1999), 28-29.

16 Taken from the Nicene-Constantinopolitan Creed, while the Apostles' Creed speaks of "one, holy, catholic church."

17 Jürgen Moltmann, *The Church in the Power of the Spirit: A Contribution to Messianic Ecclesiology*, trans. Margaret Kohl (Minneapolis, MN: Fortress, 1993), 338-39.

18 Marjorie Suchocki, "Holiness and a Renewed Church," in *The Church with AIDS: Renewal in the Midst of Crisis*, ed. Letty M. Russell (Louisville, KY: Westminster John Knox, 1990), 115.

19 Quoted in Robert Schreiter, "Marks of the Church in Times of Transformation," in Russell, *The Church with AIDS*, 115.

20 William R. LaFleur, "Body," in *Critical Terms for Religious Studies*, ed. Mark C. Taylor (Chicago: University of Chicago Press, 1998), 41.

21 Elaine Graham, "Words Make Flesh: Embodiment and Practical Theology," paper presented at the International Academy for Practical Theology's Biennial Conference, Seoul, Korea, 1997.

22 Peter Brown has documented the variety of ways in which Christians in late antiquity found sexuality a problem. See his *The Body and Society: Men, Women, and Sexual Renunciation in Early Christianity* (New York: Columbia University Press, 1988).

23 Rowan Williams, "On Making Moral Decisions," unpublished address to the Lambeth Plenary Session, Canterbury, July 22, 1998.

24 Ibid.

25 Bruce B. Birch and Larry L. Rassmussen, *Bible and Ethics in Christian Life* (Minneapolis, MN: Augsburg, 1989), 45.

26 This story is told in ibid., 47.

27 Quoted in Jürgen Moltmann, *The Coming of God: Christian Eschatology*, trans. Margaret Kohl (Minneapolis, MN: Fortress, 1966), xi.

28 Ibid., 67.

29 Ibid., 69.

30 Ibid., 71.

31 Ibid., 71.

32 Susan Sontag, *AIDS and Its Metaphors* (New York: Farrar, Straus & Giroux, 1989), 54.

33 Ibid., 73.

34 For an explanation of these views, see Moltmann, *The Coming of God*, 87-89.

35 Moltmann writes, "The modern separation between person and nature (as in Schleiermacher) or between covenant and creation (as in Barth) does neither justice to human nature nor to the community of creation. It is an expression of the anthropocentrism of the modern world, an anthropocentrism destructive of nature. . . . The patristic church's doctrine of physical redemption was more comprehensive in its cosmic dimensions" (*The Coming of God*, 92).

36 Ibid.

37 This term is used by Letty M. Russell in many of her works to denote the eschatological implications of the reign of God.

38 Moltmann, *The Coming of God*, 105.

39 Michael Welker, *What Happens in Holy Communion?* trans. John F. Hoffmeyer (Grand Rapids, MI: Eerdmans, 2000), 43.

40 Nancy Eisland, *The Disabled God: Toward a Liberatory Theology of Disability* (Nashville, TN: Abingdon, 1994), 112.

41 Susan A. Ross, "God's Embodiment and Women," in *Freeing Theology: The Essentials of Theology in Feminist Perspective*, ed. Catherine Mowry LaCugna (San Francisco: HarperSanfrancisco, 1993), 186.

42 Welker, *What Happens in Holy Communion?* 18.

43 Moltmann, *The Church in the Power of the Spirit*, 250.

44 Ducan B. Forrester, *Truthful Action: Explorations in Practical Theology* (Edinburgh: T. & T. Clark, 2000), 96.

45 Welker, *What Happens in Holy Communion?*, 70.

46 Forrester, *Truthful Action*, 95.

47 Edward Schillebeeckx, *Church: The Human Story of God* (New York: Crossroad, 1993), 4.

48 John Chrysostom, *De Virginitate* 14.1, quoted in Brown, *The Body and Society*, 6.

49 Tim Trengove Jones, *Who Cares? AIDS Review 2001* (Pretoria, South Africa: University of Pretoria, 2001), 7.

10

DIVERSITY IN THE ANGLICAN TRADITION: WOMEN AND THE AFRO-CARIBBEAN CHURCH

Clara Luz Ajo Lázaro

The Anglican tradition is commonly seen as associated with English culture and values. But in fact, the thirty-eight provinces that make up the Anglican Communion are autonomous churches with distinct histories, cultures, and heritages. Even though the spread of the Anglican tradition was associated with colonialism and the expansion of the British Empire, the agency of local Christians has shaped how the message, liturgy, and culture of the Church has been received. Within the Anglican Communion today, many do not speak English as their first language. The Anglican tradition is expressed in many local forms, interacting with indigenous cultures and religious practices. There is much diversity and plurality within the Anglican tradition. This chapter focuses on women's experience in the Afro-Caribbean church.

The English began their connection with the Caribbean during the reign of Elizabeth I, as a result of the war with Catholic Spain. English settlers landed in Barbados in 1627, captured Jamaica in 1655, and subsequently colonized other islands in the Caribbean. The importation of slaves from Africa to work on the sugar plantations changed the demographics in the Caribbean. Soon black people became the majority of the population of the Caribbean islands.[1] The slaves brought with them their cultural and religious practices from Africa. The life of the Anglican Church in the Caribbean is shaped by the multicultural and multilayered strands of indigenous, African, and white settler traditions. In this chapter, I will use the example of the Anglican women in Cuba to illustrate the rich diversity within the Anglican tradition.

Cuba, with a population of approximately eleven million, is the most populous island in the Caribbean, as well as the largest by area. Cuba's population is approximately 65 percent white, 10 percent black, 24 percent mulatto (mixed between white and black), and a small percentage Asian. The capital city of Havana has a population of more than 2.2 million. The country has gone through prolonged struggles for independence, first from Spanish colonialism and later from American intervention. The political and economic contexts, culture, and history of Cuba have shaped the life and spirituality of Anglican women there, who have carried in their hearts the ideals of freedom and sovereignty that have characterized the Cuban people. Throughout the many years of Cuban history, these ideals have unified the interests of the many who have sought political and economic freedom and equal rights for all Cubans.

These struggles united men and women of different colors, ethnic origins, and social positions. Many Cuban women who preceded us shared the ideal of freedom. They left behind a legacy of courage, strength, dedication, love for peace, and hope for evolution of just relationships between men and women. Their ideals and aspirations have led today's Cuban women to continue to dream and struggle for a world of harmony, equity, and solidarity for all.

The Cuban culture is like the soups *el ajiaco* and *la caldosa*,[2] boiled from a mixture of different vegetables and meats, each contributing its own flavor and color, but resulting in a product that has its own distinct flavor and characteristics, as a result of the combination of its many elements. That mixture is the diversity that constitutes the Cuban culture and forms the very important religious, cultural, and social factors that characterize the Cuban people. Cuban culture, formed by way of a mixture of different races and the ideals of freedom and sovereignty, has decisively shaped and influenced the experience of faith of Cuban men and women. It is from this mixture, this diversity that characterizes Cubans, that I begin to discuss the spirituality of Anglican women in Cuba, a spirituality that has developed within a process of transculturation. The term *transculturation* was first used by the Cuban ethnologist Fernando Ortíz, in order to explain the process of the formation of the Cuban people: "It is a process in which something is always given when something is received; it is a give and take. It is a process in which both pieces of the equation result in it being modified. It is a process in which a new reality emerges, which is not a mechanical agglomeration of characters, neither is it a mosaic but a new phenomenon, original and independent."[3]

The Cuban Church as a Church of Women

The Episcopal Church of Cuba—the Anglican Diocese, as it is called—has approximately 3,000 to 3,500 baptized and confirmed members. It is a church of women. But as is the usual case, women seldom appear or feature prominently in the history of the people and communities, including the formal history of the church. Yet women are always in the background, accompanying the men, helping their husbands who are priests and lay leaders, preparing altars, and serving as Sunday school teachers.

The women are there to occupy those places that men leave behind when they decide to move on to some other activities. They are there to labor and do whatever work is necessary, like second-class citizens, much undervalued, marginalized, and disregarded. But they are there, faithful, dedicated, and engaged. The women remain there, through the good and the bad, always ready to carry forward the work of the church, like a silent and silenced majority.

In this sense, the Cuban Episcopal Church is no exception to patriarchal domination. Women do not appear in its history, although we can say beyond any doubt that the Cuban church is a church of women, because the majority of its members are women and thanks to the women, the church has functioned for many years and has developed its mission to the present day. It was the women who sustained the work of the Episcopal Church during the most difficult moments of Cuban history. During the decade from 1960 to 1970, due to problems related to the changes and transformations that occurred in Cuban society and the triumph of the Cuban Revolution in 1959, many priests migrated from Cuba, and numerous congregations were left without ministers. Women took charge and maintained the work of the church, despite the difficulties of that moment in history.

When the church of Cuba was converted into an extra-provincial diocese after it became independent from the American Episcopal Church in 1966, a period of economic crisis followed. As the church was unable to financially support the clergy, women stepped in to offer their services, contributing their ideas and working to help the congregations. The great majority of the wives of clergy began to work, in order to financially support their husbands. Many of these women also began to study, in order to open new doors and to move forward, while supporting their families and helping the congregations in which their husbands served as priests.

These women's sacrifices, tenacity, and evangelistic zeal are not recorded in the church's written history, but they are recorded in the memory of the many women who lived through those challenging times. At some point, these women's courageous actions need to be written down as a testimony to their faithfulness in following Jesus and how because of their faithfulness, the church can thankfully continue to live.

However, despite a female majority and despite the sustaining work of its women, it was only in 1986 that the Cuban Episcopal Church ordained its first three women to the diaconate. Of these, only two were ordained to the priesthood (in 1990). After that, more than twenty years passed before three more women entered the ordained ministry in 2005 and 2008.

Those who were ordained in 1986, by then diocesan bishop of Cuba the Most Reverend Emilio Hernandez Albalate, were pioneers of women's ordained ministry. However, they were ordained through a process devoid of reflection by the Cuban diocese regarding what significance women's ordained ministry had for the Cuban church. The church was only responding to the strong social pressure brought forth by the revolutionary government, which opened opportunities for women in all social strata. During those years, women were encouraged to study and to integrate themselves into the public and social life in the country and in the church. Reflecting the ethos of the time, the church joined the wider society in opening itself to women's participation in ordained ministry. It was good that it happened, but even today, women's ordained ministry within the Cuban Episcopal Church has many barriers, necessitating theological reflection and analyses in light of the challenges the church faces in developing its mission in the Cuban context.

As the years passed, those first women who were ordained in 1986 became bishops. One of them, the Most Reverend Nerva Cott, was the first woman ordained as a suffragan bishop in Latin America, and the other, the Most Reverend Griselda Delgado, was the first diocesan bishop ordained in Latin America and is in charge of the Diocese of the Cuban Episcopal Church. Even though these developments are a source of pride for Cuban Episcopal women, they do not signify a true sign of the Cuban Diocese becoming open to the inclusion of women, because the women bishops were not elected by the Church Synod but rather by the Metropolitan Council for Cuba.[4] Because they were elected by the Metropolitan Council, these women bishops caused additional discomfort on the part of clergy who did not feel comfortable being directed by a woman. The first of them, Most Reverend Cott, died three years after her election, immediately after reaching the age of retirement. She was a great woman who always stood out as a leader among women, who made improvements in the liturgy, and who accompanied the women as their chaplain and counselor. However, many times she felt devalued by members of the male clergy who ignored her status as bishop.

The second bishop, the Most Reverend Delgado, faces the great challenge of leading the Diocese of Cuba and encounters many difficulties, including, as expected, the problems caused by the fact that she is a woman. We know that ordination of women represents progress, but it is not a solution for the lack of complete inclusion of women within the Christian community. There is a patriarchal and misogynist tradition in the history of Christianity that distorts the message of the good news of the Gospel of Jesus Christ.

In the Christian tradition, there are a series of interpretations regarding evil, death, sexuality, and family and marriage, which are strongly anti-woman. From the teachings of Paul to the interpretations of the Church Fathers, the relationship between men and women has been seen as unequal. Women are to play a subordinate role because of their inferior nature as compared to that of men. Women's humanity is questioned and they are placed at the lower level of the hierarchical structures: God–man–woman–world. These structures were devised based on the experience of a past era, but they continue to form part of the liturgical expressions and interpretations that are maintained in many Christian communities. They serve as arguments for the exclusion of women because women are seen as created only to be the helpers of men in procreation, women were not members of the group of apostles, and Christ was a man.[5]

Women who participate in the Christian community have been affected by this patriarchal legacy, which has been strongly maintained, sometimes because of conservative and fundamentalist tendencies within the church and sometimes because of struggles for power. These are evils that continue to haunt the church of Jesus Christ.

Windows of Possibilities

Despite the discrimination against them, women are the ones who open the windows to allow new light into the house, and this is illustrated by Cuban women's spirituality. The diversity that shapes Cuban women and the characteristics of the Anglican tradition both contribute to the development of that spirituality. The spirituality of women in the Afro-Caribbean church offers a clear example of how diverse the Anglican family is. As part of this diversity, I want to share my experience in the Episcopal community of San Felipe Diácono in the small village of Limonar in the province of Matanzas, which has been my church for many years.

This community, which has the name of a male saint, is comprised of thirty women and one man. The majority of these women are black. Among them are divorced women, widows, separated women, single mothers, and grandmothers who have raised their grandchildren. Within this group only a small minority would fall into the category of what we would call "conventional" women—women who have husbands, children, and traditional families. They are Episcopalian by tradition and conviction; the majority have attended church from an early age. At the same time, in their homes they practice an old Cuban tradition of African origin called Santería. Both traditions form part of the life experience of these women, as they were born and have been raised in these traditions. The two traditions mix and intermingle with one another, and the Cuban culture is formed and developed out of the interaction of these traditions. The transculturation process adds to the great richness of theological elements in the faith of the church community. Throughout almost four centuries, the various cultural elements have been involved in a process of interchange, assimilation, and fusion. Against this backdrop the rich spirituality of the community of women of the Episcopal Church of Cuba has developed.

The religious expression called Santería or *Regla de Ocha* is one of the Cuban religious traditions of African origin most extensively practiced in Cuba. It arose at the end of the sixteenth century, when elements of African culture and religion were introduced to the island during the period of slavery. It was mixed and fused with elements of Christian tradition and with other cultural and social elements that have their origin in this popular religious expression, which today is practiced by the majority of the Cuban people.

This interaction between Christianity and elements of African tradition emerged through a process of transculturation that structured and formed Cuban society. This process began with colonization, when the indigenous cultures of Cuba encountered the culture of the whites who came from Spain. Later, when great numbers of African men and women of different ethnicities were brought to Cuba as slaves, African cultures were integrated into this process.[6]

African men and women were very important in molding and nourishing Cuban culture. Of all the different ethnicities introduced into the Cuban territory,[7] the Yorubas from the old Dahomey, from Togo, and above all, from the South East of Nigeria exerted the greatest cultural influence.[8] The Yorubas, who in Cuba are called Lucumíes, brought with them their religious beliefs and their divinities, called Orichas, and little by little many elements of the religious practices of the Lucumíes slaves were assimilated with elements of the Christian tradition.

The transculturation process, which involved give and take, transformed the rituals, customs, and traditions of the land. The Lucumíes slave men and women of Yoruba tradition used Christian names for their deities because they found external similarities between them, and they took elements of the Catholic liturgy to celebrate their own religious rituals. As a result, the African divinities of Yoruba tradition called Orichas were commonly called *el santo* or *la santa*. In the beginning it was a strategic act to conceal and disguise the African deities. But little by little and in the course of time, these strategies evolved to become new ways, new worship elements, and new ritualistic expressions.

As a Cuban product, Santería transformed the African elements of its origins, keeping some of them while creating new elements. The male and female saints of the Christian tradition came down from their altars to meet with the African Orichas and to share with them characteristics, virtues, defects, ritualistic elements, spiritual gifts, and energies. These saints left the Mass to go to the Wemilere,[9] entering into the humble homes of the village, participating closely in the everyday life of men, women, children, and the elderly, and hence becoming much more human. In this way, the Orichas have gradually transformed themselves by taking on a Cuban identity and becoming Cuban gods and goddesses of African origin.

The spirituality of the women of San Felipe Diácono in Limonar opens a new window in the Cuban Anglican tradition, pointing to new ways for recreating Christian theological elements by elaborating and mixing them with elements of Cuban religious expression of African origin such as Santería. For these women, there is not a duality. For them, figures such as Jesus and Mary, so important to the Christian tradition, are also Orichas, and as Orichas they participate in Santería ritual elements, eat and dance, live in the homes of the people, and share with them their everyday struggles.

At the same time, as an important part of the Episcopal Christian tradition, these women also profess that Jesus and Mary show us who God is, and that Jesus' life, teachings, and acts of love and mercy can be found in the Bible. The Bible for these women is a fountain that brings them close to Jesus and Mary, whose stories touch on their own lives. The Bible puts them in touch with the figure of Mary, mother of Jesus, and the events through which Jesus revealed himself to us as the God who walks with the people, eats and dances with them, and participates in their everyday problems. In the end, for these women, Jesus and Mary are not different from the *Oricha* divinities; they are Jesus and Mary who manifest with different names, but they are the same in both traditions.

This common road from the Mass to the Wemilere is traveled by many persons belonging to the Roman Catholic Church and the Episcopal Church in Cuba. These are two Christian denominations in Cuba that somewhat accept that their members participate in these experiences and recognize the transit from the Mass to the Wemilere.

It is interesting to note that in order to be initiated in Santería, a prerequisite is to be baptized in the church, and baptism is also the sign of belonging to the Christian community. The passage through water as a symbol of transformation and of new birth is a common element in both traditions. For that reason, it is easy to find a great number of persons who, as members of the Roman Catholic Church or the Episcopal Church, are also initiated in Santería and who travel between these two traditions without any bias. These people have engaged in interreligious dialogue and have broken the barriers between the Mass and the Wemilere, the church and the home-temple.

Jesus and Mary are images of the sacred that are important parts of the religious imagination of believers. Through establishing the relationship between these figures and the Orichas of Santería, Cuban Christians, especially the women of the San Felipe Diácono community, have deconstructed the dogmatic images and have recuperated Jesus and Mary, who walk with and share in the life of the humble inhabitants of the village, such as they appear in the Synoptic Gospels. This new window opens new possibilities for an interesting way to reimagine Christology.

Jesus and Mary, who are at the same time considered Orichas, share the completely anthropomorphic characteristics of the deities of Santería—they possess all of the human imperfections and virtues, and good and evil are mixed within themselves. These are two inseparable aspects of existence in the Yoruba tradition. That is to say, the dualism of good and evil is not present in the Santería deities; they behave as human beings behave and live with them intimately.

Jesus' image is related to the manifestations or avatars of two important religious expressions of Orichas: the Obatalá and Elegguá. The diverse forms in which the divinities manifest are called avatars or paths in Cuba. The Obatalá Oricha, in his most important manifestation, is an old man, and Elegguá is a child. It is interesting that the old Jesus and the child Jesus are two facets of Jesus that have not been explored by traditional Christology. However, Santería recuperates them. In what follows, I will discuss Elegguá in its relation to the child Jesus.

Elegguá is the Oricha owner of all pathways, the one that opens and closes the pathways of destiny for all people. We must count on him for whatever decision we make in life. He is the one that opens the pathways and furthermore he takes care of the home. For that reason, his place is usually behind the doors. Interestingly, since the time of our African ancestors, Elegguá has been seen as a mischievous child. He is as unpredictable as destiny is and he can be very good or very bad. He is the messenger of Olofi, the Supreme God[10] who said: since you are the smallest and my messenger, you are the grandest on earth and in heaven and without relying on you nothing can be possible.[11]

Elegguá has been connected with the figure of the child Jesus because some of the characteristics of Elegguá can be perfectly correlated with those of the child Jesus. This was a strategy used by our African grandparents but today is completely accepted by practitioners of Santería, who at the same time confess to be Christians and attend the Christian church—like the women of the community of Limonar.

There is an old tale about a child who arrived at a prison carrying a basket full of bread and a bucket full of water. He gave the bread and water to a large number of prisoners to eat and drink, but the basket of bread and the bucket of water remained full. According to the legend, the child was Jesus Christ himself who had come as a child to attend to the material and spiritual needs of those prisoners. This is a tale that the old African slave women would tell to show the relationship between Elegguá and the child Jesus. The child in that tale is known as the Niño Jesús de Atocha, according to a legend we have inherited from Spanish Catholicism.

This tale reminds us of the miracle of Jesus feeding the five thousand, as a result of a child who offers his five loaves of bread and two fish (John 6:1-13). Again we see the miracle of feeding, of feeding the stomachs of the hungry as a gesture that is identified with Jesus. Through this image of the child Jesus we are reminded of the words in the Gospels: "Truly I tell you, whoever does not receive the kingdom of God as a little child will never enter it" (Luke 18:17).[12]

It is significant that Elegguá is the first in all things. He is the first to eat at the hour of sacrificial ritual. He is the first to whom one makes offerings. He is the first to be praised in the Wemilere, which begins with rhythms and songs to Elegguá and finishes by singing to this playful and mischievous god. Elegguá cannot be excluded from homes, for he is the guardian, the protector of domestic spaces, and at the same time he is the first one consulted in regard to plans and future projects, when there are problems or difficulties in people's lives.

An important element in the faith of the people is the symbol of the child, which is seen as synonymous with security, future development, creativity, and spontaneity. The mysticism of the people makes newly present the messianism of the prophet Isaiah—"For to us a child is born" (Isa. 9:5-6)—and signals a messianism that goes beyond traditional frameworks. Nancy Cardoso Pereira writes: "The child that brings the new cannot be the property of the father . . . . The child is born of the newness of God in the lives of the women . . . . The newness of the child-like messianism is directly found in the necessity of always being like children and placing them at the center of our lives. Beyond childhood, we plan, propose, review, prioritize, and understand the saving presence of God through children. We are to experience the sacred always present among us in the temporariness and precariousness of our most beautiful mediators of salvation and utopia: children."[13]

With regard to the figure of Mary, the process of transculturation gives her many faces, which are represented through the feminine Orichas and the relationship between them and the saints of the Catholic tradition. Mary comes down from the pedestal and is dressed in the clothing of the women of the village and she remains among them. For this reason she is so loved and venerated. This connection between Mary and the deities of the Yoruba tradition, which are the deities of today's Cuban women, is a very beautiful one. Most prominent is the relationship between Mary and Ochún, the deity of love and sensuality.

This relationship restores the image of the modest Mary, the Cuban Mary, the Mary of the people. Ochún is one of the deities of the Yoruba pantheon that has gone through a process of transformation and adaptation to become one of the most important deities of Santería. In Cuba, Ochún stops being African and becomes a mulatta, criolla, and Cuban. She is the symbol of flirtation, of grace, of beauty, and of feminine sensuality. She is the deity of love and fertility, the patron of pregnancies, and the protector of pregnant women. Women and men Santeros say that she protects the womb and newborn babies.

In Cuba, Ochún is called "de Ìyádóle," a title also conferred to Ochún in Africa and that distinguishes her as the person who occupies the most important place among all women. Possessing great power, she is miraculous and compassionate, tender and sweet like the honey she loves, but at the same time willful and relentless when she becomes angry.

Ochún is considered the owner of the fresh waters of the earth, without which life would not be possible, and also the owner of the fresh waters of the sexes, which are also essential for life. She represents a joyful woman, free, daring, and self-possessed. She owns her femininity, but not a submissive and complacent kind of femininity—instead a powerful, free, sensual, self-possessed femininity. She also controls her own sexuality. Ochún is related to Mary through the Virgin de la Caridad Del Cobre, patron of Cuba. How has it been possible to have this connection between the sensual Ochún and the pure and chaste Virgin?

The poets refer to her as *La Virgen Morena* (the Black Virgin). She is called Virgin Mambisa by historians and by the people in general, who felt she had accompanied them through the many years of struggle for freedom. She is a mestiza, mulatta Virgin, who is fervently venerated by the Cuban people, and she reflects in her image Hispanic, Indian, African, and criolla roots. It is because she reflects the mixture of our Cuban roots that this representation of Mary is a very important part of the popular Cuban religious expression.

This fusion of Ochún and the Virgin occurred in a process accompanied by struggle and rebellion in a history in which mestizas, mulattas, white women, and black women were united, while at the same time struggling for rights to the land, freedom, and independence. They fused and mixed the black virgin and the goddess of love to the extent of integrating them into the everyday life of the people, humanizing the pure virgin and transforming her into a real woman of the people, one who breaks the traditional Western stereotypes imposed upon her such that she ceases being a saint and is transformed into a joyful, dancing, sensual, and Cuban mulatta. What was initially a purely visual connection made by the slaves, who saw in the Virgin Mary and Ochún similar physical characteristics, today becomes the fusion of these two figures as the same divinity in the process of transculturation, despite the separate origins and histories of each.

In the community of women of the Episcopal Church San Felipe Diácono, Jesus, Mary and the Orichas are united, which challenges us and points us to new windows, which allow for the illumination of new spaces and new pathways to bring us closer to an experience of faith nurtured by a pluralistic, inclusive, and ecumenical spirituality. This is an example of the great diversity in the Anglican family. The strength of Anglicanism is to always attempt to be sufficiently grand as to include this enormous diversity. As Anglicans, this diversity illustrates that a God who has diverse faces is a God who has our faces and is a God who encompasses all and includes all. For that reason we need a big-tent church.[14]

(Translated by Ema Rosero-Nordalm and Lisa Fortuna)

Notes

1 Kevin Ward, *A History of Global Anglicanism* (Cambridge: Cambridge University Press, 2006), 83-84.

2 *Ajiaco* and *Caldosa* were typical slave foods, which consisted of a soup or broth, containing different root vegetables and a piece of meat, usually pork. When the food was being prepared, the flavors of the vegetables and meat would fuse and mix together, resulting in a flavor that included that of each ingredient, but that became a new and delicious flavor.

3 Fernando Ortiz, *Contrapunteo cubano del tabaco y el azúcar* (Havana: *Ciensas Sociales*, 1983), xxxiii.

4 The Cuban Diocese was an integral member of Province IX of the Episcopal Church of the United States until 1967. For political reasons, the Cuban Diocese was allowed autonomy that year. Today, the Cuban Diocese is an extra-provincial diocese. For that reason, the Metropolitan Authority is under the guidance and ruling of a Metropolitan Council formed by the Primate of the Anglican Church of Canada, the Archbishop of the Church in the Province of the West Indies, and the Presiding Bishop of the Episcopal Church of the United States. One of the functions of this Council is to authorize the elections of bishops and to make provisions for the episcopate when necessary. This means that if the Synod of the Diocese meets to elect a bishop and falls short of an election, the Metropolitan Council may appoint a bishop from among the priests who meet the requirements for election. Both Bishop Cott and Bishop Delgado were elected by the Metropolitan Council and not by the Diocesan Synod.

5 See Peter Brown, *The Body and Society: Men, Women, and Sexual Renunciation in Early Christianity* (New York: Columbia University Press, 1988); Kari Elisabeth Børresen, ed., *The Image of God: Gender Models in Judeo-Christian Tradition* (Minneapolis, MN: Fortress Press, 1995); and Rosemary Radford Ruether, *Women and Redemption: A Theological History* (Minneapolis, MN: Fortress Press, 1998).

6 Ortiz, *Contrapunteo cubano*, 243.

7 Ortiz mentions ninety-nine different ethnicities. See Fernando Ortiz, *Los negros esclavos*, 3rd ed. (Havana: Ciencias Sociales, 1975), 100.

8 All of the villages and tribes situated in this region that spoke the Yoruba language were identified with this name. For that reason, Yoruba is "a basic linguistic denomination, even though these tribes were related through the same culture and belief in a common origin." See Natalia Bolivar Arostegui, *Los orishas en Cuba* (La Habana: PM Ediciones, 194), 3.

9 Wemilere is one of the liturgical rituals that Santeros celebrate, through a festival of dance, songs, and tambourine playing. These rituals are meant to evoke deities that are believed to become present in the bodies of initiated persons through trance possession.

10 For Santeros, the Supreme God is of such magnitude that human beings cannot speak of him, either in philosophical or theological discussions; this God is so great for human beings that he cannot be explained. For Santeros, this is the same God of the Christian church; there is no significant difference. He can be called Yahweh, but also by other names such as Olofin, Olorun, or Olodumare, which are all names for the supreme God in the Yoruba tradition. It is interesting how this fusion does not pose difficulties for believers. With time and in the process of transculturation, the characteristics of the Christian God were perfectly blended with those of the God of the Yorubas, without problems or religious discussions.

11 Pierre Verger, *Orixás: Deuses iorùbás na Africa e no novo mundo* (Sao Paulo: Editora Corrupio, 1981), 27.

12 See also Matt. 19:13-15 and Mark 10:13-16.

13 Nancy Cardoso Pereira, "El Mesías siempre debe ser Niño," in *Por unas Tierra sin Lágrimas*, Revista RIBLA No 24 (Quito Ecuador: Editorial DEI, 1997), 22-23.

14 Adrian Chatfield, *Something in Common: An Introduction to the Principles and Practices of Worldwide Anglicanism* (Nottingham, UK: St. John's Extension Studies, 2007), 8.

11

ANGLICAN WOMEN WITNESSING IN A MUSLIM CONTEXT: EXPERIENCE IN MALAYSIA

Judy Berinai

The study of Islam has become very popular in the past twenty years, becoming the focus of extensive research not only among Muslims but also among Christian scholars. Beginning with the resurgence of Islam in the 1970s, fundamentalists have stressed the importance of Islam and Islamization or re-Islamization of society, rather than modernization or Westernization. Consequently, many Western-oriented authors interpret fundamentalism as a violent reaction of Muslims against the West. For instance, V. S. Naipaul, a Trinidad-born British novelist of Indian background claims that fundamentalism is anger against the West as a consequence of the West's imperial history, monopoly of resources, and political manipulations.[1] Likewise, Robin B. Wright, in her book entitled *Sacred Rage: The Wrath of Militant Islam*, states that terrorism is a manifestation of Muslims' anger against the West.[2] This interpretation has become more prominent since the attack against the United States on September 11, 2001. As a result of the attack, unfortunately not only Western-Muslim relations have deteriorated but also Christian-Muslim relations. Further, the war against international terrorism stresses the dangers of militant Islamic fundamentalism and the necessity of defeating it everywhere in the world, including in Muslim countries. Sadly, the misunderstandings and prejudices between the West and the Muslim world have intensified and caused violence and injustice, which have affected Christians, especially women, living in Muslim contexts.

Since the nineteenth century, issues concerning the status and role of Muslim women in society have been widely discussed among Muslim intellectuals and religious and political leaders in the Muslim world because of their diverse views on the subject. Women often are not treated equally to men in Muslim societies which, sadly, incites violence and injustice against women. Women have to struggle in order not only to be recognized but even to survive in some Muslim societies. It is therefore crucial for Muslim scholars and religious and political leaders to reread and reinterpret Islam's teachings concerning the status and role of women and to challenge male dominance in their societies. There is a need to challenge discrimination against women with an eye toward creating a more egalitarian society.

This chapter discusses Anglican women witnessing in Muslim contexts, using Malaysia as a case study. In order to search for relevant approaches to witness to Muslims, it is critical to understand Islam and its impact on society, particularly the resurgence of Islam and Islamization. I will discuss here the multicultural context of Malaysia, the challenges of Islamization for Christianity, and the ways Anglican women can witness to Christ.

Malaysia in a Multicultural Context

Malaysia is a federal constitutional monarchy and a multiethnic and multicultural country[3] with a population of 28.3 million, of which 91.8% are Malaysian citizens and 8.2% noncitizens. Of Malaysian citizens, ethnic groups known as "Bumiputera"[4] (Malays, Orang Asli, and indigenous ethnic groups in East Malaysia) constitute 67.4%; Chinese, 24.6%; Indians, 7.3%; and others, 0.7%.[5] However, despite Malaysia being a multiethnic and multicultural country, the Malay majority (more than 50% of the total population) dominates Malaysian government, power, and politics. Furthermore, Islam is Malaysia's official religion and the Malay language is the official national language.

Geographically, Malaysia sits in the heart of Southeast Asia, sometimes called the Malay Archipelago, and contains two distinct lands: Peninsular Malaysia (neighboring Thailand, Singapore, and Indonesia) and the Eastern states in the northern part of the island of Borneo. Peninsular or West Malaysia consists of eleven states: Perlis, Kedah, Penang (Pulau Pinang), Perak, Selangor, Melaka, Johor, Negeri Sembilan, Pahang, Terengganu, and Kelantan; whereas East Malaysia consists of Sabah and Sarawak. There are three federal territories in Malaysia: Kuala Lumpur (the capital city), Putrajaya, and Labuan. They are governed directly by the federal government. The Federation[6] of Malaysia was formed in 1963 and included the eleven states in Peninsular Malaysia (which gained its independence from the British on August 31, 1957), the two states in the island of Borneo (Sabah and Sarawak),[7] and Singapore.[8] Because of political and economic matters that caused internal and external threats to Singapore, on August 7, 1965 the leaders of Malaysia and Singapore signed an agreement that resulted in Singapore becoming a fully independent country on August 9, 1965. In the following section, I will describe the resurgence of Islam in Malaysia, as background for discussing the challenges to witnessing Christ in a Muslim context.

Islam and Islamization in Malaysia

According to A. H. Johns, Sufis had the most significant role in bringing about the Islamization of the Malay Peninsula in the fourteenth century. Their influence had grown significantly in the Muslim world in the thirteenth century, and their teachings appealed to the mystic tendencies of the Malays and their rulers.[9] Similarly, according to Samuel Bryan, *Mohammedanism* (a name for Islam used by historians and missionaries in the past) was brought to the coastal settlements of the island of Borneo over several centuries by Arab traders and adventurers. He asserts that it was a great economic force that caused the influence of Mohammedanism in Borneo.[10]

Islam has always been an essential element in Malay identity and Malay nationalism.[11] Shanti Nair states, "Islam made significant contributions in legitimating the earliest forms of political authority in the Malay society."[12] In spite of Malaysia being multiethnic, multicultural, and multireligious, Islam occupies a position of some consequence in its sociopolitical landscape. According to the Malaysian Constitution, Article 160(2), Islam is a central feature of Malay identity. Consequently, Malays are supposed to be Muslims, and apostasy is considered a serious offense. Furthermore, since Malays constitute the majority of the population, Islam is crucial to Malaysian politics.

The Islamic revivalist *dakwah* movement in the early decades of the twentieth century was a fundamental factor in forging anticolonialist and nationalist reactions among Malays. Some scholars state that the main purpose of the movement's pioneers and activists was to challenge many of the concepts on which Malay identity depended: the centrality of sultans (kings of the Malay states) to the social order, *adat* (traditional customary law), and animist-inspired Malay superstitions. Islam became the state religion of the Federation of Malaya in 1957 and of the Federation of Malaysia in 1963. Islam in Malaysia has long been operating in a context of Malayness and been subordinate to it. In fact, Article 160(2) of the Malaysian Constitution defines a Malay as a person who professes Islam, speaks Malay, and conforms to Malay customs. Malay identity is therefore culturally defined.

Patricia A. Martinez states, "The Islamic resurgence was not intended to convert non-Muslims to Islam; it was rather about targeting Muslims to have deeper Islamic knowledge and stronger Islamic identity, and to bring the practice of Islam under closer government control and scrutiny."[13] Nonetheless, the Islamic resurgence has created an oppressive atmosphere for the non-Muslim population of Malaysia. Moreover, its impact has increasingly placed them in a subordinate position to that of the vast majority of Muslims who are Malays.[14]

Article 3(1) of the Federal Constitution states: "Islam is the religion of the Federation but other religions may be practiced in peace and harmony in any part of the Federation."[15] According to the Malaysian Constitution, the head of state, the king who bears the title of Yang di-Pertuan Agong, is obliged to pledge to protect the religion of Islam, and the sultans (Perlis, Kedah, Selangor, Perak, Negeri Sembilan, Pahang, Kelantan, Terengganu, and Johore) and governors (Penang, Melaka, Sabah, and Sarawak) act as the head of Islam in each state. There is room for *Syariah* (the spelling of Sharia, Islamic law, in Malaysia) within the constitutional framework, but it is only applicable to Muslims, and then mainly in family and religious matters. The role of Islam as outlined in the Constitution has a symbolic character. In light of Article 3(1), it is apparent that Malaysia is constitutionally not an Islamic theocracy, despite the elevation of Islam and irrespective of the strong claim to the contrary made by then Prime Minister Mahathir Mohammad in September 2001 (discussed later in this section).

However, despite the statement in Article 3(1), the Islamization process has been implemented in various forms over the years. Islamization in the 1970s was, to a large extent, a grassroots phenomenon of nongovernmental organizations, but since the beginning of the 1980s, it has become a government policy. The implementation of Islamization[16] by the Malaysian government was most intensive during Mahathir Mohammad's regime as the Prime Minister from 1981 to 2003 through various political and economic policies and programs that were designed to highlight Muslim's religious identity, impose Islamic traditions and values, and regulate Islam.

In the initial stages, the implementation of Islamization was quite subtle and did not cause major threats to the non-Muslims in Malaysia.

For instance, in the first phase, Islamization included some initiatives in education,[17] focusing on Islamizing architecture of new government buildings and reforming the dietary and dress practices of Muslims. The second phase focused on establishing and expanding Islamic institutions, such as Islamic banks, Islamic centers, and mosques. During these two phases, the Malaysian federal government launched programs for building more Islamic schools, offering more Islamic courses in local universities, and sending more students to the Middle East to become Islamic scholars. The state-controlled portion of the media also increased their selections of Islamic television and radio programs. Subsequently, the Islamic Centre was created under the sponsorship of the Prime Minister's Department, which played a major role in implementing Islamization programs.[18]

By the third phase of Islamization policies and programs in the late 1980s, non-Muslims had become marginalized by the national culture, which was geared toward Malay culture and Islamic teachings and values, such as expanding the capacity and jurisdiction of the Syariah courts and legal apparatus and standardizing various state "Islamic" organizations.[19] In 1988, the situation intensified even more when the Malaysian Parliament approved amendments to the federal constitution and added Article 121(1A), which reads: "The [civil courts] shall have no jurisdiction in respect of any matter within the jurisdiction of the Syariah courts."[20] Islamic resurgence followed in all other states when in September 2001, then Prime Minister Mahathir Mohammad declared Malaysia to be an Islamic state.[21]

These changes severely impacted non-Muslims in Malaysia. The state government followed the state religious departments' precedent by implementing initiatives that reflected Syariah values at the highest levels of government. Furthermore, the state governments also began curtailing non-Muslim places of worship[22] by refusing them building permits and land allocations and by proactively destroying them. In addition, on a national level, the civil courts began refusing to consider child custody cases when any party was a Muslim, claiming that jurisdiction in such matters lay solely with the Syariah courts. Sadly, the Islamization policies were regarded as part of internal Malay-Muslim policies and programs and therefore exempt from critical assessment by non-Muslims.

In 2003, Abdullah Ahmad Badawi succeeded Mahathir Mohammad as Prime Minister and pursued his predecessor's Islamization policies and programs, but by moving from the concepts of "modern" Islam (or "moderate" Islam) to "Islam Hadhari"[23] (or "civilizational Islam"), which highlights the glories of Islamic civilization and aspires to reach such heights

again.[24] This pursuit of Islamization through Islam Hadhari led to the introduction of a new history syllabus and a new series of history textbooks into
all secondary schools across Malaysia. Thus, instead of focusing on world
civilization, Islamic civilization was imposed upon students in Form Four
regardless of their religion. In addition, history became a compulsory subject.[25] The imposition of an Islamic metanarrative was a deliberate attempt
to impose a new form of identity on both Muslim and non-Muslim children. Islamic education is compulsory for all Muslim children in national
schools with five or more Muslim pupils, and courts have confirmed that
no exception will be granted for personal reasons or parental wishes. Thus
the Islamization process has permeated the entire school experience for students who attend national schools. This definitely does and will continue to
influence the worldview and identity of the younger generation of Malaysia,
which can be alarming for non-Muslims.

Reflecting on the implementation of Islamization by the Malaysian
government over the years reveals how Islamization clearly has impacted
both Muslims and non-Muslims in Malaysia. Furthermore, it reveals
how the direction and spirit of the entire religious nationalistic project
in Malaysia is to locate Islam and the Muslim community at the center
and non-Muslims, including Christians, in a subordinate position. The
religious resurgence has contributed to increased polarization, and the
dominance of Islam has had substantial implications at all levels of
Malaysian society. Muslims are expected to abide by Islamic laws reg-
ulating their daily lives. The lives of non-Muslims are affected in ways
not in accordance with their worldview and religious beliefs, and their
religious practices are often hindered or interfered with. For those reasons, in order for Malaysia to be a truly multiethnic, multicultural, and
multireligious nation, as it is often portrayed in tourism advertisements
and reflected in cultural and religious ceremonies and festivals, it is crucial for the Malaysian government to reexamine its laws and policies.
Multiculturalism need not be a mere commodity for the nation. It is critical to reinvestigate the history of the country in order to treat all citizens
equally and with integrity, regardless of their ethnic and religious backgrounds. Ethnic diversity should be acknowledged and respected by providing an atmosphere where people from diverse backgrounds can meet
and dwell together in unity, without having to politicize and racialize
their ethnic identities for inter-ethnic rivalry or for dignified survival.
Historically, members of every ethnic community in Malaysia have the
right to be Malaysian citizens and therefore need to be accepted and
treated equally politically, economically, and socially. Furthermore, in

spite of the fact that Islam is the state religion, other religions are equally significant and enriching. The diverse ethnic communities in Malaysia need to work together toward realizing a nation where there is equality of opportunity and social justice for all. Only then will every ethnic community find it unnecessary to turn an ethnic identity into an emblem for stimulating ethnicism, nationalism, or religionism to rally internal solidarity against an external real or imagined rival or enemy or against the oppression of the state or imperialist power. As a minority living in a multicultural and multiethnic society, Christians in Malaysia face challenges and opportunties, to which I shall now turn.

Christianity and Challenges of Christians in Malaysia

After the advent of Islam in the fourteenth century, successive Christian colonizers such as the Portuguese in 1511, the Dutch in 1641, and the British in 1786 followed. In Sabah and Sarawak, Christianity arrived in the late nineteenth century. Historically, it is undeniable that the Christian presence in Malaysia is the consequence of missionary efforts that were made possible through the provisions of the colonial powers. Nevertheless, the number of Christians has grown since independence. The churches are autonomous and the leadership of the churches is now entirely indigenous. Hence, although the Malays are the majority group and profess Islam, the Christian community is made up of Chinese, Indians, and many indigenous peoples of Sabah and Sarawak, comprising 9.1% of the total population. The majority of Christians reside in Sabah and Sarawak, forming one-third of the population.

The Merdeka (Independence) Constitution that was accepted at the independence of Malaya on August 31, 1957 devotes substantial attention to issues pertaining to religious freedom. The Constitution grants a great deal of religious freedom to its citizens, although it does include some limitations—restricting propagation of non-Muslim religions among the Muslim population and not allowing minors to choose their own religion. It in no way prohibits a Muslim from converting to another religion. However, as discussed in the previous section of this chapter, Islamization has been implemented in different ways over the years through government policies and programs intended to boost and secure the place of Malays and Islam in society. Albert Walters, a Malaysian Christian theologian, claims that "political, socio-economic, cultural and theological factors have combined to polarize Muslims and Christians into mutually antagonistic communities."[26]

In view of the Malaysian Constitution's provisions related to religious matters, Christians face many challenges that, in some ways, can be a hindrance to the Church's mission in Malaysia. For instance, in 1981, Indonesian Bibles, called the *Alkitab*, were confiscated and destroyed, and all importation was banned under the Internal Security Act (ISA). This was due to the word "Allah" being used in the *Alkitab* to translate the word "God." In addition to the word "Allah," there are three other Arabic words—*Kaabah, Baitulallah,* and *Solat*—that the Malaysian government forbids non-Muslims to use, due to theological issues concerning the words' Arabic origin. These words also are perceived to be confusing to Muslims and authorities were suspicious that they could be part of plans to subtly convert Muslims. In addition to confiscating Christian Bibles, Christian books were and continue to be confiscated and banned under an act prohibiting the use of words of Islamic origin.[27]

The Malaysian government continues to employ the ISA against any person or event perceived by the Minister of Home Affairs to be a danger to the country's security. As a result, the Act has instilled unnecessary fear in Malaysian citizens, particularly non-Muslims. For instance, in 1987, one hundred sixty people were arrested under the ISA, and in March 1988, the Malaysian Parliament introduced a document entitled, "Ke Arah Memelihara Keselamatan Negara" (Toward preserving national security).[28] Olaf Schumann, a well-known scholar in Islamic studies, explains:

> The Internal Security Act (ISA) was originally promulgated in 1960 as a tool for the government to use in dealing with the Communist insurrection. Later it was repeatedly used or misused to tackle political crisis. It allows the detainment of a suspected person for up to sixty days without legal procedure, and the detention may be prolonged for another two years by consent of the Minister of Home Affairs without explanation. Political justifications nowadays usually refer to a danger to the integrity of the federation. Thus a considerable numbers of the opposition were and are detained under this Act.[29]

Anglican Women Witnessing Christ in Malaysia

In the past fifty years, women have made significant contributions to social and economic development in Malaysia. By achieving a higher level of education, they have increased their participation in the labor force as doctors, dentists, lawyers, architects, businesswomen, politicians, educators, and so on. Similarly, women have contributed enormously in Christian ministries, particularly through women's organizations and fellowships, both at the local and national levels. However, despite this progress, women in Malaysia, irrespective of their ethnic and religious backgrounds, still face difficulties, discrimination, and violence at all levels of society. As a matter of fact, only forty percent of women are employed, and their involvement in decision-making roles is still very low. In view of women's limited participation in the labor force and in decision making, which has adversely affected women's well-being and welfare in many ways, the Ministry of Women, Family, and Community Development was set up to consider women's affairs more seriously and to find solutions for some of the related issues. In some ethnic communities, a girl child is considered less valuable than a boy, and as a consequence, many women suffer violence without protest. In fact, even in some Christian communities, women are still discriminated against due to gender issues. There is an urgent need for theological reflection.

In recent years, Malaysia has become one of the largest destination countries in Asia for migrant workers; in turn, trafficking of persons has become a sophisticated and organized operation. In response, different organizations—including Christian women's organizations, such as the Women's Commission in the National Evangelical Christian Fellowship (NECF),[30] the Young Women's Christian Association (YWCA), Malaysian Women in Ministry and Theology (MWMT),[31] and the like—have been formed to work against human trafficking and violence toward women and to teach the value of women. It is critical for women in Malaysia, including Anglican women, to work together with concerted effort to protect women, particularly those who are being marginalized or discriminated against, regardless of their ethnic and religious backgrounds. This is a way of showing solidarity, love, and concern. For instance, *Tenaganita* (Women's Force) is a grassroots organization committed to promote and protect the rights of women workers and migrant workers in a globalized world. They established three main programs, namely, Anti-Trafficking in Persons, Migrant Rights Protection, and Health and HIV/AIDS.[32] There are also other women's groups in Malaysia that work to protect the rights of all women and migrant workers by providing shelters for those who are victimized.

Christian women in Malaysia have taken on the challenge of pursuing theological education and becoming theologians, Christian educators, and church pastors. The number doing so may not be so impressive in the

Anglican Church, due to its reluctance to recognize women's leadership role in the Church. Nonetheless, this has not hampered the involvement of Anglican women, both those theologically trained and the laity, in witnessing Christ in their own contexts: families, neighborhoods, communities, workplaces, and society.

Reflecting on the conditions in Malaysia discussed earlier in this chapter and on the issues specifically faced by women living or working in Malaysia, it is critical for Christian women, including Anglicans, to be more intentional in their Christian witness. They must be more aware of issues affecting Christians and well-informed about Islamic doctrines, the Malaysian Constitution and its restrictions regarding political and religious matters, and national security matters associated with the ISA, and yet not be intimidated and not limit their witness to only Christians. Christian witness goes beyond borders and is unconditional. It is therefore a challenge for Anglican women to be prepared, bold, and willing to "take up one's cross" in witnessing Christ in a Muslim context.

It is indeed distressing to learn that the Islamization process is imposed on the educational system of Malaysia and how it clearly affects Christian children and youths who are studying in the national schools. They are exposed to Islamic beliefs, practices, and values. It is therefore critical for the church in Malaysia to strengthen its Christian education programs, which involve children and youth ministries as well as parenting programs, so as to witness Christian's beliefs, teachings, practices, and values to children and youths as well as to provide them a Christian environment. It is equally important to equip and support parents and parents-to-be for the challenging task of bringing up and educating children in a Christian way in a Muslim environment that can be hostile and unfriendly at times. Strengthening Christian homes and family institutions is also a good way of witnessing Christ in a Muslim context—witnessing Christ through Christian families that are committed and united with one another, stable, and living in peace and harmony. Women are often considered "natural" educators and nurturers. They are normally passionate in educating and nurturing the younger generation. For that reason, they can collaborate and design programs and activities related to Christian education, which are needed because Christian children are deprived of Christian teachings in the national schools. Although there is a subject called "morals," it is actually an Islam-oriented course whereby non-Muslim children are expected to learn the Islamic worldview and its values. Thus, in the local church context, Anglican women can encourage, support, and inspire one another in facing challenges related to Islamization, discrimination, and other contemporary issues.

Christians are commanded to love God and to love one's neighbor. In the Malaysian context, the spirit of *Muhibbah* (goodwill) is often promoted and encouraged among community members. For that reason, it is an opportunity for Anglican women to witness, love, care, support, and show concern for women of other faiths so as to express and share the first and second commandments in the Bible. Witnessing among non-Christian women, specifically battered wives, sexually abused women, single mothers, abandoned children, elderly and lonely ones, ill-treated foreign domestic workers, and victims of human trafficking includes offering them psychological and social support as well as advocacy. These are some of the ways of showing solidarity and offering unconditional friendship, support, care, and encouragement and sharing Christian love, which, it is to be hoped, can restore their lives and help them regain feelings of self-worth and dignity. Accordingly, ministries of healing, hospitality, and economic empowerment can be major ways in which Anglican women can witness to others and reflect the ministries of peace and reconciliation.

There are various approaches to witnessing Christ in a Muslim context such as Malaysia. First, Anglican women need to be aware of the challenges to a wider and deeper understanding of Christian witness. They must see nation building as promoted by the Malaysian government as the area in which God is at work through the Holy Spirit. Anglican women need to come out of their comfort zones and exercise a more caring attitude toward issues of national interest and take their rightful place as the salt and light in Malaysian pluralistic society. In this sense, Anglican women need to be alert and sensitive to contemporary issues in Malaysia in order to become effective witnesses.

Second, the situation in Malaysia calls for and challenges Christian and church unity. The Malaysian government will listen to one "church" voice rather than to a host of voices from divided churches. More concerted efforts at transcending denominational, cultural, racial, and linguistic barriers should be made to unite Christians in Malaysia to further effective Christian witnessing. Accordingly, to become effective witnesses in Malaysia, Anglican women are encouraged to unite and work with other Christian women across denominations.

Third, it is essential for Anglican women to be aware of and to learn new approaches to and strategies for witnessing. They are called to cooperate with other women for the common good in addressing issues such as social ills, moral decadence, and social and communal injustices. It is crucial to have a deeper understanding of one's faith in a pluralistic context. This will help Anglican women to witness Christ more confidently through daily encounters and interactions with neighbors,[33] in workplaces, and in the public sphere.

Fourth, due to the nature of Malaysian society, there is an urgent need for a serious attempt to understand Islam and other religions. Christian witness most probably will not be relevant and meaningful in a multireligious context, such as Malaysia, unless Christians in Malaysia, including Anglican women, formulate a contextualized and relevant theology of religions.

Fifth, the second commandment, "loving neighbors," can be a tender and yet powerful way to extend and build friendships and live out the love of Jesus with Muslim neighbors in Malaysia. Malaysians are generally friendly and courteous and it is therefore not difficult to befriend our Muslim neighbors to seize any opportunity for witnessing through words and deeds.

Sixth, praying for Muslims in Malaysia and across the globe, especially in the Arab world, which is in turmoil, is another powerful way of witnessing Christ in a Muslim context. We need to acknowledge that God is at work using many different ways to make Himself known among Muslims. Thus, Anglican women need to create awareness and promote prayers for Muslims among Christians, specifically with other Christian women. Besides praying for Muslims and the Malaysian government, Anglican women need to pray for Christians to open up their hearts to their Muslim neighbors and to be a blessing to them in practical and concrete ways, to pray for more divine encounters to occur among the Malays (see Acts 10:17-48), and to pray for Christians to be courageous while extending the hand of fellowship and assistance to new people and new believers.

In conclusion, remember that Jesus said, "This Gospel of the Kingdom will be preached in all the world as a witness to all the nations, and then the age will come" (Matt. 24:14). Jesus's statement is a challenge to Christians, including Anglican women in Malaysia, to witness Christ by "preaching the Gospel in all the world as a witness to all nations." Anglican women in Malaysia are in fact blessed to be in a multiethnic, multicultural, and multireligious society, which provides a glimpse of "all the world" and "all nations." For that reason, Anglican women in Malaysia need to aspire to a global vision "to witness Christ to all the world and to all nations," and yet not necessarily uproot themselves to other nations: there are many possibilities for realizing the "global vision" in their own local context, which consists of different ethnic communities. Nonetheless, although Malaysia's multiethnicity has added to the rich heritage of its land and people, it obviously is not a land of milk and honey, as it has also given rise to many problems and challenges. However, justice for all was the hope and prayer of women all over the world during the Women's Day of Prayer on April 2, 2012. "Let Justice Prevail" was the theme for the Women's World Day of Prayer 2012 and the focus was on Malaysia. Let this urgent call, "Let Justice Prevail," be realized in Malaysia through the witness of Anglican women and other Christian women and men and "the Gospel of the Kingdom be preached in all the world as a witness to all nations."

Notes

1   V. S. Naipaul, *Among the Believers: An Islamic Journey* (New York: Knopf, 1981), 143, 167-68, and 178.

2   Robin B. Wright, *Sacred Rage: The Wrath of Militant Islam* (New York: Simon & Schuster, 2001), 79 and 191.

3   We can trace the development of a multicultural society in Malaysia back two thousand years. However, it intensified in the twentieth century as a result of British colonial policies, which encouraged the immigration and settlement of large numbers of people (mainly from China, India, and Indonesia) to meet the demand for labor in public works as well as in primary production sectors, provided excellent prospects for trade and commerce, and offered the law and order associated with British rule. By the end of British rule, Malaysia had become an Asia in miniature, representing people from almost every part of Asia.

4   "Bumiputera" literally means "sons of the soil," referring to the indigenous ethnic groups in Malaysia. The Malaysian government gives the Bumiputera, especially the Malays and Muslims, certain privileges intended to promote their economic standing.

5   See the Distribution and Basic Demographic Characteristics 2010 published by the Department of Statistics of Malaysia in 2011, http://www.statistics.gov.my.

6   A federation is a group of states united under one central government, with each state having its own state government.

7   Sabah and Sarawak became British Crown colonies in July 1946.

8   Britain gave Singapore internal self-government in 1958. On May 27, 1961, Tunku Abdul Rahman, the first Prime Minister of Malaysia, proposed a merger between the Federation of Malaya and Singapore and the creation of a new federation, to include other British colonies in the northern part of Borneo, such as Brunei, Sabah, and Sarawak, in order to avoid possible Chinese dominance in the new federation. A referendum on September 1, 1962 revealed that seventy-one percent of the population was in favor of the merger. However, the Sultan of Brunei did not support it. The Cobbald Commission, formed to learn whether the people in Sabah and Sarawak supported the federation, reported in August 1962 that two-thirds of the people agreed, in spite of opposition from the Philippines and Indonesia.

9   A. H. Johns, "Malay Sufism," *Journal of the Malayan Branch of the Royal Asiatic Society* 30, no. 2 (1957): 5-11. See also Robert Day McAmis, *Malay Muslims: the History and Challenge of Resurgent Islam in Southeast Asia* (Grand Rapids, MI: Eerdmans, 2002), 17.

10 See Samuel Bryan, "Mohammedanism in Borneo: Notes for a study of the local modifications of Islam to the extent of its influence on native tribes," *Journal of the American Oriental Society* 33 (1913): 313-44.

11 For a discussion on the historical and political development of Islam in West Malaysia, see Michael S. Northcott, "Christian-Muslim Relations in West Malaysia," *Muslim World* 81, no. 1 (January 1991): 48-71.

12 Shanti Nair, *Islam in Malaysia Foreign Policy* (London: Routledge, 1997), 15.

13 Patricia A. Martinez, *The Islamic State or the State of Islam in Malaysia* (Singapore: Institute of Southeast Asian Studies, 2001), 477-78.

14 For further discussion of the Islamic resurgence, see Northcott, "Christian-Muslim Relations in West Malaysia."

15 "Constitution of Malaysia," http://confinder.richmond.edu/admin/docs/malaysia.pdf. See also Dato (MS) P.G. Lim, "Towards National Integration: of the Constitution, Governance and Ethnicity," *Journal of Malaysian Bar* 32, no. 1 (2003): 1-24.

16 For a definition and discussion of the term "Islamization," see Jerker Alf, "Islamisation in Malaysia and its Effects on Churches," *Swedish Missiological Themes* 91, no. 3 (2003): 429-30.

17 In fact, Mahathir Mohammad had planned to "Islamize" the educational system in Malaysia in the 1980s and 1990s.

18 R.S. Milne and Diane K. Mauzy, *Malaysian Politics under Mahathir* (London: Routledge, 1999), 84-85. See also Karminder Singh Dhillon, *Malaysian Foreign Policy in Mahathir Era, 1981-2003: Dilemmas of Development* (Singapore: National University of Singapore, 2009), 227-48; Shanti Nair, *Islam in Malaysia Foreign Policy* (London: Routledge, 1997); Hussin Mutalib, *Islam in Malaysia: From Revivalism to Islamic State* (Singapore: Singapore University Press, 1993); and Barry Wain, *Malaysian Maverick: Mahathir Mohomad in Turbulent Times* (Hampshire, UK: Palgrave Macmillan, 2009).

19 Kikue Hamayotsu, "Politics of Syariah Reform: The Making of State Religio-legal Apparatus," in *Malaysia: Islam, Society and Politics*, ed. Virginia M. Hooker and Noraini Othman (Singapore: Institute of Southeast Asian Studies, 2003), 56.

20 In addition to the dual system of law established in Article 121 (1A), Article 3 provides that Islamic law is a state law matter, with the exception of the Federal Territories of Malaysia.

21 Martinez, *The Islamic State or the State of Islam in Malaysia*, 474.

22 This had a particularly great impact on churches in West Malaysia, which is Malay/Muslim dominated, compared to churches in East Malaysia.

23 The basic principles of Islam Hadhari are officially set out as follows: "Faith in and piety towards Allah, a just and trustworthy government, free and liberated people, a rigorous pursuit and mastery of knowledge, balanced and comprehensive economic development, a good quality of life for the people, protection for the rights of minority groups and women, cultural and moral integrity, safeguarding of the environment and strong defense capabilities." See Department of Islamic Development Malaysia, *Islam Hadhari: An Explanation* (Putrajaya: Department of Islamic Development Malaysia, 2005), 12.

24 Department of Islamic Development Malaysia, 2005.

25 In 1997, Mahathir Mohammad tried to introduce and make the study of Islamic civilization compulsory for all university students in Malaysian universities, but the policy was opposed by non-Muslims. See Milne and Mauzy, *Malaysian Politics under Mahathir*, 89-90.

26 Albert Walters, *We Believe in One God? Reflections on the Trinity* (New Delhi, India: ISPCK, 2000), 98.

27 For instance, in 1997, 230 different Christian books were confiscated and banned.

28 "Dikemukakan dalam Dewan Rakyat/Dewan Negara menurut perintah," in *Dewan Rakyat/Dewan Negara 1988* (Kuala Lumpur: Jabatan Percetakan Negara, 1988), 18-29.

29 Olaf Schumann, "Christians and Muslims in Search of Common Ground in Malaysia," *Islam and Christian-Muslim Relations* 2, no. 2 (1991): 242-68.

30 The Women's Commission in the National Evangelical Christian Fellowship aims to raise the profile of the contributions and concerns of Christian women in Malaysia through networking with churches and organizations.

31 Both Malaysian Women in Ministry and Theology (MWMT) and the Asian Women's Resource Centre (AWRC) are determined to raise awareness, especially among the churches in Malaysia, regarding issues related to gender roles and power sharing. As ecumenical women's organizations, they share

work in advocacy and raising awareness with other women's groups, such as Sisters in Islam. They also promote interfaith solidarity among women.

32 See http://www.tenaganita.net.

33 In Malaysia, it is normal for different ethnic and religious groups to live in the same neighborhood. Furthermore, it is also becoming normal for families to be multicultural and multireligious due to intermarriages.

EPILOGUE

Judith A. Berling

In February of 2009 the editors of this volume attended a Global Consultation of Anglican Women in Theological Education at the International Studies Centre at Canterbury, United Kingdom, organized by the Anglican Communion Office. This consultation was different from many others because the majority of its participants were women from Asia, Africa, Latin America, and the Pacific Islands, with less than half from North America and Europe. Not only did women's voices and perspectives shape and construct this consultation (our only male interlocutors were a bishop from Sri Lanka and Archbishop Rowan Williams), but concerns and issues of women from the two-thirds world were front and center, reminding those of us from the global North that the Anglican Communion no longer radiates from the global North, but from all corners of the globe. The conversations at the consultation painted a distinctive portrait of the Church as seen through the eyes of a global group of theologically educated Anglican women. After the consultation, the editors planned the present volume to ask Anglican women scholars from across the Communion to explore Church and mission.

What difference does it make to have a sustained conversation from educated and thoughtful Anglican women from across the globe about the history of the Church, its present tensions and issues, and its future potential? What are the implications of this volume for the life of the Communion? In this epilogue I will lift up a few significant themes or principles that deserve further reflection.

The first theme is contributed by authors who bring voices from the global South, from countries and cultures whose introduction to Anglicanism was inextricably embedded in the domination of the British Empire. At the 2009 consultation, Kwok Pui-lan named the implications of this particular history well when she confessed that she was ambivalent about seeing England (Canterbury/Lambeth) as the "center" precisely because of the colonial history of the Church. Anglicans in former colonies need to understand and deconstruct the particular histories of the Anglican Church in their countries and to disentangle the threads of colonial domination from the core mission of the Church. Gulnar E. Francis-Dehqani's chapter explores how women who worked for the Church Missionary Society were caught between colonial aspects of mission and the gender constraints of Victorian British society, thus complicating the early models for and instruction of women in the Anglican Church in Iran. Cordelia Moyse explores the history and evolution of the Mothers' Union as conceptions about the roles of women and family evolved historically. Unless we understand the complex forces shaping the history of women in the Anglican Communion, particularly in the former colonies, we will not have an adequate understanding of the present and the potential futures of the Church.

Second, although this should be evident to churchgoers, these authors remind us that the Church is largely made up of women—women who do much of the day-to-day work of the Church in the world. Clara Luz Ajo Lázaro, writing of the Afro-Caribbean Anglican Church in Cuba, reminds us that it is primarily a church of women:

> The Episcopal Church of Cuba—the Anglican Diocese, as it is called—has approximately 3,000 to 3,500 baptized and confirmed members. It is a church of women. But as is the usual case, women seldom appear or feature prominently in the history of the people and communities, including the formal history of the church. Yet women are always in the background, accompanying the men, helping their husbands who are priests and lay leaders, preparing altars, and serving as Sunday school teachers.[1]

As Ajo Lázaro notes, the centrality of women's work in the Church is very nearly universal, but because women have not until recently been included in ordained orders or in the church hierarchy, their contributions have been largely invisible. Women historians are working to retrieve and describe the significant contributions of women to the work and the mission of the Church in the world.[2]

Scholarly attention to the work of women in the Church, be it in the Mothers' Union or behind the scenes in local parishes, entails a notion of the Church as primarily comprised of the people (*laos*, the laity) rather than primarily as a hierarchy of ordained orders. Remembering that the Church is primarily the baptized people of God bringing God's love into the world keeps our attention focused squarely on the desperate needs of that world. Esther M. Mombo's chapter passionately argues for the need for the Church to effectively address issues of poverty in Africa in ways that will empower African people themselves to move beyond poverty. Denise M. Ackermann uses biblical interpretation to underscore the urgent need for the Church to address the AIDS and HIV pandemic. While both of these authors appreciate Anglican Communion initiatives, the thrust of their chapters calls on local churches—on the *laos* of the Church—to recognize and address these problems.

Ellen K. Wondra's chapter on authority draws out the ecclesiological implications of understanding Church as the *laos*—the people of God. She argues that there is a crisis of authority in the contemporary Church as it struggles over a number of contentious issues, in part because these issues are being debated and decided within authority structures that pay scant attention to the voices of the *laos*, to the diversity of believers that comprise the Church. She writes:

> Difference matters. Gender matters. Race, ethnicity, sexual identity, social and historical location relative to social structures including colonialism—all these matter. Yet little attention is paid to any of these, let alone to their central role in forming the very traditions of theology and practice that are at the Church's foundations.[3]

Even when women and representatives from the former "margins" of the Communion are absorbed into the hierarchical structures, they are incorporated in ways that tend to erase the distinctive voices, perspectives, and experiences they could bring; they function primarily as part of the hierarchy (within its traditional structures) rather than as voices of the particular contextual experiences of their local churches. She argues for a different vision of the Anglican Communion and of Anglican authority that is more attentive to and welcoming of its diversities, that listens more carefully to the diverse voices in the Communion.

The authors of this book implicitly or explicitly challenge the adequacy of the practices by which reports on issues are settled. Wondra writes:

> Officially commissioned church reports, resolutions, and actions reiterate the conviction that the Church as it is, is justified and sanctified by its founding traditions, themselves cast as the revelation and inspiration by God for the Church's good. Beyond that, the response has often been to incorporate a few persons into dominant forms that

change little, thereby in large measure denying that difference is of much real importance at all.[4]

Such practices suggest an implicit understanding of the Communion
as a hierarchically controlled organization, a club or guild, whose boundaries, ethos, and principles are guarded and controlled by those who have
risen in the authority structures. There is virtue in conservation of tradition and a careful evolution of the Church based on time-honored principles guided and interpreted by those who have been elected into the
collegium of the bishops. But an implicit understanding of Communion
as hierarchy/club/guild can also devolve into top-down stipulation and
enforcement of principles of Communion in ways that exclude or alienate
particular sectors of the global Church.

The chapters of this book, featuring women's voices and perspectives
from across the globe, see the Communion not as hierarchical structure,
but rather as community, enduring and reciprocal relationships that are
more central than particular interpretations of doctrines and teachings.
Kwok Pui-lan cites an example of Anglican women affirming ongoing
relationships in spite of differences over doctrine:

> For example, while some African and other conservative
> bishops threatened to boycott Lambeth 2008, a group of
> Anglican women attending a United Nations Conference
> reiterated their commitment to remaining always "in com-
> munion" with and for one another amid deep divisions
> over sexuality in the Communion. The more than eighty
> women from thirty-four countries acknowledged global
> tensions in the Church, but did not "accept that there is
> any one issue of difference or contention which can, or
> indeed would, ever cause us to break the unity as repre-
> sented by our common baptism."[5]

One of the key contributions of women's voices to the understanding
of Church and mission is their tendency to honor relationships as having
priority over doctrinal debates and differences. Understanding the
Communion as a community built on relationships founded in shared
baptism is one way to live with and through our debates over doctrine
and biblical teachings.

Differences exist within the global Church, and they matter. No longer
can any one corner of the Communion dominate all the other parts.
Kwok argues strongly that we need a more inclusive church that embraces

north and south, male and female, differing histories and understandings of Anglicanism. She writes:

> This means reimagining a Communion that is truly global, multicultural, respecting differences and remaining in conversation and fellowship even when it becomes difficult. It means asking the difficult question of how the Church can come together as "disciples of equals,"[6] given the massive inequity of wealth and power in the world. If the Church can find a way to live out its commitment to mutual responsibility and interdependence, it can offer hope to a broken world and offer a foretaste for God's Kingdom. Many Anglicans would like to see the birth of such a new church: a church that is more concerned about God's mission than policing sexuality. A church that is not afraid of cultural difference, but welcomes diversity as its strength. A church that is not centralized or hierarchal, but celebrates democracy and participation of all who together constitute the Body of Christ.[7]

The authors of this book argue not on behalf of women only, but for the inclusion of many diverse voices in and across the church and an emphasis on church as the people of God, the communion of the baptized.

I have experienced the aspiration for and work toward an inclusive church at work in my local parish, St. Mark's Episcopal Church in Berkeley, California, where I am an active lay leader (currently Senior Warden). St. Mark's has long been a parish with strong and active women; we were the first church in the Diocese of California to elect a woman to the vestry. The women of St. Mark's have strong voices and participate actively in leadership in all levels of the church. We have just elected our second woman rector. But the leadership and voice of women in St. Mark's by no means exclude or displace the men: strong women and strong men lead together. The inclusion of women's voices and perspectives brings distinctive issues to the attention of the church; it challenges unconcious patterns of male authority and privilege; it opens up conversations to include a diversity of views and voices. My parish is characterized by an ever-lively exchange of views: if there are ten of us in a discussion, there will be at least twelve different opinions. This diversity of views and voices opens space for yet more views to be expressed from those representing as yet unheeded perspectives. In this sort of church—in this community—one does not experience an orderly parish based on time-honored traditions authoritatively interpreted by the ordained (male) leadership, although we appreciate—indeed expect—education about Anglican history, issues, and traditions from our clergy. We are always seeking to think more deeply about our Anglican/Episcopal heritage. Instead of an orderly hierarchical community, St. Mark's is characterized by a vibrant conversation about and exploration of the implications of the Christian life; we are bound together not by shared opinions but by baptism and by vibrant worship based on faith in God and Christ and the traditions of Epsicopal/Anglican worship.

My parish is a particular and localized example of the Anglican Communion in a corner of a university town in California. Like the authors of this book, we are reflecting critically on the history of Christianity and the Anglican Communion, are discussing with deep concern issues and tensions within the Episcopal Church and the Anglican Communion, and are praying about the future of our parish and of the Communion. We are increasingly clear about the need for intentional inclusion of a full range of voices in our parish (men and women, persons from many cultural heritages, lifelong Anglicans and those from other denominations and traditions, persons in interfaith families and marriages). And we believe that to do so effectively we need to understand Church as the baptized people of God, who enter into mutual ministry and engagement with the ordained clergy. In our particular context and on a very small scale, we are seeking to understand the history of the Church, its present context, and its future potential as presented by the authors of this book: as an intentionally inclusive community of baptized believers seeking to live the Gospel in recognition of the specific needs of a suffering world. The essays in this volume can help parishes like mine think more deeply—ever more inclusively—about Anglican Church and mission.

Notes

1 Clara Luz Ajo Lázaro, chapter 5 in this volume, 171.

2 Cf. Ellen Wondra, chapter 2 in this volume, 23.

3 Ibid, 21.

4 Ibid., 21–22.

5 Kwok Pui-lan, chapter 1 in this volume, 14. "Solidarity Statement," Anglican Women's Empowerment, http://anglicanwomensempowerment.org/?page_id=46.

6 Elisabeth Schüssler Fiorenza, *In Memory of Her: A Feminist Theological Reconstruction of Christian Origins*, tenth anniversary ed. (New York: Crossroad, 1994), 140, 150.

7 Kwok, chapter 1, 18.

INDEX